My LIFāSANA

François Raoult

PRAISE FOR My LIFāSANA

It's a delight that you are doing wonderful work in the field of Yoga and Music. Your association with Noëlle Perez adds to our bond. She was a remarkable student of Guruji. I have all appreciation for your work.
—PRASHANT S. IYENGAR

Śrī Prashant S. Iyengar is the son of Yogāchārya B.K.S. Iyengar and an authority in Yoga and the ancient yogic texts. He is presently the director of Ramamani Iyengar Memorial Yoga Institute in Pune, India. He is also an accomplished musician.

*

Reading this book was a more intriguing and engaging experience than reading most typical Yoga books. That is because François Raoult teaches us about Yoga and its practices by sharing the story of his life, instead of only instructing us in techniques. He weaves together riveting stories about years spent visiting remote and sacred places, about meeting all types of sadhus, famous Yoga teachers and musicians, and about crazy bus trips and train rides through remote lands in the dark of the night. He also shares his unique and often humorous take on things. As we read, we begin to understand how he absorbed the magic of Yoga from all his travels by willingly embracing everything and rejecting nothing.

François is a mystic who questions all of life with an open heart and a sense of adventure while trusting his own intuition and leading with his heart. Thank you, François, for taking all of us on these trips with you. What you have written inspires me to practice my own Yoga and to choose to live my own life right now with more enthusiasm and joy and wonder. —JUDITH HANSON LASATER

Judith Hanson Lasater has taught Yoga worldwide since 1971 and has written eleven books on the topic, including Teaching Yoga with Intention: The Essential Guide to Skillful Hands-On Assists and Verbal Communication *(Shambhala Press, 2021).*

*

The Sanskrit word, āsana, derives from a verb meaning "to sit quietly," "to persevere in a course of action," and "to celebrate." The title of this groundbreaking book then couldn't be more apt. François' life is an "āsana," his Self sitting quietly, watching intently, as he with single-minded dedication pursues the supreme goal, realization of that Self, in a spirit of celebration. To call François a "Yoga teacher" is something of a misnomer; he's rather a teacher of life who uses Yoga as one of his modalities. —RICHARD ROSEN

Richard Rosen has taught Yoga since 1987 in the San Francisco Bay Area, and has authored five books. Since being diagnosed with Parkinson's Disease in 2002, Richard has worked with many people dealing with the same condition. Richard happily lives in Berkeley, California.

*

François, a world traveler, has studied deeply with many renowned masters of yoga and meditation. He has translated his life experience, personal insight and extensive understanding of the physical and metaphysical body into a wonderful book. There is no lack of wholehearted humor, which is sometimes impish, sometimes self-deprecating. It only enhances the knowledge François imparts, which ranges from observations for everyday life, to instruction in the fundamentals and complexities of the deep practices of Āsana, Ayurveda, Prāṇāyāma, and Nāda Yoga. This book is a must read for student and teacher alike. —BAIRD HERSEY

Baird Hersey is a composer and author of The Practice of Nāda Yoga. *He studied with The Gyuto Monks and Bobby McFerrin and leads the overtone singing choir Prana.*

In the quarter-century since I first met François Raoult I have watched his practice and his teaching continue to evolve in a direction substantially different from that of most modern "Yoga." As François rightly notes in My LIFāSANA, "At this point in history we don't even know where Yoga begins or ends!" What we can be sure of is that whatever genuine Yoga may be, it does not include that rigidity of practice or attitude that has become so popular among Yoga instructors and practitioners. This book distills the experiences of decades of study and practice into the fundamentals that every student of Yoga needs to know and embrace: refine the perception of all your senses, reconnect with nature, develop aplomb, work with sound, learn to laugh. Written in the informative, humorous style that characterizes his Yoga teaching, this book illuminates the path toward self-transformation that the author has followed so successfully, a path that can benefit any serious student of Yoga. —ROBERT SVOBODA

Robert E. Svoboda is the first Westerner ever to graduate from a college of Ayurveda and be licensed to practice Ayurveda in India. He lived in India for more than a decade, and while there was tutored in Ayurveda, Yoga, Jyotish and Tantra by his mentor, the Aghori Vimalananda. He is the author of more than a dozen books.

*

François' stories are far more than reminiscences of a life well-lived in the worlds of Yoga. He writes of an India that in so many respects no longer exists, one that can no longer be found and certainly not revisited. It is difficult to compare his experiences to the realities of modernity, but it is not difficult to uncover in these stories the heart of Yoga itself. It is a story of lifetimes, not only one life, but like those Yogis who tell their own stories, François tells of multiple lives, journeys in the world, in the body and mind, and from the depths of the heart. Here is the work about life's possibilities and purpose where goals must remain unfinished even as journeys conclude and years pass. Yoga is deep engagement with life in the emergent forms of consciousness made manifest, personal, revealed, and concealed in words, practice, and artistry. If you seek to understand Yoga, then you should journey with François, for that is the pilgrimage to soulfulness, what in Sanskrit is called sahrdaya, to be "with the heart." The heart itself has taken its seat, its Āsana in these words and images and stories—and François has made that gift ours to experience through his own experience. —DOUGLAS BROOKS

Douglas Brooks is a professor of religion and chair of Asian Studies at the University of Rochester in Rochester, N.Y. One of the world's leading scholars of Hindu Tantrism, he earned his doctoral degree from Harvard University. In addition, he lived for many years with his Guru in India, receiving a classical Sanskrit education.

*

One of the gifts of François Raoult's My LIFāSANA is that this book reads like its title. Readers are invited into the wanderings of this great Yogi's mind, clearly shaped not just by his teachers (Noëlle Perez-Christiaens and B.K.S. Iyengar) but all the life experiences that imprinted on François to date.

The book reads like an extended playlist into François' mind and teachings. Having trained under François, it is a reminder of the days in his company and humor, as well as his continual renewals (e.g., Drinking from the Source). Except herein, you can savor the Source in all its glory.

In a section on teaching, in a letter to a student, François writes, "What a blessing to teach you. To teach you how to teach. For you to be a bead on this mala of transmission." For that's what this is, transmission down from the ages. And so, too, is this book: transportation down from the sages. Wiser for having read this, like the fount that it is, this is a book I will return to again and again. Within these pages, François shares how to journey into Life well-lived, LIFāSANA. —ELLEN HOROVITZ

Ellen G. Horovitz, is a psychotherapist, certified Yoga therapist and Yoga teacher. Ellen has authored nine books including Head and HeART: Yoga Therapy & Art Therapy Interventions for Mental Health Practitioners *(Handspring Publishing, 2021).*

My LIFāSANA

A collection of essays, poems and aphorisms on Yoga and Life

by François Raoult

Open Sky Editions

This book reflects the author's present recollections of experiences over time.
Some characteristics may have been changed and some dialogue recreated.

The ideas and practices in this book are intended for information purpose only, not to be a
substitute for the medical advice of a licenced physician. The author and designer disclaim
any liability arising directly or indirectly from the use of this book.

Copy Editor: Thibault Raoult
Cover and Book Design: Susan Etu
Illustrations: Karina Alvarez
Cover Photography: François Raoult
Photography on page 202, 203, 227 and Back Cover: John Myers
Sanskrit Consultant: Richard Rosen

www.openskyyoga.com

To my Muse Nathalie,

For giving me space and time to write my life and practice āsana,

For inviting me to teach in her school "L'École du Corps-Conscience,"

For sharing the Venice Carnival, the Sources of the Ganges,

For making the retreats in Crete and India creative and transformational,

For accepting me as I am, with my Pitta-ness,

And, above all, for her unconditional support and Love.

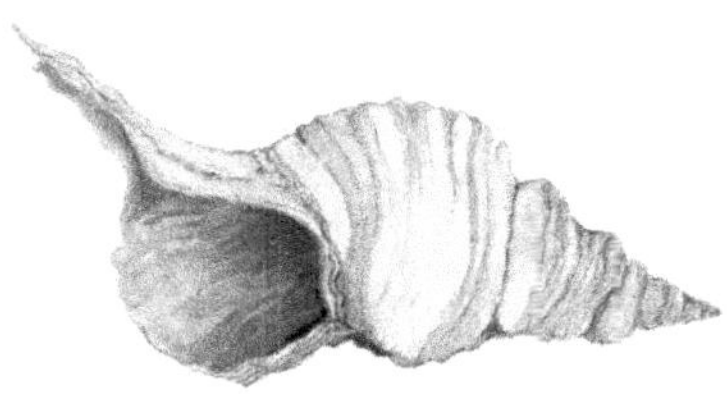

TABLE OF CONTENTS

PART TWO: ĀSANA

PART THREE: TEACHING

PART FOUR: MISCELLANY

PART SIX: ŚAVĀSANA

PART SEVEN: NĀDA YOGA

Music of Yoga of Music of Yoga of Music of . . .

SANSKRIT PRONUNCIATION GUIDE

Translation is the rendering of one language to another, for example, Sanskrit to English. Transliteration, on the other hand, is the rendering of one alphabet into another, for example, the Sanskrit alphabet to our Roman alphabet. The English alphabet has 26 letters, Sanskrit has 46. Therefore, diacritical marks are used over or under certain letters. Some of these English transliterations are only approximations. Asking for forgiveness from the past and present Paṇḍits, we did not italicize the Sanskrit words, we added -s for plural and capitalized all āsana names.

VOWELS

a	like the *u* in c*u*t
ā	like the *a* in f*a*ther (the macron means it's held twice as long as its short companion)
i	like the *i* in p*i*n
ī	like the *ee* in s*ee*
u	like the *u* in p*u*t
ū	like the *oo* in f*oo*l
ṛ	like the *ri* in *ri*m
e	like the *a* in g*a*te
o	like the *o* in g*o*
ai	like the *ai* in *ai*sle
au	like the *ow* in h*ow*
ṃ or ṇ	(anusvāra, "aftersound") a resonant nasal sound pronounced with an open mouth like the *n* in the French word *bon*
ḥ	(visarga, "sending forth") a final *h* sound that echoes the preceding vowel, e.g., *ah* is pronounced *aha*, *ih* is pronounced *ihi*

CONSONANTS

k	as in *k*ite
kh	like the *k* in *K*ate
g	as in guitar
gh	as in dig-*h*ard

ṅ as in si*ng*

c as in *ch*urch

ch as in staun*ch-h*eard

j as in *j*oy

jh as in he*dgeh*og

ñ as the n in ci*n*ch

The retroflex letters (also known as cerebrals, indicated with underdots) are pronounced by turning the tip of the tongue to the roof of the mouth and then "flicking" it off. The corresponding dentals are pronounced with the tongue against the teeth.

ṭ, t as in *t*ub

ṭh, th as in ligh*t-h*eart

ḍ, d as in *d*ove

ḍh, dh as in re*d-h*ot

ṇ as in n in ti*n*t

n as in *n*ut

p as in *p*ine

ph as in u*p-h*ill (not pronounced as f)

b as in *b*ird

bh as in ru*b-h*ard

m as in *m*other

y as in *y*es

r as in *r*un

l as in *l*ight

v as in *v*ine
(when the *v* follows a consonant, it's pronounced something like a *w*)

ś (palatal) as in *sh*in (similar to the german *ich*)

ṣ (retroflex) pronounced with the tongue-tip curled further back than *ś* as in bu*sh*

s (dental) as in *s*un

h as in *h*ome

ACKNOWLEDGMENTS

To **Śrī B.K.S. Iyengar**, for blinking his eagle eye toward me during a Yoga intensive in Pune, India, for making me learn English in 1977, for creating a bridge between Haṭha and Rāja Yoga and for being an unconventional, unpredictable and human Guru, Merci.

To **Jean-Claude Garnier**, member of L'Arche Community, Yoga pioneer, my very first teacher in Nowhereland, Normandy, in 1972, at a time when people still confused Yoga with yogurt, and, by a karmic twist as he moved out of town, for leaving me with all his 100+ students to teach with no warning at the age of 22, Merci.

To **Noëlle Perez-Christiaens**, for her pragmatic and mystical approach to Yoga; for including Africa in the East-West centric equation, for making carrying on the head a practice accessible to all, and for her stunning Aplomb until her last exhalation, Merci.

To **Marguerite Duvauchelle**, eccentric, autodidact philosopher and music teacher, for being my first piano mentor, for those long nights of deep listening in her small attic, from Stockhausen's *Stimmung* to Glenn Gould's Bach *Partitas*, and for being curious, Merci.

To **Judith Hanson Lasater**, for being a mindful and strong feminine voice in a too often macho yoga world; for driving with me across France at high speed, co-teaching memorable retreats near Nice, for always answering my crazy questions with grace, and above all for sharing an unconditional, absolute love of Mozart, Merci.

To **Thich Nhat Hanh**, 'Thay' for the close circle, for trying to make me smile and slow down in Plum Village's Mindfulness Summer Retreats with limited success and for inviting the Bell to resonate forever in our hearts, Merci.

To **Thibault Raoult,** creative writer, neo-dadaist poet, blues player, for being the laser sharp, visionary, respectful editor of this very book, Merci.

To **Karina Alvarez**, visual artist, for the inspired drawings of my dreams and illustrating the yogic Journey of this book, Merci.

To **Susan Etu**, visionary graphic designer, for co-creating the Open Sky Yoga logo and so many flyers with such refined sense of aesthetics, and for creating the cover and design of this book, Merci.

To **Monica Alanna DiCesare**, for sorting out thirty years of my writing in Yogawaves Newsletters and other sources, for answering the call beyond the norm of duty, Merci.

To **Yvonne Millerand**, dancer, explorer and disciple of Śrī Krishnamacharya, who was my mentor at L'École Nationale de Yoga in Paris, Merci.

To all **Open Sky Yoga teachers** and Open Sky Airlines Crew, ecclectic yet homogeneous, especially to **Mary Aman, Michael Amy, Carla Anselm, Christianne Asper-Contant, Thomas Battley, Joshua Bryant, Andrea Escos, Heidi Friederich, Ellen Horovitz, Kinga Kondor-Hine, Rick Lynch, Rebecca Lyons, Meg Ruby, James Thompson, Josephine Vittoria** for creating a virtual, spontaneous Sangha and a lively creative yogic subculture over the last few decades, Merci.

To all **Upa-Gurus**, people, places, events for giving me inner pranic showers and Haṃsa (goose) bumps, Merci.

To **Edwin Bryant**, for his humble and sharp commentaries of the sacred texts of India and for trying once the three-in-one drink, chocolate powder, chai and one shot of espresso at the Starry Night Café, Merci.

To **Sonam Targee**, for his clinical and practical knowledge of Ayurvedic science, and for his wild kirtan, Merci.

To **Ojo Calientes** and the **Posi Pueblo** in New Mexico, for the lithium and arsenic pools, the mud baths, the ancestral adobe and for welcoming my father's ashes on the Mesa, Merci.

To **Dr. Robert Svoboda**, for his brilliant marathon, Indian-style lectures on Ayurvedic science; for his crazy wisdom and for his friendship, Merci.

To **Douglas Brooks**, for his revolutionary and traditional teachings, for telling the Truth about the Origins of Yoga, the timelines, what we know and don't know, for being a Boogie-Yogi, Merci.

To **Thomas Myers**, for coming many times to Rochester, New York, in the late Eighties at the time when fascia was not fashionable and for not cancelling a workshop during a Siberian blizzard, Merci.

To **Michael McGrath**, for knowing so many archaic Chinese ideograms, Merci.

To **Roshi Kapleau**, Zen master, art collector, for loving Yoga and allowing us to teach in the Buddha Hall, Zendo of the Rochester Zen Center since 1987, and for dying one day with great spirit in the garden in his wheelchair, with his sunglasses on, Merci.

To **Sólbjört Guðmundsdóttir** and **Unnur Einarsdóttir**, my Icelandic friends for welcoming me in their shamanic land of glaciers, geysers and volcanos and for trusting me to share my teacher training Journey with great people from the North, the South, the East and the West, Takk Fyrir, Merci.

To **Zoreh Afsarzadeh, Gloria Alcaide, Laura Allard, Lorraine Arsenault, Mario Battistel, Barbara Boris, Vero Coeman, Jennifer Cooper, Nicole Couloubaritsis, Susan Emery, Nesta Falladown, Audrey Favreau, Dominique Fugère, Gabriel Halpern, Supriti Kotler, Sandra Kozak, Vicky Labbé, Julie Laurence, Martine Le Chenic, Elise Miller, Kelly Moore, Carol Nelson, Gaëlle Nicot, Steven Norber, Margaret O'Grady, Burt Peeters, Tao Porchon-Lynch, Richard Rosen, John Schumacher, Kim Schwartz, Laura Spaulding, David Sunshine, Patricia Walden, Dipti Woltz** and many more dedicated yogini and yogi across Europe, USA, Canada, Mexico, India and other planets, for taking the risk of hosting me, for giving me a wildcard to teach what I love in their cities and Centers, Merci.

To **Patrick Bismuth**, virtuoso baroque violinist for recording Biber's *Passacaglia*, for co-teaching a Yoga retreat for string players in the late Seventies at a Dieppe public music school, Merci.

To **Richard Rosen**, true seeker and poet, for helping with Sanskrit ḍilemṁmās beyond the norm of duty, Merci.

To **Baird Hersey**, underestimated overtone singer and composer, for coming out of his cave to give out-of-this-world concerts at Open Sky Yoga, Merci.

To **Bobby McFerrin**, for his patience, compassion and a divine week of Song Circles, Merci.

To **Triopetra**, the three rocks facing Pavlos Place where we go every year to treat and retreat; to **Petros** and **Georgios** who make it possible, Merci.

To **Nestor Kornblum, Michele Averard, Mehtab, Eric Bredard, Davorin Jagodic**, and **Jacques Petit** for their love of Music; for gonging, composing, toning, overtoning and to help me dive and swim in Nāda, the Sound of the Universe, Merci

To **Linda Leclerc,** for making me roll on the floor, for losing it, laughing for no reason for 72 hours, Merci.

To **Joellen** and **Fred Kentner**, for their non-possessive hospitality, for the years at the Farm with the deers and the wild turkeys, Merci.

To **Jibu**, my Indian brother, to the mysterious **Madam** and the selfless Ayurvedic **Dr. Sheela** at Chamundi Hill Palace, Kerala, for helping to regenerate my cells, Merci.

To **Krishna Das**, for hanging out in my house for a few days with his gang of musicians including **Wah!**, way back, before he became mainstream, Merci.

To **Pandit Mukesh Desai**, classical Indian singer, disciple of Pandit Jasraj, for saying to me once: "François, you are not really a musician, you are musicalized," Merci.

To **Dr. Tiwari**, Head of the Lonavla yogic hospital, for welcoming me as a guest to study and sharing some gulab jamun in secret, Merci.

To **Pradeep Kumar**, nominated best Kathakalī actor of Kerala for his brilliant rendition of a Vampire in the Māhabhārata and for his loyal friendship, Merci.

To the **Stromboli** Volcano, for its major eruption, only three weeks after climbing to the top of it at night with a group of lucky out-of-their-minds Yoga students, Merci.

To **Dave Vogler**, Grand Webmaster of the Shadow, Vāta Wizard of the Yogawaves Newsletters, which became a fertile ground for *My LIFāSANA*, Merci.

To **Marie Madeleine Davy**, philosopher, for being a radical Christian mystic, Merci.

To **Emily Conrad** and **Bonnie Bainbridge Cohen**, for a few literally mind-blowing somatic retreats and for helping me to think outside the Iyengar box, Merci.

To **Deborah Granger Raoult**, for introducing me to Emily and Bonnie, Merci.

To **Diane Lebo Wallace**, yarnbombing expert, for proofreading (soundproofing!?) the text, Merci.

To **Margaret Braun** and **Christy Lesher**, for reading The Book with a yogic eagle eye, Merci.

To **John Myers**, director of Myers Creative Imaging in Rochester, New York, recipient of many Gold Addy Awards, for taking the magical headshots with the giant conch, Merci.

To **Natalie Schorr**, for translating my French poems into English and English poems into French; and for sharing the poem "Le Pont du Gard" by her late husband, Mark Schorr, Merci.

To **Rebecca Lyons**, for moving her spine like a dolphin in Triopetra, Merci.

To **Emma Divita**, for assisting a Renaissance man with social media and for flying the drone, Merci.

To **Roland Shön**, scenarist extraordinaire, for playing the quena together in Paris, for sharing theatrical adventures in the streets of Europe for a decade with no shame and great success; creating a bridge from the Théâtre-en-Ciel to the Open Sky Yoga, Merci.

To **Tachi**, my Tibetan terrier of noble descent, who should have died when he was six months old from a severe heart murmur but lived 11 years, for keeping me company and for practicing passive backbends like a true yogi, Merci.

To my three children, **Maïwenn, Maël** and **Thibault**, for bearing with a traveling Yoga father and for keeping the lineage alive, Merci.

To **Marie-Françoise**, my big sister, for her intellectual curiosity and for opening before me the doors of another culture, Merci.

To my parents, **Marcelle** and **Jean**, for giving me the love of vacationing with no plans, for sharing their love of Nature, gathering chestnuts, daffodils, wild blueberries and mushrooms, and for getting a piano before buying a car when they were broke, Merci.

To **all my students**; the fanatic, the curious, the moderate, the unconvinced, the ghosts, the absent-minded, the challenging and rebellious ones, bodhisattvas in disguise, to those from the four continents, from all ages, walks of life, genders and races, to those who know much more than the teacher, to the pregnant midwife, to the deaf actress and the blind organists I taught, for keeping me on my toes and on my head until today, Merci.

To **Mother India**, for welcoming me as a challenging teenager, for making me feel at home, no matter what; for Her extended family and friends, known and unknown. Merci, Mercy!

I have spent my days stringing and unstringing my instruments
while the song I came to sing remains unsung.
—Rabindranath Tagore

I didn't want to tell you, but since you've forced the issue,
I just don't want to belong to any club that would have me as a member.
—Groucho Marx

The purpose of art is to lay bare the questions
which have been hidden by the answers.
—James Baldwin

Prelude: THE LOST HORSE

A man who lived on the northern frontier of China was skilled in interpreting events. One day for no reason, his horse ran away to the nomads across the border. Everyone tried to console him, but his father said, "What makes you so sure this isn't a blessing?" Some months later his horse returned, bringing a splendid nomad stallion. Everyone congratulated him, but his father said, "What makes you so sure this isn't a disaster?" Their household was richer by a fine horse, which the son loved to ride. One day he fell and broke his hip. Everyone tried to console him, but his father said, "What makes you so sure this isn't a blessing?"

A year later the nomads came in force across the border, and every able-bodied man took his bow and went into battle. The Chinese frontiersmen lost nine of every ten men. Only because the son was lame did father and son survive to take care of each other. Truly, blessing turns to disaster, and disaster to blessing: the changes have no end, nor can the mystery be fathomed.

I've always loved this story of "The Lost Horse."
A few personal examples will show how and when that story came alive in my life.

Curse: First Confinement in March 2020 with the Covid-19 pandemic.

Blessing: More time for writing this book.

Curse: I had leg surgery to remove the saphenous vein just before the confinement.

Blessing: Gave me time to recover my full potential.

Curse: I had to cancel all my workshops around the world.

Blessing: More space to regain my yoga practice.

Curse: I contracted hepatitis in 1985 in India. Barely made it back home. I was sick as hell with eyes like kumquats. Had to be in bed for weeks.

Blessing: I built a giant city in LEGO, all day long. It was touching the ceiling, with the airport on the windowsills. All I could do energy-wise. My son, still very young, had the best time of his life, playing with his father. He still remembers.

Curse: A few decades ago. The train stopped for six hours in a blizzard in the Hudson Valley on the way to New York City.

Blessing: I ended up being in the same wagon as some of the Twyla Tharp Company dancers. They were looking for an Iyengar Yoga teacher to go on a world tour with them.

Curse: Had severe nose bleeds in classes with B.K.S. Iyengar in Pune. Due to genetics, fatigue, heat and Śīrṣāsana overdose.

Blessing: They transferred me to a medical class for a couple weeks where I learned a great deal about Yoga therapy and appreciated for the first time the value of Restorative Yoga.

Curse: Marrakech, Marocco, 1970. Sleeping outside in a park near the train station (not a good idea). In the morning, realized everything was stolen from me: money, backpack, even my shoes.

Blessing: I still had my passport.

Curse: Had to beg for coins at the border in Tangier to cross the Mediterranean Sea, Spain and France. Had to eat leftovers on restaurant terraces at the end of the service.

Blessing: Collected enough money in a few days to catch the ferry to Gibraltar. On the boat, I found a ride with an artist painter driving an old Citroën Two Horses all the way back home. I even paid for his food and gas!

What are your stories of curses turned into blessings?

PART ONE

Travels

TALISMANS

During an interview in January 2016, a journalist asked Barack Obama to put on the table all the things he had in his pants pockets. The photo was then published in a weekly French magazine. Surprisingly enough, he had a little Hanumān that an Indian women gave him, a little Buddha, a rosary that Pope Francis offered him and he said, "When I am feeling tired or discouraged, I can put my hand in my pocket and tell myself, yes, I can transcend this because some people gave me the privilege to work on problems that directly affect them."

For as long as I can remember, I have also traveled with a little bag of talismans—a small leather purse clicked to my belt next to my trekking pocket watch. In the middle ages, El Camino pilgrims carried one filled with small ex-votos, a few gold coins or whatever they received while begging.

Here is what's inside:

- A medal from Chambord castle, where King Francois I used to live (not me). A salamander is engraved on one side. It was the totem animal of the king associated with the motto: "*Nutrisco et extinguo.*" Translated: I am nourished by good fire and I extinguish the bad one. Quite appropriate for Pitta doṣa.

- A Śrī Yantra coin, complex maṇḍala of nine interwoven triangles, symbol of the manifestation of the cosmos.

- A Minoan coin from Crete with a labyrinth. Life is a maze, a spiral . . . we have to travel roundtrip to its secret Center.

- As a joke, a token to enter Long Branch Saloon in Dodge City, Kansas. I found it in an antique shop in Sedona. It says: Food, Whiskey. Kind of the opposite side of Patañjali's path of renunciation! Is there a Middle Way?

- A sitting Buddha with a seven-headed snake behind his head, like Viṣṇu—what I call a protective satellite dish. I feel this shield often in sitting meditation, a psychic hood.

- A miniature statue of Nandi, the vehicle of Śiva. My wife has a collection of Nandi of all sizes gathered in India over the years.

- A small wood painting of Saint Francis of Assisi. He is the one. Talked to the birds like Messiaen. His *Canticle of the Sun* is close to the Gāyatrī mantra. Deep ecology ahead of its time. Makes me proud of my first name, after him, François. Not to be confused with the other Saint Francis (Xavier) who mingled with the Portuguese inquisition in Goa!

- One LEGO human. It can only bend from the hips and shoulders, keeping the torso in Tāḍāsana! Can perform Vīrabhadrāsana 3 perfectly! A reminder that the spine should not be used first in āsana. Instead: use the limbs!
- An unroasted cashew nut. Given to me in South India by an old lady, part of a nomad family, roasting cashews on the side of the road. Looks almost like:
- A little black lava stone from Iceland. Ancestral vibration. Apparently, these stones were given by midwives to women for safe birth. Reminds me of Iceland and Stromboli island, both beginning and end of the *Journey to the Center of the Earth*—places I have visited many times and close to my heart.
- A generic vertebra. Sculpted in brass. Such a marvel. To see the space for the spinal cord is a silent homage to the notochord.
- A seal of Mohenjo Daro. Made of clay by my father from a bronze copy bought in Mumbai Art

Museum. Represents a horned human figure in a seated posture with signs written in a yet undeciphered alphabet. Probably Dravidian. A symbol of the unending Indo-Aryan debate. Neolithic layer has shaped early Yoga. And a seal is a Bandha!

- A mini *Kāmasūtra* book. Sexuality is important. If it gets repressed, abuse of all kinds could appear later in history. As a bonus, a long list of āsana names. For some, it's a confusing matter, for others a way to see God; go figure it out!
- A Gaṇeśa amulet, made of gold and silver with a secret love message hidden inside.
- A USB flash drive, small memory key to the United States of Being.
- A brass scallop micro-pendant—a symbol of the pilgrimage of Compostelle. Our house is built on one of those mythical trails. Via Arelatensis, from Arles to Santiago.
- A roly-poly toy, always going back to center. Given to me by a teacher trainee at graduation. Sometimes when we sit on our seat, āsana, we experience a pendulum-like micro movements in deep stillness. A sign that we are getting back to where we once belonged and that we are at the right time in the right place.

All these items are very small and create a mini (but powerful) art history museum! It all fits in my little pouch and might provide protection while traveling. Who really knows!?

PILGRIMAGE TO INDIA

The shortest way from ourselves to ourselves is the Universe.
—MALCOM DE CHAZAL

I remember way back in the intense heat of the Afghan summer in Kabul, cooling off with a chilled cucumber soup. Divine! Walking for a few weeks across Afghanistan to enter Mother India near the Golden temple of Amritsar.

I left Normandy for Kathmandu a few weeks earlier by foot, hitchhiking East a couple months before. Eating raw root vegetables, stolen in gardens at night in Yugoslavia, crossing Turkey, catching the longest ride ever to Iraq with rally pilots testing a car for long distance (this was before Saddam Hussein.) Then Iran where the Shah was still ruling; Afghanistan—the King was still in charge; another long section with a truck of socks through Pakistan before crossing the Indian border. And literally finished the trip in a truck of coal from Patna to Kathmandu. My white suit was black when I knocked at the cheapest hotel near the Pashupatinath Temple.

Surprisingly enough, according to his wonderful biography *Words Without Music*, Philip Glass and his girlfriend followed the exact same route, hitchhiking as well a few years later…can you imagine we almost met!

The return Journey, from Kanyakumari, India's most southern point to France was rough. With only a few rupees left, I took the third-class train with the goats all the way back to Amritsar. Crossed the Indo-Pakistani border again by foot.

Pakistan was heavily flooded by the monsoon. I got really sick with dysentery and fever near Quetta. Had to stop and rest a few weeks near the place where Bin Laden was shot years later. Only ate plain rice and yogurt.

Then a three-day bus and train ride via the South Iranian desert. Three drivers relaying themselves day and night. I was teaming up with a Swiss hippie who only had a few possessions left. A passport, a parrot, and some opium. Not sure he made it to the Swiss paradise . . . I arrived in a Tehran youth hostel exhausted with swollen ankles the size of my thighs. Kapha inertia and heat.

From there to Austria, it's a blur. One late night in Germany, I took refuge in a tent, which was part of an outdoor camping exhibit. Sounded like a great opportunity at first but I got kicked out early morning by a German Shepherd.

It was November by then. Ended up with a motorcycle ride out of hell, picked up early morning, freezing my way on the backseat across Normandy, back to the womb of my cozy parents' home.

I defrosted myself and slept twenty-two hours non-stop. I went back to architecture school, only two months late. *Those were the days, my friend . . . we thought they'd never end . . . for we were young and sure to have our way . . . La la la la . . . la la . . . La la la la la . . . la la . . .*

SHORE TEMPLE

What if you slept? And what if, in your sleep, you dreamed? And what if, in your dream, you went to heaven and there plucked a strange and beautiful flower? And what if, when you awoke, you had the flower in your hand? Ah, what then??

—NOVALIS

This episode took place towards the end of my first Indian pilgrimage. Mahābalipuram is a mythical and historical place, south of Chennai on the coast of southern India. The bas-relief of Arjuna's story there is one of the wonders of the world. The tsunami of December 2005 flattened everything on that coast but the Temple of the Sea, which is at the core of this story. This is a literal translation from my 1972 journal.

Sunday, July 29, 1972:
Traveling alone, towards Mahābalipuram, in an antique bus. Palm trees of the lagoons, setting of the sun, vision of peace intensified by a rainstorm. The night falls. I eat some very spicy rice in a giant

banana leaf, which replaces the plate. And, because of the rain, find a small hotel, let's say a shelter for three rupees, for the rest of the night. The degree of humidity can be up to 95%. In Normandy, that would be a thick fog! Tomorrow—the flying temples on the beach.

Monday, July 30, 1972:
Finally, alone. The Temple of the Shore at sunrise. Built in the eighth century. Another crazy dynasty, to build a sanctuary on sand! The stone is just a shadow of stone, eroded by the salt, sculpted by the wind, polished by the tides of the Indian Ocean. It looks like a tight fabric, petrified in its folds by supernatural forces. The color and texture of the temple resemble the Celtic sanctuaries of Brittany, calvary crosses of rose, gray, green, and rust-color granite. They have a desolate feel, solitary, almost the end of the world on the shore, but they belong here, no doubt. Embossed in the stone, impregnated by the faith of man and by the serenity of the Beyond, lions and dragons, grossly cut, share the friezes, the corners and the summit of the temple. In the center, in a dark crypt, a man or a king, a God maybe, of impressive size, seems to suffer on the stone bed. With an anxious gesture he attempts to stand up, supported by one hand. He seems to want to tell me the last words, the ultimate message of the last solar living beings.

The sun on the beach gives the energy of life. Women walk, draped in their bright colorful saris, garlands of flowers in their ebony hair. They collect shells for offerings. A few meters from me, the Temple of the Shore. Immobile. I will sleep inside it this very night.

Mahābalipuram (puram, the peacock) is a very small fishing village where you can eat succulent sweets perfumed with ginger or coconut. It was the port of Kanchipuram, under the dynasty of the Pallavas, whose empire expanded all the way to Vijayanagar, the sacred city. Anyway, I settle down slowly on the beach, next to the temple, and I fall asleep. Tomorrow, I think, I will leave for Pondicherry and visit Śrī Aurobindo's ashram. On Sunday morning Mother gives Darśana from her balcony . . . I will be there.

Tuesday, July 31, 1972:
I sleep on the beach. It rained heavily during the night. Early morning a deluge of thick rain. An unbelievable amount of electricity, a sky of fire. So, I take refuge inside the temple and fall asleep on a sarcophagus-like stone bed. I dream, encircled by dragon spirits and then sun spirits. Like a nativity. I wake up just ahead of the sun. Fiery sky again, golden overtones at the horizon but other colors also. Pirogues (dugout boats) are at sea like Chinese shadows, their sails backlit. I bathe in the ocean with the autochthons, the local people. Naked. I run on the shore. Free. And finally take the bus for Chingelput for one rupee. Then the daily chai, a spiced milk tea.

I look at my hands. I have an orange "stigmata" on one of my hands, as if the sun itself came to settle in the dream, and stamped the center of my palm. No idea how it happened! That is a true story. The orange flower-like print in my palm stayed for a few days. No cleaning, no washing would erase it. I

Shore Temple, Mahābalipuram
Where purā yogānuśāsanam

draw it in my little notebook. This temple is one of the most sacred places in India.

February 2005:
One of my students was traveling in India for a few months before the tsunami hit. I asked him by email if he would visit the sacred sites of Mahābalipuram for me. A few days after the tsunami, he wrote that he was supposed to go there the very day of the catastrophe, but that his guide changed his mind, so they went inland. This saved their lives. But then he told me that he saw something about that temple in the *Hindu Times*, describing how the people who took refuge there were saved and everything else was destroyed.

His story made me reconnect with my past, how the temple created an aura of protection for me as well. After researching the archives, I found the article and a photo of the temple. I jumped with joy, returned to my journal's old, beat-up pages, and here was the same photo, one of the very few I took thirty years ago. Also, the tsunami ocean reflux revealed other parts of the temple, small shaped pagodas, now under water again.

Maybe that night shaped my life in some strange way, asking me to let go of rational beliefs and to accept the protection of the God who sleeps forever in the Temple of the Sea. For once, I had to leave the mental plane for an astral one! Did I receive a message? I learned later that the reclined statue is a representation of Viṣṇu's cosmic sleep.

August 2007:
Heavy rain from the monsoon. Visiting the temple of the Shore again, this time with Nathalie. Needing to share the magical vibration. But we are shocked to see fences built around the whole area. A Lourdes-like bazaar selling a bunch of junk is now booming next to the temple. We can no longer access it from the beach and have to pay an entrance fee. That is the price to pay for spiritual tourism! Still, the connection is there, beyond the commercial aspect. Wooden doors have been installed in front of each entrance, so no way into the Sanctum Sanctorum. They have barricaded the Gods.

January 8, 2009:
Got confirmation from a village historian that everything was wiped out by the tsunami, even the "new temple" from the 1940's. Only the Shore Temple remains intact. We are visiting as a group of Yoga students and teachers from Open Sky Yoga Center. Early morning again, still dark when we reach the sacred place. Wild horses on the beach. Women in colorful saris walk down the beach, carrying pineapple and mangoes on their heads. They seem almost to be falling backwards, their posture is so open. Liberated psoas, strong lordosis, high sternum, vertical axis, harmony versus aesthetics. It's an eternal vision of Mother India. The infinite ocean, the timeless sacred maṇḍala of the temples. We are the first pilgrims of the day at 6 A.M.! Some had been complaining about waking up early but now—no regrets! As soon as I entered the Gate, I burst into tears, instantly, waves of Kuṇḍalinī rising. More tears. Passing through a Gate is like that, a form of initiation. Why do I feel that I belong—as

if an essential part of me was born here? The light of the rising sun caresses the eroded granite, the Gods in their sanctuaries are still lying down in their cosmic sleep or sitting in meditation. Oh, the potential of a new life, a new Creation like deep in Śavāsana!

January 2011, 2013, 2015, 2017, 2019:
More visits at sunrise in Mahābalipuram. To be yoked again and again . . . taking refuge, hugging the stone lion on the temple grounds. I may have a telepathic connection with him. A bit like the stone circle of Outlander in Scotland! Durgā in the form of Mahiṣāsuramardinī is climbing on its side.

This lion has a strange niche carved in his chest, reminding me of Magritte's painting. An empty space for a heart, a birdcage or a piece of sky. A cosmic mailbox? I have to be alone. Karmic tears of release, enstasis, not sadness or grief. Oceanic tears out of the Blue. Feeling protected. Invincible.

The End. (No End.)

FULL CIRCLE. India 1972–2019

To go forward means to go far. To go far means to return.
—TAO TE CHING

I am grateful to my teacher Jean Claude Garnier, who introduced me to Iyengar Yoga in 1971 in Rouen, Normandy (the middle of nowhere). Shortly after, I left for a six-month Indian pilgrimage including a cathartic experience in the Mahābalipuram Shore Temple. Jean Claude, a disciple of Lanza del Vasto, introduced me to one of his teachers at the time, Noëlle Perez-Christiaens. She invited "Guruji" in 1975 and 1976 to the Paris Iyengar Institute, where I studied for a decade, way before the Yoga fashion madness. So, I got exposed right away to the intensity and authenticity of Yoga after studying with disciples of Krishnamacharya like Bernard Bouanchaud and Yvonne Millerand.

A technical and mystical correspondence was going on between East and West, between B.K.S. Iyengar and Noëlle Perez, about surrendering in Tāḍāsana, blanket support in Sarvāṅgāsana, Christ and Yoga, the spirit of Prāṇāyāma. In 1976 in Paris, after an intense day of Yoga and dinner with him in a crêperie, ending with the usual ice cream sundae he loved, I nervously asked him, walking side by side on the sidewalk, how I could further my Yoga journey. He just responded, laughing, "Come to Pune!" Things were simpler and more direct back then.

A few months later in February 1977, I did go to Pune. I had the honor to present him with Noëlle's book, *Prāṇāgnihotra*. We were only a dozen students at the Ramamani Iyengar Memorial Yoga Institute that month. I stayed in the cheapest hotels with the Sādhus, no running water or electricity, biking to class early morning from the other side of the city, bumping into black cows in the dark! So, the Dīpikā, the little light, got lit. I went back numerous times to India, sometimes to study Yoga, other times to research Shadow Puppet Theater traditions in the temples of Karnataka and Andra Pradesh or to record music in the Himalayan provinces of Ladakh or the Kingdom of Zanskar for my Masters in Ethnomusicology. All because of my first teacher!

In 2019 I found out Jean Claude was giving retreats and living part of the year in Mahābalipuram. So, I knocked at the door of the so-called Yellow House and sure enough he opened the door! We had a great visit, forty-seven years later, reconnecting in such a wonderful way, beyond the teacher/student relationship.

Full circle, India to India, in the village of the Shore Temple!

NEAR EAST & FAR WEST

The East of the East is the West! And vice versa. Go West, young man! You will find India eventually. Actually, there is no specific place on earth where East meets West. It can be anywhere. If you keep going West, you will never go East! Saying Yoga is not for the "Westerners" does not make sense at all. Or to say that they are more heady and the Indians are more intuition-based. India has a body of sophisticated philosophical texts and they argued over centuries about concepts, words, visions of reality. All schools are represented from nihilism (Śūnyavāda) to non-dualism (Advaita). Finally, since Yoga, in addition to its Dravidian origins, has proto-Indo European roots, Europeans and American immigrants are not that far apart from Indians, yoked by genes and languages. Irish from Ire-land (land of the Aryans) and Aryans who migrated towards India have a common ground. Icelandic is the oldest Indo-European language related to Sanskrit. Sanskrit is a big sister to Greek and Latin, not a mother. Nationalist Hindus don't like the idea. Yoga could be universal! But wait a minute! Where do the African Boshimans or the Australian Aborigines fit in the East-West dialogue?! They are often forgotten. Same in art and music. Another ethnocentric view, (East-West-centric?) where the North and the South (especially the South) are forgotten one more time?

PILGRIM'S FOOT

Breathing in, I know Mother Earth is in me.
Breathing out, I know Mother Earth is in me.
Kiss the Earth with your feet.
—THICH NHAT HANH

Tāḍāsana, all the standing and balancing āsanas, reset our feet for the practical journey of Life, an embodied one. In India and in many cultures in the world, countless pilgrims still walk step by step for a month with bare feet. A pilgrimage is a guide, providing a way to meet yourself and generate a deeper sense of belonging.

May your feet be alive and take you on that Path. Look at the foot of a newborn, how much life there is, the potential arch! Emotions are expressed in the toes as sign language. The symbolic foot of early Buddhist sculptures, facing the sky with printed lotus flowers, reflects that esoteric alchemy of pilgrimage and cosmogony. Look at your own feet, did they lose the connection with the earth? Are they hammered, "hallux valgused," collapsed, frozen, repressed, tired, wounded, sad? Or can they sing and dance? Can they really walk the walk and walk the talk?

How will they carry you for the rest of life?

SĀDHU

A remote monastery in the French Alps is connected to the legendary Mount Athos in Greece. On the chapel walls are beautiful icons and paintings of saints. The one that struck me was Saint Onuphrius. He was a fourth-century desert ascetic, reminding me of the Naga Sādhus in northern India. They have the same vibration; they have nothing left, not even clothes. When we went a few years ago during the pilgrimage to the Sources of the Gaṅgā, Gaṅgotrī and Gomukh, we met a few of those wandering monks. Westerners have invested in ski poles, Vibram sole shoes, and Under Armour special wear, and they still are cold and struggle. The Sādhus have just ashes on the skin, and they do well. Yoga in that tradition is more about inner fire, Bhastrikā, Nauli, etc. No sun salutation here, no hot Vinyāsa flow. Just being in Vṛkṣāsana for ages, or Prāṇāyāma all night with long Kumbhaka.... I met one of them who just conveniently broke a vow of silence. I was a little self-conscious to tell him I was a Yoga teacher. "What is your favorite Prāṇāyāma?" I asked. He answered with a strong musical voice and retroflex Indian accent: "Intake, only intake! Exhale, you die!" That is all I got from him. Means Viloma, long interrupted inhalation with retentions, all night. That is probably why some books warn you about Prāṇāyāma hazards.

VIMALA THAKAR

Mount Abu, Rajasthan

Not sure how I found out that Vimala Thakar, a poet, philosopher, yogini, social activist was becoming frail, but I had a calling to see her. She usually received students or pilgrims to have a conversation about life and sacred texts. She was old school.

She retired in Mount Abu, Rajasthan, a tradition for sages and spiritual teachers, after teaching worldwide— more in Europe and Australia than on the American continent. That is why she is less known by the American Yogasphere. Well, Donald Moyer, an inspired Yoga teacher from Berkeley, CA, did publish *Glimpses of Raja Yoga* along with *Sparks of Divinity* from Noëlle Perez on Rodmell

Press before he died.

Her books and poems touched me deeply. And her life. Her parents were jailed as followers of Gandhi so she was like an orphan. She followed their steps, marched with Gandhi and also became very close to Krishnamurti. A good combo.

We (my wife and myself) arrived late afternoon after a few hours driving across the desert. We were finally guided to her house, quite high on the hill. We knocked at the door.

A servant opened the door. We asked, "Is it possible for us to visit and talk with Vimala?" She said that she was too weak to come to the front door. The servant went to her bedroom and mentioned our request. We heard a feeble voice coming from far: *God bless you*, she whispered.

A few days later, she died.

MIRA ALFASSA

Śrī Aurobindo Ashram, Pondicherry, Summer 1973

I was invited to stay a few weeks with a friend on the grounds of the future Auroville. Only a few tents and the very beginning of construction. I had read Śrī Aurobindo Integral Yoga books and Satprem as a teenager, so hearing Mother giving a Darśana on Sunday morning from the balcony of the Pondicherry Ashram was mind-blowing, literally. I realized it retroactively. A major blessing and special moment. She left her body a few months later in November.

MANI

Kataragama, Śrī Lanka, August, 1972

After traveling alone for six months around the coast of India like a western Sādhu, I finally crossed by ferry at Rameshvaram to reach Śrī Lanka. It was possible back then, just a few miles of ocean to cross. After a few days, south of Colombo, I was in the bus towards Tissamaharama when I met a Buddhist monk who suggested I visit Kataragama.

Coincidently, I heard before I left for India that the German composer Stockhausen went to Kataragama two years before and had a cathartic experience. He got inspired by it to compose part of his twenty -nine-hour long mystical opera *Aus Licht*. I was a big fan of his music, especially *Stimmung*, his overtone vocal piece for six singers a cappella, composed in 1968. So that is what triggered this little adventure and confirmed that I was on the right track.

August 9
I arrived late evening at the Rāmakṛṣṇa mission, a pilgrim's place where they provide food and shelter

to everyone. I had very few rupees left, so it was perfect! Kataragama has a dense concentration of sacred temples, chapels, shrines, one for every major religion. It is not a true synthesis, more a small religious shopping mall where they are all represented. I met another monk on the sacred grounds who guided me. He thought that I was a Buddhist, so I was allowed to enter all shrines and follow the various ceremonies. In a Hindu sanctuary the trident of Śiva was aligned at night with the lights of the distant mountain top. After many pujas I was covered with sweet water, dirt, flowers . . . so many deafening bells going that I felt I was losing my mind (that was the point). Clouds of incense made it difficult to see the painting of the gods and goddesses on the walls.

Some devotees were walking around with their tongues pierced with a knife blade (they were not bleeding because they chewed on Ayurvedic plants and potions before). Others were hooked by a butcher hook to a pole. Advanced tapas in a special festival, somewhat similar to the self-flagellation of the Catholics, including John Paul II and the crazy fellow of Opus Dei in *Da Vinci Code*, to be closer to Christ! You get the drill? A tsunami of sound petrified the crowd of pilgrims. The officiant chanted with a scorched and passionate voice. Presence and devotion matter more than aesthetics. His eyes were illuminated, he still has candlewax on his shaved head! I ended up with massive amount of sandalwood powder on my forehead. In Kataragama, all religions are merging. Followers of Rāmakṛṣṇa, Vivekānanda, Christians, Muslims and Buddhists all attend puja, ritual, mass on their respective days. You can imagine that it wasn't a quiet restorative session.

After a traditional meal on a banana leaf served on the floor, a yogini from Jaffna gave everyone little pieces of sweets. At night, I was sleeping on the marble floor in a large hall with all the pilgrims.

August 10
Waking up with a chai, I befriended Father Arthur Perreira, who guided me further. He was not that old but had trouble walking. He had been living here for years and had the role of a caretaker, literally, taking great care. He gave me a mission.

There is a small ashram at the top of a mountain, he said, where Mani, my guru, a holy woman versed in Jyotish, lives in a hut, maybe ten miles away and I am too much in pain to walk up the trail to pay my respects, would you be willing to bring her flowers on my behalf? Forests all around were planted with trees from Burma, he said, and all kinds of beautiful flowers are cultivated like jasmine. So, we collected tons of flowers, made a giant bouquet. And the morning after, he took me to the beginning of the trail. I began ascending . . . monkeys and snakes were abundant in the rocks. Trees had tortured trunks. I kept climbing for a few hours in intense heat and soon I could see the ocean and more mountains in the distance. White stupas in the valley and roads. Felt like I was flying above the clouds. I arrived at the top drenched in sweat, drank water from a coconut offered by an ageless man. Then I began to look for the Mother. A young monk took me to her. After bowing, I offered her the flowers from Father Perreira. She smiled, nobody spoke a word of English, so smiling was the perfect language. They offered me a meal with delicate curries, pancakes and grilled bananas.

On the way down the mountain, I met a sage in the jungle, Śrī Ganeshan, officiating in the small temple. He offered me jasmine water to drink. His eyes were blue and white like the sky.

Oh, I forgot to mention that Mani gave me two precious stones, unpolished rubies, to thank me. She remembered Father Perreira very well (thank God! otherwise, I would have been the fool on the Hill!) and she was grateful for his gift of flowers. I kept those precious stones in a little silver box I bought in Syria later on the way back to France and I still have it on my altar at home almost fifty years later. Maybe it's time to polish the precious stones and insert them on a ring or a shamanic power stick!? I believe they assisted and protected my journey into the long inner trekking of Yoga.

Summer 2014 (just before B.K.S. Iyengar's passing)
Went back to visit with my wife Nathalie. All sacred areas are now fenced and you need a ticket to enter. Pilgrims are still there but the whole place has lost its soul. No more Life. Father Pereira died years ago. I could not remember where the beginning of the trail was. They built hotels and shops everywhere, so I could not go back to climb that mountain and see if the small ashram was still there. But in any case—Mani, a remarkable women and Jyotish astrologer—would have vanished.

NOËLLE PEREZ-CHRISTIAENS

In the spring of 2014, I felt the urgent need to meet with Noëlle, whom I had not seen since 1985.

She received me in her small studio in Paris, not far from the Eiffel Tower. Halfway between a cave and an anthropological museum. The mythical place of a hermit and a seeker. We talked for a few hours, looked at photos of Aplomb, daily life postures around the world, which I've collected over decades. She was very generous with her time and comments.

From 1975 to 1981, I would come to Noëlle's classes in Paris every Friday, hitchhiking from Dieppe, about one hundred miles away. Sometimes I would not make it or would arrive late. The door was closed at class starting time. That is old school! Or I would get stuck overnight back to Dieppe where I was teaching Yoga and also where our theater group, *L'Atelier de L'Arcouest*, which became *Le Théâtre-en-Ciel*, was based. Noëlle's line-up: a one-hour class on Tāḍāsana only, one-hour session of Prāṇāyāma sitting and then a two-hour āsana class for teachers. She asked me a few times to bring my string puppet Gwendal to Prāṇāyāma class to demonstrate complete surrender. The surrender of the puppet to the manipulator. Surrender to Gravity, a Higher Force. Let the breath be or go through us instead of controlling it.

Iyengar and she were very close like a mythical platonic couple, guru and disciple. She studied theology, comparative religions, anthropology, Sanskrit with Anne Marie Esnoul and had a very rich correspondence with Mr. Iyengar.

Noëlle was like my mother of transmission. She died in simplicity with no possessions. Everything she owned she donated to her anthropological Museum in Portugal. In Setubal she fell in love with her late husband, an illiterate fisherman, because of the way he carried on the head.

Karma is such that I was programmed to be very close in time and location to the place where she was cremated in France. I had an appointment in Béziers at 3 P.M. I made the appointment a few months before and her cremation was at 5 P.M. in Perpignan (the center of the world according to Salvador Dali!). We were only seven in attendance—like the cakras. I played the quena in the huge dome of the crematorium of Perpignan as she was traveling on the other side. The sound system was defective, and I just happened to have my Bolivian flute handy. At the center of the Dome, we could see the Sky through a small circular opening.

I also felt compelled to write Mr. Iyengar a few months before his passing, to let him know that Nöelle Perez, in her own way stayed very close and loyal to him and probably was the closest disciple by spirit and essence to his teaching. More than some official senior teachers who later took over the world like conquistadors. He responded quickly, despite his frail condition in March 2014. I had the chance to read his message to Noëlle so they both left in peace and reconnected as their path diverged in the nineties for mysterious reasons. One of them maybe is that they were equally absolute and stubborn! Mission Reconciliation impossible?

FOR NOËLLE

Reclaim the vertical axis
A good idea for all the non-aligned people on the planet!
And under Noëlle's guidance one claims it at the Lost and Found
It was lost without any doubt
But good news (Noëlle tells us)—
To climb Mont Meru
No need to travel to Peru
The thread of Aplomb is in us
It is our birthright
An architecture of verticality
From quadrupedy to bipedy, what a trip!
And how marvelous, when it is revealed
To affirm it with Aplomb
Cultivate, re-create, and respect the lordotic arch

To place its keystone
Above the secret Sacrum
And reset our humanness
Open that psoas paralyzed by sedentariness
Widen that precious diaphragm, one between Heaven and Earth
Which is longing for freedom
Anchor the calcanei, flamenco-like
Walk on virtual stilts
As Basque shepherds do
In perpetual equilibrium
For all of the above and in the name of all
Who had the privilege to meet you
Thank you! thank YOU Noëlle
Beyond physical and spiritual
Noëlle, you never cared for fashion
And you found the noble side of functional
Thanks to the Eiffel Tower
So close to the Iyengar Institute
Which guided your steps
As you were walking your beloved dog Panta
That tower where you saw in watermarks, as a Rishi would, the eight limbs of Yoga interwoven,
Fading into one another from earth to sky
From the four pillars of Yoga, Yama, Niyama, Āsana and Prāṇāyāma to the parabolic antenna
That emitter-receiver, that Samādhi
That you embodied, which gave you strength and inspiration
To receive, assimilate and transmit the fabulous teachings of Africa, Portugal and India
Especially those of Bellur Krishnamacharya Sundaraja Iyengar
With whom you had, as a dance, a mystical correspondence
You also met your husband, Miguel, whom I don't know but whose name rhymes with yours
With your simple and mystical words, you knew how to water those faded spines
And let them fly toward the sky like sunflowers
You offered us the synthesis of animal nature
And all the lost arts of ancient cultures
From Celtic prehistoric menhirs to ecstatic Khmer Buddhas of the Guimet Museum
Thank you for giving us the keys
To live our lives fully

Because of your infinite energy
That energy always renewed
That eternal force
Which is in us
And in Her
And just is.
—François, March 2014

POUR NOËLLE

Retrouver son axe
Bonne idée pour tous les desaxés de la Planète!
Alors, allez, sous la houlette de Noëlle, le réclamer aux objets trouvés!
Il a été perdu sans aucun doute
Bonne nouvelle, nous dit Noëlle,
Pour retrouver le Mont Meru
Pas besoin d'aller au Pérou.
Ce fil de l'Aplomb, Il est en nous!
C'est notre droit de naissance
L'Architecture de la verticale
De la quadrupédie à la bipédie, quel voyage!
Quelle merveille, quand il est enfin révélé,
Et de l'affirmer . . . avec aplomb!
Cultiver, recréer, respecter la cambrure
Reposer sa clef de voûte
Au dessus de ce sacrum secret
Affirmer par elle son humanité
Ouvrir ces psoas paralysés par la sédentarité
Élargir ce diaphragme, ce dôme entre ciel et terre
Qui ne demande qu'à être libre
Ancrer les calcanea comme en flamenco
Marcher sur des échasses virtuelles
Tels les bergers basques
En équilibre perpétuel
Pour tout cela, et au nom de tous ceux et toutes celles
Qui t'ont rencontrée

Merci, merci à toi Noëlle
Au dela du physique et du spirituel
Noëlle, tu n'as jamais suivi les modes
Et tu as retrouvé, du noble fonctionnement, le Mode!
Merci aussi à cette tour Eiffel
Qui a su guider tes pas, Noëlle
Quand tu promenais Panta, ta chienne bien aimée
Cette tour où tu as vu, en filigrane, comme un Rishi, les huits membres du Yoga
Tissés de la terre au ciel en fondu enchaîné
Des quatre piliers, représentant Yama, Niyama, Āsana et Prāṇāyāma
Jusqu'à l'antenne parabolique
Cet émetteur-récepteur, ce Samādhi
Que tu as incarné et qui t'a donné la force et l'inspiration
De recevoir, assimiler et transmettre les enseignements fabuleux de l'Afrique,
Du Portugal et d'ailleurs . . . et bien sûr de l'Inde,
En particulier ceux de Bellur Krishnamacharya Sundaraja Iyengar
Avec qui, comme une danse, tu as entretenu une mystique correspondance
Qui t'a permis de rencontrer ton cher Miguel que je ne connais pas,
Mais dont le prénom rime avec le tien
De tes mots simples et mystiques,
Tu sais arroser nos colonnes vertébrales fanées qui ont tant besoin d'eau
Appelées vers le haut comme les tournesols vers le soleil
Tu nous offres la Synthèse de la nature animale
Et de tous les arts merveilleux de ces civilisations disparues
Des menhirs de la préhistoire celtique aux Bouddhas Khmer extatiques du Musée Guimet
Merci de nous donner les signes, les clefs,
Pour vivre pleinement nos vies,
Par ton énergie, Noëlle.
Cette énergie toujours nouvelle
Cette force éternelle
Qui est en nous
Et en Elle
Et qui Est.

—François, Mars 2014

ST PAUL DE VENCE

During a week of vacancy (vacuum, vacation), I had space to visit the magical foundation Maeght in Saint Paul de Vence. Terry Riley played *A Rainbow in Curved Air* on the roof in 1970, inventing the feedback loops. I saw the Giacomettis and Miro's Cosmic Egg in the garden conceived by Miro himself, who has affinity with early tantric art and Navajo petroglyphs. If you have a chance, at least virtually, visit that special place!

SO LONG GURUJI

Śrī Lanka, August 20, 2014

Amazingly, we were staying in Śrī Lanka that night in Galle in a small guesthouse, reminding me of the Seventies and my first Journey to India. I woke up at 3:45 A.M. not knowing why, whereas I usually sleep like a log through the night. Later that morning we learned the news of Iyengar's passing. I'd had the feeling since March that the end was near and I'd even written him about recurrent dreams I had. I wrote with a sense of urgency. I also wanted to reconcile him with one of his first pupils, Noëlle Perez-Christiaens.

> Dear Guruji,
>
> I had a dream recently and I had a call to share it. You were standing giving a talk on Yoga to a big gathering of students.
>
> They were organized in Yoga hall like a Śrī Yantra. Each person was divided into three persons standing behind one another, their superficial self on the outside circle and their deeper Essence closer to the center of the maṇḍala. You were standing at one of the gates of the maṇḍala. A young child came with a procession of children with masks, puppets and offerings. I was sitting watching the whole scene like a great movie.
>
> Maybe it means that your teachings bring people closer to the Center, to their true Self. I don't know, but I know dreams are dear to your heart, as you yourself had premonition dreams, as did your beloved wife earlier in life . . .
>
> May God and Patañjali bless you like you blessed all of us with your brilliant and charismatic presence for so many years. May the light of your eyes illuminate the world like a laser beam of consciousness and awakening and become a shooting star in the Open Sky.
>
> With Love and respect,
> François Raoult
> February 20, 2014

He answered the same day he received; in fact, it looks as if he answered before he received it, according to the dates on the mail! Here is his precious answer:

Ramāmaṇi Iyengar
Memorial
Yoga Institute

1107-B/1, SHIVAJINAGAR,
PUNE : 411 016, (INDIA)
PHONE : 25656134

3-3-2014

My Dear Francois Rault,

I just received your letter and read about your dream. Hope this dream acts as a value in the field of yoga. I am running 96, and as such it is hard for me to guess your form of opinion. So do excuse me.

Also I am happy to know through you that Noelle Perez is keeping well and may God bless her with that same type of mind.

Actually my job is to part with what I have and people may use my art for the good or for self enhancement. This is human nature which you have to accept and continue the work which is close to one's heart. That is what I am doing.

With all my best wishes to you.

Yours sincerely,

(B. K.S IYENGAR)

I read *The Times of India's* great article on the following Thursday in New Delhi airport, a full page all over India, where He was finally recognized by his countrymen, a bit late actually (like the Mime Marceau in France) but still I know he would have felt good about it— from darkness to light.

MOONBATHING

Plum Village, France

Years ago, I had a private consultation with Dr. Robert Svoboda, one of the world's leading Ayurvedic experts. After looking at my chart in Vedic astrology, Jyotish, we found out that Rāhu was in charge! He suggested, in addition to drinking some magic Ayurvedic potions, that moonbathing and especially playing the flute under the full moon would be beneficial to my health.

A year later, in the next summer retreat at Plum Village, a day before the full moon, Thich Nhat Hanh heard me practice my classical flute outside and asked me if I would play for the Full Moon festival, which is very dear to Vietnamese tradition. I made French crêpes all day for two hundred people to contribute to the feast, and others prepared mung bean and sticky rice mooncakes. In the evening we were invited on the wooden terrace of Thay's small hut in the next valley. Everybody was sitting or lying down in the grass. A few people played before me, a little girl played *"Three Blind Mice"* in a loop on a mini violin, then an older Vietnamese man played the đàn thran, a sixteen-string zither traditional instrument and finally I played my transverse flute into a small sound system, so I could color the wind sound with amplified harmonics. It was reverberating all the way to the other side of the valley and the full moon began to rise.

I had just fulfilled Dr. Svoboda's prescription!

LAZY DAY, PLUM VILLAGE

France 1987

(Memory of Plum Village month-long meditation retreat)

Thich Nhat Hanh, the Vietnamese Zen master, had planned as part of the retreat, one formal Lazy Day each week. That means no mandatory sitting meditation, no fixed meals, etc., no schedule that day. That was the most challenging day for participants, and even more so for Americans! How difficult to be detached from a fixed routine, even or especially a healthy meaningful one! One possible interpretation of the Patañjali Sūtra on Abhyāsa and Vairāgyābhām could mean to be detached from practice itself and then be detached from detachment as well! We know from being in Śavāsana, in Yoga Nidrā and in silent sitting, that there is a deeper space inside behind the layers of tension, agitation, behind the to-do list. When all those twisted Vṛttis finally vanish—if they ever do—we can experience, as they say in India, that the silence is the cause of all sounds. Similarly, deep rest can be the source of all actions. Sometimes laziness is a medium for it.

After that powerful retreat in the south of France, I appreciated a sharpness of perception, the vibrancy of colors, the presence of air on skin, the coolness of water, the vastness of the summer sky—similar to the one Van Gogh painted a century ago. Sometimes beauty is so intense, it almost hurts or makes you cry. That is why I have been so moved when reading Krishnamurti's *Notebook* over and over again, out loud:

"Everything became more intense, every colour, every shape and in that pale moonlight all the wayside puddles were the waters of life. Everything must go, be wiped away, not to receive it but the brain must be utterly still, sensitive, to watch, to see. Like a flood that covers the dry parched land IT came full of delight and clarity, and IT stayed."

POSI PUEBLO

Every time I visit Ojo Calientes, New Mexico, I meditate in a little canyon on the way to Posi Pueblo, high on the Mesa. I created a miniature land art project in memory of my father with stones, driftwood, plants and little pieces of polished glass. It includes some of his ashes. A few years ago, I went back in the early morning, played the quena (Bolivian flute) and this little text came to me afterwards.

Life must come back, like wild grass, naturally
So don't practice too formally
Don't pass more time learning how to live than living!
We must blend into Nature with a spiritual camouflage
Not overcontrolling our breath so Nature can guide us
Natural breath is the Mantra
Natural Posture is the Yantra
Natural Nature is the original Land Art
Let us listen, see and vanish

La Vie doit reprendre ses droits comme l'herbe sauvage
Donc ne pratiquez pas trop formellement
Ne passez pas plus de temps à apprendre a vivre qu'à vivre!
Il faut se fondre à la nature dans une sorte de camouflage spirituel
Se rendre invisible. Ne pas contrôler la respiration afin qu'elle puisse nous guider

La respiration naturelle est le Mantra
La posture naturelle est le Yantra
La nature est le land-art originel
Écoutons, voyons et disparaissons!

GET BACK, GET BACK TO WHERE YOU ONCE BELONGED

Life is a spiral, a vortex. We return to old places with a fresh, more evolved, more in-volved point of view. It could be where we were born but also just where we feel we belong, if you have been adopted for example. The Source can be a country, a place of power, a mountain, a temple or cathedral, a vacation spot from childhood—maybe a place inside ourselves, deep in our hearts and genes.

For me, Mahābalipuram in South India, the Celtic forest of Brocéliande, and the Mont Saint Michel are on the list. What is at the Center of your spiral? When will your next pilgrimage be? When will you get back to where you once belonged? Life is short, but it is wide.

CITTASLOW

Yoga should be part of Cittaslow, a movement which started in Orvieto, Italy, in the nineties following the Slow Food movement, founded to counter McDonald's store opening near the Spanish steps in Rome. Slow food, slow cities, slow travel. Slow Restorative Yoga and Prāṇāyāma should also be part of that movement. And Cittaslow gives a new meaning to the second Sūtra: yogaś *citta*-vṛtti-nirodhaḥ!

AIRPLANE YOGA

Note: This article was written for a magazine to address jet lag and flying side effects, but the prescription can be applied to virtual flying on the internet or any Vāta aggravation, for example, if you feel as grounded as popcorn on a trampoline.

Every time I fly somewhere to teach a Yoga seminar, visit my parents in France, or study in India I open a magazine and find an article on what to do to minimize discomfort or jet lag from traveling. One airline even publishes a "Yoga/meditation" flyer that is actually quite good and lighthearted. The subtitle is, "How to look like a real weirdo to your fellow passengers." The meditation part is deeply influenced by Thich Nhat Hanh (they forget to credit him, so I do). The brochure ends on a light note: "As the mind is brought into stillness, you will feel stable, yet tranquil . . . almost as if you're flying. Oh wait, you are flying. Well, see, it's working already."

I am not sure we can call it Yoga, but at this point in history we don't really know where Yoga begins or ends! There is airplane Yoga, office Yoga, Yoga butts, even Elvis Yoga with Elvis hits in the background. Yoga is spreading in the culture of fitness and in the business world at the speed of light. So, let's surf the wave and see if we can improve the lifestyle of travelers. Yoga or not Yoga, it will at least minimize pain and help people stay focused.

Before you travel by plane, the best choice is to practice being more relaxed and adaptable. Knowing that you will be in flexion and crunched for many hours with knees bent almost in a fetal position, mild backbends and spinal traction are a great option. Practice the locust, the bow, downward facing dog, lunges, decompressing your spine with your hands on a support like a wall or a table. Any release for the back of your legs is welcome. Just a well-rounded, simple Yoga practice will do.

During the trip, in the plane itself, you can practice shoulder openers and walk often up and down the aisle even if people think you are restless. A few times, I did Śīrṣāsana in the back of the plane but that is more adventurous. A more reasonable option is to place your elbows on the seat in the front of you to open your triceps and intercostal muscles (that is, if the person in the front of you is short!). Now I've tried placing my Achilles tendon or heels on the head rest in front of me, but be sure the other passenger is asleep. If you have two seats and a window, Viparīta Karaṇi Mudrā is possible or at least legs up vertically against the window. If you have three seats, almost everything is game, Setubandha Sarvāṅgāsana, Supta Pādāṅguṣṭhāsana, seated forward bends, etc. Massaging the feet is always great. Take as many pillows and blankets as possible to support your lower back; maintaining the natural lordosis is good to avoid pressure on the discs, especially between sacrum and fifth lumbar. Support your neck. I always take a window seat to have better support against the wall or the window. The downside, of course, is that if you need to go to the bathroom, you have to jump over the next person if they are asleep, but that even gives you more exercise and an interesting challenge. I have done it many times successfully. For sleeping, cover your eyes with an eye bandage or t-shirt. Earplugs can also help. Although you may look like a mummy, you will rest in your little cave almost in a state of regression like a little kid under the blankets smiling to yourself. It is at least emotionally nurturing if not perfectly comfortable for your body. Also, surrender to the seat after creating a support system with blankets and pillows.

Don't over-adjust. See how children and animals seem to fall asleep blissfully in any position, even in a noisy environment. Learn from them, they are great teachers. I remember being in Śavāsana on the floor in Victoria Train Station in Bombay, one of the busiest places on earth—people walking over me, screaming tea vendors. After that, anything is possible!

I also suggest finding out if the airport has a playground area; that is a great place to practice, with toys to play with and bars to hang from. Chapels (usually non-denominational) are great for sitting meditation or Prāṇāyāma. They are always in remote places, and empty. Finding them will also give you a little adventure.

After the trip, in transit, do more backbends on those molded plastic chairs, which are not so good for sitting anyway. Use counters to release your spine. Stretch the hamstrings.

Also, after the trip, to minimize jet lag, practice Prāṇāyāma daily, Ujjāyi, Viloma or Nāḍī Śodhana. My teacher, Mr. Iyengar, suggested five minutes of inversions per time zone to erase the negative side effects of jetlag, such as spaciness and fatigue. He also suggests reversing circulation through inversions, since some people tend to retain fluids.

Finally, from an Ayurvedic point of view, Vāta doṣa is aggravated by traveling. Dryness of skin may occur or mild headaches. So, consistency of practice, even a minimal one, with deep breathing and a few mindful āsana, goes a long way to give you stability in a time of transition if not turbulence. Drink enough fluids and stay away from airy foods like popcorn, since you have been in the air already. And now you need to be grounded. Time for stews and soups with good bread. Or maybe a bath after oiling the skin with a Vāta-pacifying oil.

Try these things next time you travel.

LIVING STUPA

I have always been fascinated by stupas. Their symbolic, sacred, archaic architecture. Viewed from above, it is a maṇḍala. In the Center of a stupa, inaccessible, hide ritual objects, bones or relics. All we can do is walk around clockwise and identify with its Center. Same in sitting meditation. The center is mysterious, untouchable but we can experience it. Is it the Center of Gravity, the cave of the Sacred Heart, the Hara, the Ātman ? Is it a virtual place?

Some of the most beautiful stupas are in in Nepal and Śrī Lanka. Those in India have been destroyed or are not very well maintained, as, sadly, Hindu fanatics did not appreciate their anti-caste philosophy. Buddhism deeply influenced Yoga but is no longer alive in its birth-place.

I did a pilgrimage to Sārnāth and Sanchi in the Ganges Valley. Only one monk was left in Sārnāth, sweeping the grounds, and he was from Śrī Lanka. In Sanchi, the Jataka tales are sculpted on every wall like beautiful lace. I made a special trip one year to take photos. That was before the digital era. I took hundreds and was going to offer them to my friend Rafe Martin, a Zen Buddhist, Jataka tale specialist, and inspired storyteller. My camera cover was not sealed well so when we developed the film back home, they were all blank. Another tale of impermanence or just Buddha blinking an eye?

In 1972 I stayed for a few weeks on the hill of Swayambu stupa in Kathmandu. I rented a little room in a simple local house, ate pancakes once a day, the favorite breakfast of the American hippies and the monkeys. The following is an excerpt of the travel journal I wrote at the time:

Pilgrims from all countries, monks, nuns or families deambulate around the stupa, humming the sacred mantra. Dogs are sleeping, monkeys are fighting. Gods and goddesses are meditating behind golden curtains or hidden in the stone. Children are playing. Ashes are dispersed in the wind in all directions. Every morning, when we approach the Stupa, we are petrified. In the four directions, on every side of the harmika, two lotus eyes bloom in the stone. The undescriptable gazing of those eyes penetrate each and every atom. You cannot have eye contact with a Buddha. Transpersonal, He will transpierce you, looking at Nothing or gazing towards the Infinite.

Every morning, two probes auscultated us. Beyond language, concepts and images, they penetrate the depths of our being.

The stupa emits the fundamental Sound. Every day, we accord ourselves with the tuning fork of the Universe.

A transversal cut of the torso in anatomy books shows the central channel of the spine and concentric layers around it. With the power of mind and imagination you can enter by the gates—of palms, soles, fontanelle, perineum—or by osmosis from the outermost layers of the skin to the core.

We are a living stupa. We are Maṇḍala.

PART TWO

Āsana

NORMAL IS RELATIVE!

For a while I had a bumper sticker on my old 1967 Volvo: *Normal is relative.*
How do you know normal is normal?
Sometimes just the absence of pain is normal.
How do you know your neutral is neutral?

When a teacher or a book uses the term neutral spine, for example, what do they really mean and how does the student respond? In French, neutral gear is called dead point, le point mort. Can you find it when you are alive? Means the engine is not running, you are flying like a glider. Neutral cannot be something you hold or do. The practice is proactive and it reeducates. Then you have to accept, to let go. You cannot keep holding your belly in or Mūla Bandha all day long for example. Tone and let go.

How do you know balanced is balanced?

What is a "balanced pelvis?" I have seen videos where they demonstrate a pelvis too far forward, too far backward and then balanced in the middle! Balanced is actually a forward tilt but then again what is a normal forward tilt? Same for the feet, you will see teachings where they make you put more weight on the toes, then more weight on the heels and then "good posture" is in the middle, like 50/50. Whereas we know more weight on the heels is the way. More weight towards the toes aggravates falling arches and amplifies hallux valgus. In traditional cultures, the greater trochanter and the external maleolus are on the same vertical line viewed from the side. Even if we know the facts, there are ethnocentric views, fitness compulsive overtones, twisted body image ideals playing in the cultural background.

How do you know natural is natural?

Is breathing natural, when there is unconscious stress and the weight of the world on your shoulders? Is natural orange juice really natural?

On which pair of opposites is your middle way based? Balanced is not necessarily in the middle! My middle way is not your middle way.

Neutral, normal. Balanced, natural. Use these words carefully, not casually. They are seductive but loaded.

UPRIGHT OR UPTIGHT?

The course of every intellectual, if he pursues his journey long enough
and unflinchingly enough, ends in the obvious,
from which the nonintellectuals have never stirred.
—ALDOUS HUXLEY

Writing this very book and using the computer more and more these last few years, flying worldwide and driving across Europe as projects and business opportunities have increased, my psoas muscles have been shrinking proportionally and my upper back's kyphosis has become more pronounced (more hunched). It's likely that the vertical axis when standing and walking has also been altered. This invites greater awareness and more mindful Yoga practice. Now that the -dote has been diagnosed, the antidote can be applied! In Yoga āsana we have counterposes for this. I strongly suggest practicing them sooner as prevention (antidote before the dote) rather than later merely to get back on track (after the damage has been done). Of course, as we will explore, there are many factors contributing to the negative impacts and side-effects of lifestyle on posture, some of which are beyond the physical plane. All this to say, it's important to cultivate awareness, and then act on that awareness.

You have perhaps come across articles in mainstream magazines giving you tips and to-do lists, urging you to get a flat tummy and a flat everything, which supposedly would improve your postural alignment. Or maybe you have been verbally abused by parents and teachers about not slouching at the dinner table or in classroom. "Stand up straight!" they say. But what really is "good" posture? Is it natural or cultural? Ruled by instinct or by influence? Surely it is distorted by our belief systems, and body image issues, which is why it is not easy to change the existing patterns and even more difficult to envision a positive blueprint for posture as it manifests in lifestyle. Indeed, most anatomy and fitness models are ethnocentric.

How did we lose integrity of our postural balance and the vertical axis of our spine? And how can we find our way back to freedom, lightness of being and ease in posture? Is there a way to reverse the Psyche's side effects via Soma, to discover a reverse psychosomatic path? Yoga can go both ways. I believe this on a fundamental level. I teach and write, hoping more human beings will wake up and practice what is truly essential. Wherever there is life there is potential for reversibility. At worst, my outlook is that of a proactive, pragmatic pessimist. At best, I am an engaged and inspired optimist. For example, I believe that even with a difficult genetic history there is hope for rehabilitation, minimizing or delaying issues with a mindful consistent practice.

At the mall or airport more often than not we see the norm as a general collapse of body structure, closed ribcage trapping the lungs and heart, vertical sternum and sacrum, compressed if not vanished necks (belonging to what I call the "no neck" tribes), trapezius of steel, anxious diaphragms, fallen arches, tight bellies, and flattened spines. What is missing is pure, true integrated Tāḍāsana, a noble posture we see as a natural state in most traditional cultures still to this day. When one properly executes Tāḍāsana, known to Yoga practitioners as Mountain Pose, this means one is also in Aplomb. When people are tired, overstressed and underslept, depressed and uptight, posture becomes distorted. Most of us are literally ahead of ourselves, with the head ahead; and it shows. (See in the Verticality prescription page for how to bring your head back on the top of your shoulders or, more precisely, bring your whole body back under your head!)

At times I even wonder if the head might fall off like a bowling ball. We may see a center of gravity pushed forward from the hips as sexual innuendo (like with John Wayne); some would mislabel this as overarching or hyperlordosis. Sometimes the whole body falls forward like the tower of Pisa, as tension and angst govern all systems. Giacometti's sculpture serves as a symbol of this pattern.

There is a long list of hypotheses on how and why this shift happened: hyper-technology, virtual reality, lack of roots or connection with ancestors, steering our life toward myopic forms of success, intellect trumping instinct, culture trumping nature, dysfunctional extended families, mainstream religions moving away from spirituality, fundamentalism of all kinds, including, sadly, certain branches of Yoga (are they even branches?), repressed sexuality, following aesthetic criteria at the expense of harmony and poise, having a bizarre list of priorities (for example matching the color of your socks to the color of your car), fear of aging and death, layers of make-up covering suffering and fatigue, plastic surgery being accepted as a natural or almost spiritual evolution whereas most of the time it is simply masking existential anxiety, paralyzing the skin into artificial smiles and fixed robotic expressions instead of exploring Śavāsana and deep release of the braincells and the nervous system, overexercising versus using your body functionally with moderation and mindfulness in daily tasks. All these factors contribute to the shift away from the vertical axis and cosmic dharmic integration. But any of these can be minimized with Yoga and somatic practices, psychotherapy, deep relaxation, and by reinventing your life mission and making different life choices. Indeed, Yoga is a framework for this fundamental decision-making.

A few generations ago, my grandparents, living in the heart of rural Brittany and the Loire Valley, had wonderful posture: solid, extending from the earth, with the spine erect. I remember my grandmother sitting for hours at picnics in what is known in Yoga as Daṇḍāsana, Staff Pose or Upaviṣṭa Koṇāsana, Wide Angle Pose. She would be lacing and knitting with excellent posture, meaning with a natural dose of lordosis in the lumbar spine. She certainly hadn't taken any Alexander technique workshops; hadn't even travelled more than fifty miles from her house, ever. In fact, she had zero knowledge of what "Yoga" is. She didn't have Pilates workout on Tuesday night (or Wednesday!). She simply was perfect by instinct. In a few generations we went downhill. Cars and computers, car seats and airport molded seats all contributed to this gradual move away from intrinsically good posture. Technology has overruled our instincts, by adding more sedentary mental activities: driving, flying, etc . . . which all contribute to depressed flexion of the torso, osteoporosis, loss of tone, etc . . .

So why not, when you have a chance, reconnect with nature, your first nature, hike up sacred trails to mountaintops or walk the trail of the Appalachians, Saint Jacques de Compostelle, or the ones leading to the sources of essential rivers. Why not experience fully love, air, water, and food (in that order, if possible) as priorities. Why not see beauty everywhere as sacred in simple things, walk in the woods instead of running in the malls or biking indoors, stationary.

Of course, it is not just the fact that we are sitting more or that we are more sedentary, having drifted from our ancestral nomadic origins, that affects us in our posture and daily rituals. The whole civilized world suffers. Sure, traditional, untouched cultures—when they still exist (some in the Amazonian forest do not yet distinguish between labor and play)—have more structural integrity, but that doesn't mean they are "happier" or have a "good time." In reality, it is an even deeper paradox. We have all the technology, the food that we need (and supplements!?), while they have nothing and still have stunning postures, be it the women of South India, the Masai warriors from Africa, Tibetan or Peruvian shamans. Almost everyone who visits India is shocked by the hellish poverty and chaos they encounter but also amazed by the sheer spontaneous joy, laughter, and deep kindness that are almost omnipresent amidst such difficult living conditions.

Though we might wish for a romantic golden era, which, as we know, was not necessarily so golden, we cannot go backwards. Twelfth-century Europe was a battlefield of rape and murder; we know little about pre-Vedic India, and certainly next-to-nothing about postural habits in those times. As philosopher Douglas Brooks pointed out in a lecture, "Just because prostitution and slavery are old does not make them great or better!" The Western mind is so idealistic. We praise "back to nature" and "deep ecology," many times forgetting how education and literacy have helped entire populations to be aware, for instance, of what documents they may be signing. While the beauty, not to say functionality, of traditional posture is to be honored, one would be hard-pressed to wish for it at the expense of being manipulated by abusive landowners or dictatorial regimes. It is true, unfortunately, that many do not have this choice. Of course, the binary of good posture/literacy is not an absolute. Looking in America, and beyond, moreover, one sees manipulation and coercion being carried out regardless of the recipients' literacy or education. Nevertheless, given our resources, we must work to improve literacy around the world, while at the same time furthering our awareness of posture. Posture can inform life, as much as life can inform posture. We have the opportunity to restore some of this joy; if we can do so, it opens us back to the world.

So, witness as much as possible what is left from traditional cultures, with realism not voyeurism. Take advantage of the spreading of world music (a result of globalization) to appreciate differences. But also, for those of us with higher income per capita or education level: let's rediscover and reclaim standing, sitting, moving, walking, breathing—functional integrity—the same can be said for experiencing sexuality in its sacred and orgasmic song without guilt or shame. If you have a chance, explore again the texts of Wilhelm Reich, Thérèse Bertherat, Alexander Lowen, Karen McHose and Andrea Olsen to name a few.

Finding the balance between animalism and culture, instinct and education, is still a challenge and a work-in-progress. How can we combine the advantages of "civilization" without ruining our animal dimension? As Carl Jung once wrote, "Too much of the animal disfigures the civilized human being, too much culture makes a sick animal." Teachers, coaches, therapists of all kinds, philosophers and sages, friends and your own practices and explorations are here to assist you in your quest by offering you the signs, the access codes to be in "aplomb!" An informed repertoire of specific āsanas contributes to your potential as a radiant cell in a greater harmonious organism. Oh, to be integrated harmoniously in the widest ecology of life!

LESSONS IN PUPPETRY

In the mid-seventies, I worked as a puppeteer in an avant-garde theater troupe, *L'Atelier de l'Arcouest*, directed by Jean Dutour (who worked with Philippe Gentil, a world-renown puppeteer), touring the theaters and the streets of Europe, guided by insightful, visionary partners-in-play. Later, a few friends and I created our own troupe called *Théâtre-en-Ciel*. I was introduced to Yoga through the art of string puppets. In order to create desired movement and expression, I had to determine a corresponding center of gravity, recognize how many strings there were and where they attached. In all this I explored the relationship between the manipulator and the manipulee, subject and object, distance and fusion (all mystical and yogic topics indeed). I learned that it was up to me to choose how much to control and let go, how much yin in the yang, and vice versa, in order to create the illusion of life and death on stage. And now, as a Yoga teacher, these are all still options, only the floor of the Yoga center is the stage, and I the puppet. Geeta Iyengar has an amazing chapter in *Yoga for Women* on Yoga Kuruṇṭa in which she writes "Kuruṇṭī is a puppet, a doll made of wood. And in Yoga Kuruṇṭa one learns to manipulate oneself in the various Yoga postures by means of a suspended rope as if one were a puppet. Here the puppeteer and the puppet are one, performing their own puppet-show."

Usually, there's a string at the very top of the head, the fontanelle for human beings, (the Śirṣā of Head Balance). If you have been to Rajasthan in the northwestern part of India, you may have seen simple folk puppets that, with a few strings, almost walk, dance and perform all kinds of remarkable feats, given their limited resources (i.e. strings!). Secondary strings that come from the ears and in the back of the skull, at the occipital protuberance, can make the puppet say yes and no.

So, when you are standing yourself in Tāḍāsana, can you imagine and feel this invisible string, in Indian philosophy, the string of Brahma, the Brahma Sūtra, like a higher force, a cosmic magnet pulling you up and moving you like a chess piece on a board!? Gravity will be the counterforce. The vertical axis is essential in most cosmologies. Axis mundi refers to various mountains from Mt Kailash to Mt St Michel and the Black Hills of the Sioux and it becomes the spine and the central Nāḍīs in the human body. In classical Indian dance, Bharatanāṭyam or Kathakalī theater in South India, and in African dance as well, the space of the heart is always open. Hips and shoulders are the hubs for movement of the limbs and the vertical axis of the spine is not compromised. In fact, this is also validated in Yoga when we say shoulder and hip openers are prerequisites to prevent compensation in the spinal curves and to create a healthy, integrated āsana.

CULTURAL CONTRAST

Every time I come back from India, especially rural Southern India or Himalayan areas like Ladakh and Zanskar, and enter the dark underground world of the subway in Paris or New York, I am able to better see how culture has been embodied in both places. How almost everyone wears a mask of tension, somewhat paralyzed (and not necessarily from Botox injection), is depressed, hunched over, looking down and tired, sad, older than their biological age, with a gray aura despite abundance of food and wealth in a so-called civilized world! Actually, I have the feeling almost everybody falls forward, walking becomes an endless succession of falls that creates tight hamstrings, calf muscles, back and neck muscles, and extra tension in the whole superficial back line which Thomas Myers describes so well in his book *Anatomy Trains*: "The superficial back line, SBL, connects the entire posterior surface of the body from the bottom of the foot to the top of the head . . . as a continuous line of integrated myofascia." Other side effects include breathing anxiety and impact on the vertebral discs. In India we have the impression that they are falling or diving backwards so open are they in the front. No impact when walking; beyond this, there is gliding, lightness…

In India, Africa, South America but also in Europe up to the beginning of the century, being on a vertical axis, being "d'Aplomb" was a natural and undisturbed state. The energy ascends, is upright, not in an uptight (military-like) but rather in a fluid way. Keeping integrity of posture in very difficult living conditions is a miracle, to say the least. Tāḍāsana (Mountain Pose) is the foundation of human life. How can we cultivate or regain this integrity in a "natural" way? Not with some kind of posture police or over-controlling teachers who impose upon the body their limited version of good posture. Mindfulness and somatic intelligence have to be developed gradually. So, re-educating posture, reclaiming verticality, (if it has been lost), is a noble, essential, and, best of all, possible mission!

I still have this image of an Indian woman carrying a huge basket of pineapples on her head and also carrying my eldest son on her hip, walking gracefully on the beach of Mahābalipuram next to the Temple of the Sea. She likely walked miles and miles every day with that heavy load, and yet her smile was still so light and shining. This is the definition and execution of Grace . . . Harmony, poise, aplomb, effortless effort, it is all there. It is beautiful and functional, as Bauhaus architects insist that something is beautiful only if it is functional. We can say the same for animal and human beings! All those people carrying on the head should be on the cover of Yoga magazines and they may not even know what the word *Yoga* means.

YOGA OF VERTICALITY

[Description]

Let us look at what a harmonious, vertical posture is like when standing or walking.

- APLOMB: Virtual plumbline aligning vertically the outer ankle bone (maleolus), the greater trochanter, the acromioclavicular joint, and the inner ear.
- ENERGY VECTORS: Up the front of the torso, down the back releasing the trapezius muscles, up the back of the skull and down the facial muscles, releasing the lower jaw. So, the auriculo-nasal line is descending.
- FEET: More weight on heel than toes. Natural space between toes. Minimum or no pronation. No hallux valgus. Second toe (or more precisely midline between second and third toe) pointing forward. Feet parallel, with a natural tendency to externally rotate.
- LOWER LIMB: Vertical legs like stilts. Grounding or anchoring the head of the femur in the hip sockets, also called bringing the top of the thigh back.
- LUMBAR SPINE: Natural lordosis. Sacrum tilted forward about thirty degrees, no tucking of the tail. To tuck or not to tuck, that is the question!

- ORGANS and PELVIC FLOOR: Good residual tone needed in the pelvic floor to promote and ensure continence, good tone of deep abdominal wall to support the organs and good tone in the sole of the foot to guarantee propulsion in walking. But not a permanent holding in the name of peer pressure, the media in general, and poor self-esteem. Good residual tone is not driven by willpower and may require active practice and rehabilitation but then it will stay with you even in your sleep!

- RIBCAGE: Sternum high and uplifted, responding to the sacrum angle, wide open costal arch and diaphragm. You are the tallest and most vertical when the distance between the front of the sacrum and the top of the sternum is optimized. The chest cavity is no longer a cage but a three-dimensional elastic structure, protecting the heart and the lungs. Adaptable. I love to see the clouds and the birds inside the chest in the Magritte paintings *The Healer* and *The Therapist*. Maybe if you open the door of the cage, the bird of anxiety will be set free and vestigial wings of shoulder blades will fly again.

- RELAXATION: Find a good space, sukha, with a fluid body, child- and cheetah-like as opposed to being a freezer on wheels or a block of concrete with a broomstick as a spine. Being at ease with yourself invites instinct of balance and natural alignment. Stress tends to cloud the mind and make the body off-center. Of course, psychosomatics, life stories and challenges, traumas and accidents of all kinds play a huge role in the density and texture of the tissues. Standing is not much work in a state of equilibrium, when Tāḍāsana is passive, practiced with effortless effort. Weights and counterweights balance each other spontaneously in relationship to gravity. Āsana is a mobile becoming stable. If you regain harmonious posture or are in "Aplomb," collapsing and shrinking would take effort and feel like work. That would be being in literally good shape and good content.

YOGA OF VERTICALITY

[Prescription]

So many options to explore, practice and be aware of. Observation is key. As the French photographer Bresson once said: "See then act." Even Saint Augustine wrote that "Action follows being." So sometimes when you enter meditation in a pose, the pose holds you, the same way music plays you when you are in the zone. But you may also build and rehabilitate parts that have been wounded or have lost tone, flexibility or juice. What follows are a few proposals, chosen carefully for accessibility and efficiency. Sequencing here does not matter; it is less a Yoga Vinyāsa than it is a meditation. Theme and variation on cultivating the vertical axis. Feel the before and after in every practice. This is the best way to learn and integrate what works and what does not.

- Carry an object on the head (a small, round sandbag is ideal). Alternate squatting and standing in slow motion, go up and down steps, etc. Vertical axis guaranteed.

- Press the wall with the back of the head. It is the most direct way I know to reset the head. Stand about a foot or two away from the wall, then be in Tāḍāsana as if the floor was slanted. Only the back of the skull, slightly higher than the occipital protuberance, presses the wall, and the upper thoracic spine moves into the body, minimizing flexion of the upper back and lifting the sternum. This effectively tones the back of neck muscles, releases the throat, prepares you for inverted poses, and brings you back into balance. Watch for the lower ribs poking forward or bringing the hip joint too far forward, too anteriorly over the feet, both instances of compensation.

- Gastrocnemius and soleus stretch, Achilles tendon release. Roll a blanket and place your feet on it keeping the back heels on the floor and the feet parallel. Use the blanket as an arch support. Stay like this for a few minutes. You can explore flexing the knees a little to release and lower towards the Achilles tendon. Then stand again floor level, walking a step back off the blanket, closing your eyes. Don't you feel like you are falling backwards? Then you are truly verticalized! More experienced or flexible practitioners can forward fold and walk fingertips forward towards Downward Facing Dog, feet on the rolled blanket as if wearing extreme earth shoes with negative heel, without losing the contact of posterior calcaneum with the floor.

- Stand with one sandbag in each hand (as if you are carrying two identical suitcases), then drop them and take off like a rocket! Remember how, when you take off a heavy backpack after hours of hiking, you feel like flying!?

- Lift one or two sandbags in a Piñcha Mayūrāsana (Forearm Balance) pattern. Again, watch for compensation in hip joint. Ground the femurs and engage Mūla Bandha if needed to stabilize the pelvis from inside as well.

- Backpack belt. Start by placing an unlooped belt across your back, thread the belt under the armpits and then up, over the shoulders. Cross the belt on your back, just below your neck and pull the ends downwards and sideways. This will clear the trapezius tension, ground the shoulder blades, lift the sternum, bring inhalation into the upper lobes of the lungs that are often atrophied. It can be done in downward dog with a partner, what I call Husky-āsana, as if ready for the Iditarod race.

- Pādāṅguṣṭhāsana with concave back. Can be done with hands at the wall or belts if forward bending is limited. But most people will have a blind spot anyway, not seeing the flexion of the lower lumbar vertebrae when taking the big toes. Practice it facing a mirror. First question: do you see your lower back? Second question: is there a natural lordosis still!? Then you will realize how difficult of an āsana it is for those who have lost Aplomb, maybe have a mini-awakening or an ah-hah! moment and begin practice releasing the hamstrings and toning the back muscles, a great combination.

- All standing poses, Trikoṇānasa/Ardha Candrāsana for toning the back muscles and stretching the back of the legs, Vīrabhadrāsana 1 for opening the psoas, Vīrabhadrāsana 2 and 3 to sculpt the torso and open/stabilize the hip joint, if done mindfully without compensation, will contribute to a healthy integrated Tāḍāsana. After all, they are called standing poses for a reason. You access the blueprint.

Backbends and Forwardbends. In most backbends the sternum is lifted as in Setubandha Sarvāṅgāsana. In most forwardbends the tailbone is grounded and released like in Child's Pose or is naturally tucked like a fiddlehead so the combination of both merge into a functional standing pose. You can even do āsana algebra (Algebrāsana?!). For example: Piñcha Mayūrāsana + Paripūrṇa Nāvāsana = Śalabhāsana + Ardha Navāsana = Śīrṣāsana + Sarvāṅgāsana = Tāḍāsana! Practice each set as a polarity, let's say for one or two minutes in each pose and resolve the equation in Tāḍāsana. Notice the positive side effects locally and globally, images, visions, roots, state of the mind, etc.

- Passive backbend over a chair, a railing, a table, an airport counter, an upright piano, etc . . . to lift sternum and minimize kyphosis. This will be best to minimize aging of the spine and osteoporosis.
- Sit on your toes extended. Stretching flexors of the foot and plantar fascia. Then stand up. More weight on the heels? Good.
- Śavāsana with Prāṇāyāma support. Widen the costal arch, lift sternum, release trapezius, etc. Lie down for five or ten minutes (or more) to rest or practice Prāṇāyāma then stand up, after rolling on your side and go on with your life, renewed and realigned.

ADVENTURES FOR MORE EXPERIENCED YOGIS

- Go from Halāsana to Tāḍāsana through Cakrāsana, Adho Mukha Śvanāsana, Uttānāsana, rebuilding the vertical axis backwards! Rewind the tape and be in Tāḍāsana heaven, feel like a genie coming out of the lamp!
- Tāḍāsana/Śīrṣāsana/Tāḍāsana roundtrip. One of my students said recently, as we were practicing in class, "I wish we could go directly from one to another, roundtrip like a ninja!" So, stay in Śīrṣāsana with more weight on the Śirśā, the back of the fontanelle, for one minute or more then gradually come down with straight legs, land on your toes and if possible, go directly into Uttānāsana by pushing with your hands and up in Tāḍāsana. Can also be done by hanging in the ropes in Śīrṣāsana for a few minutes and gradually transition to Tāḍāsana through a forward bend. Appreciate how this gives you another chance to be cosmically reintegrated.

TĀḌA & ŚAVA

Why is Tāḍāsana the first pose in *Light on Yoga* and Śavāsana the last pose? Initiate a journey through all āsanas from Tāḍāsana to Śavāsana, from Alpha to Omega, from A to Anusvāra in the mantra AUṂ. Tāḍa and Śava truly are the two main challenges of the modern era Western world— functional standing posture and deep relaxation, verticality and horizontality. How they mutually influence each other is part of the quest.

Is standing on two feet still work-in-progress for human beings? How did we move from quadrupedalism to bipedalism, from water to land? How did the curves of the spine emerge, turning digitigrades into obligated plantigrades? Life as a sea cucumber, horseshoe crab, walking stick, jellyfish, or a turtle may be pleasant but standing would be a challenge!

FIRST ENCOUNTER WITH ŚRĪ B.K.S. IYENGAR

Besides the ongoing puppetry, my interest in posture fully peaked by assisting my Yoga teacher in Paris with her research. Noëlle Perez-Christiaens, at the time one of the most influential teachers in Europe, was also an anthropologist and historian of religions. We started to look at postures in daily life like you might in Alexander Technique. We asked, from an evolutionary perspective: what is it truly to be a human being, a biped, vertically oriented? How does it interfere with Yoga āsana, especially standing, seated and inverted postures that have Tāḍāsana as a blueprint? To her credit, we looked at other cultures than Indian. We looked beyond the East-West cliché, to Africa and the rest of the world. Collecting images and documentaries of how humans dance, stand, sit, bend forward, carry babies and baskets. We tried to see how the imagery could help us to practice Yoga more mindfully— closer to our original blueprint— using the balancing instinct, the way nature intended. All those years of practice and research are still a filigree in all I see and teach.

When Mr. Iyengar visited Paris in 1975 at Noëlle's invitation I received a shock. I was so taken by his ideas and his presence that I asked to become his student. (Shortly thereafter I was in Pune, India, where Iyengar lived and taught, to begin formal studies that would last more than three decades. At the time, there were no politics at his school, no ego, no fashion, no certification, just Yoga with a simple, joyous man and a creative teacher!) In Paris, we took him to visit a couple art exhibits at some of Paris' great museums, the Guimet Museum I recall, where he admired a Rājanāga in pink sandstone, and then a day later to a show on Ramses and Egyptian art. Relative to Indians, in Iyengar's mind, Egyptians were Westerners. He remarked, more or less, that in Indian art posture goes upward whereas in occidental art it falls forward as if the sculptor wanted us to look at the feet. It's true, if you look at some of the Egyptian sculptures, like the famous seated Scribe, the chest is collapsed, not as open as in Indian art, where you find majestic torsos, high sternums, wide open diaphragms, be the great early Śivas or the Apsaras of the Khajurao temples. Consider, too, the Buddha statues of the early Khmer civilization that you can see also in the Guimet museum in Paris (just cross the bridge from the Eiffel Tower!). So, one brief remark from the guru triggered a whole movement of research on Tāḍāsana, Head and Shoulder Stand. Indeed, through an ongoing dialogue between Noëlle and Mr. Iyengar the use of blanket supports came into being to respect the verticality of the human spine.

Should we carry objects on our heads again, relearn a lost tradition? Did we actually carry on our heads in our old European cultures and until when? We know that bakers still delivered breads on their heads in Paris during World War II. All of Southern Europe (Portuguese fisherman, Greek islanders, etc.) at this time still carry on the head. Then cars and bikes appeared and unless you had an open sunroof, head carrying was too challenging! So, the senior students and teachers, myself included, at the time at the Iyengar Institute (which became the Institut Supérieur d'Aplomb) were assigned various missions in various parts of Europe and the world. We took photos, documented and studied how people were behaving both in the media and in real life. We found a sort of pre-Yoga, consciousness-based practice that ultimately is also Yoga.

We need to tune the body and mind before entering the āsana, as well, and erase previous habits (if this is even possible). We must examine what is genetic, what is environmental, changeable, less changeable, or not changeable from an Ayurvedic point of view. If a musician plays on an out-of-tune instrument, no matter how skilled and aware he or she is, the music will be off-key (unless there is no awareness or denial, which is another matter altogether!). So, we need to go both ways. Formal practice of Yoga can improve posture, yes, but also awareness in daily life tasks can become an access code to the underlying sacred architecture of Yoga āsana. A sort of ping pong goes on between passive and active, conscious and unconscious Tāḍāsana. And sometimes the bridge is closed: this explains how some dancers, gymnasts, and even yogis might have great posture, acrobatic skills, and poise when on stage or performing but at the dinner table, afterwards, might be depressed, closed, retracted. On the surface, this is paradoxical; but don't we all have multiple personalities, one overconfident, poised, defiant, and ascending, while another is depressed and neurotic!? Nevertheless, in Open Sky Yoga, we can creatively explore our contradictions, feet on the earth, head in the sky.

WALKING GAMES

Here are a few ways to reset walking and find lightness of being in every step. All standing āsanas and many other classical Yoga postures will help indirectly to walk more efficiently on the vertical axis. But I find also the following walking games very helpful.

BACKWARD WALKING SLOW MOTION

Tracking the parallelism of the feet, the rolling from toe to heel. There is also backward running, good concept but actually dangerous! Some records of the mile and marathon retro-running are held by Indians of course. By the way scallops can also move backward . . . Walk ten to twenty small steps backward, then reverse it, walk forward again at normal speed and feel the amazing shift. It sounds crazy but after walking backward, you won't fall forward anymore when you walk forward!

STILT WALKING

Walk on the back of the heels with locked extended knees, with maximum dorsiflexion of the foot, foot and toes off the ground. But keep the feet themselves in deep plantar flexion as if you were picking up something. The deep flexors are the "engine," the turbo reactor of the walk! What would happen if we were walking with no ground underneath? Our feet would be moving like jellyfish or diaphragms in water! So, stilt walk with very short steps, in fact if you have real stilts you need to keep moving! Then let go and walk normally . . . again, observe the shift.

CHEAP BUDGET CARTOON WALK

Imagine that you are rolling the floor backward proactively with your feet. As if the floor was moving backward when you walk forward. Relativity walk. To stimulate the wheel/push scooter action of the feet. This will propulse your foot higher in space. This is why in India or other traditional cultures we see the entire bottom of the back foot of the person walking in front of us, hanging vertically. Allowing us to read the future in their soles!

GLUTEUS FOCUSED WALK

At every step, add strong gluteus contraction to the existing one. Gluteus power allows psoas opening and speed as well as a fantastic sacroiliac 3D micro-massage. You can actually place your fingertips along the sacro-iliac fault and feel it. You will have alternative buttock squeezing action! It will propel you faster forward. You can combine with the previous one for a high-speed walk.

POST WARRIOR ONE WALK

Practice Vīrabhadrāsana 1 for about one minute, on one side keeping back foot in the sagittal plane. Then walk. Compare both sides. Repeat on the other side.

NATURAL WALK

Enjoy walking like an animal. With no plan! No walking meditation, no fitness walk, forget all exercises. Just walk in a state of innocence.

HOW TO SIT

We are the only species on earth to have so many options for standing, sitting and eating, etc. Maybe it is a poisoned gift, since we also have the possibility for the intellect or the mental layers of ourselves to interfere with, if not overrule, primal instinct, reflexes and animal nature. Sometimes it is a good thing to be civilized; sometimes it is oppressive. That is why we have to be educated or reeducated, a noble task. We also have to reclaim our instincts, our sense of the natural buried under layers of belief systems (education, religion and politics).

Originally, Yoga was about focusing, being conscious or just being. Being in touch with the source of life. Sitting was probably the first and only āsana.

On the practical side, we pass a lot of our lives sitting at desks, driving, flying, playing music, writing, emailing, eating, etc. Our lives are lived mostly in unconscious patterns of flexion—forward bending in the sagittal plane—and then when we die, we shift to the ultimate deep relaxation, Śavāsana.

So first let's say that there is a lot of casual, informal sitting in daily life. If I am hanging out with friends, listening to Bob Dylan, I don't care so much about form or alignment. It is casual sitting. I cannot police myself all day long. That would be compulsive—and even mindfulness can be compulsive! I am hoping that my formal practice in Yoga will allow my body to have healthier patterns on its own. Being relaxed and receptive is most important.

But as soon as mindful breathing is involved—when you are doing formal meditation practice in any tradition, or when you need internal focus to dwell in the present moment—then the vertical axis and the alignment of the spine are essential. Energy (Prāṇa, Chi, Life Force) can flow more harmoniously and breath can reclaim its full territory. Freedom of the diaphragm and the pelvis are crucial in Yoga, since these are places where physical and emotional tensions are stored (along with the hamstrings, the hip flexors, the trapezius, scalenes, jaws, etc.). Everything, the story of your life, is printed in the body.

Sitting on the floor is challenging for non-squatting cultures. And because our level of awareness is sometimes low, we don't realize the negative side effects of sitting patterns until full-blown sciatica pain is shooting down the leg, or a disc becomes paper-thin, or trapezius muscles become like steel! Some of us are also too idealistic and think that living at the floor level is going to be healthy and so much better than chairs for our backs, where even in India they like to sit on something and in Zen monasteries they use a Zafu. So, let's look at some guidelines for sitting effortlessly and with maximum structural integrity.

I believe that you can re-pattern the whole body, erase or erode old dysfunctional habits, by being supported and by mindfully adjusting various components of the body in relationship to gravity. Sitting is a balancing act, like any pose on earth. So, you have to balance weights and counterweights of the body.

Here are some guidelines for sitting in a simple crossed-legged posture or in the beginning stage of half-lotus:

1. Make sure your knees are lower than your hip joints. Sit on the front of the sitting bones but not excessively (center front of the ischial tuberosities). Don't sit too close to the front edge of the seat, or you will have too much weight bearing on your knees.

2. Maintain a healthy lordosis. Lordosis (concave lower back) is not a problem, but a lack or an excess of it is. And that is quite subjective according to your belief system or even culture. Ballet,

aerobics, tai chi, African dance and various Yoga schools all have different takes about "tucking" the tailbone or not, contracting the abdominal wall or not, Mūla Bandha or not, etc. In my experience releasing the belly is good, as is accepting a forward tilt of the pelvis to create or maintain our humanness through the lumbar curve.

3. Let the upper body, chest and shoulders act as a natural counterweight to the pelvis and the belly. If you were against a wall, your shoulder blades would touch the wall. That will prevent hunching the upper back. It will open the heart center and release the solar plexus. In more marketable terms, it will prevent aging—or, as some wellness gurus say, "promote youthfulness."

4. Center your head at the top of your spine. This will happen spontaneously (you can consider the skull a giant vertebra with a mutation) unless the spine has been distorted by a genetic pattern such as a deep kyphosis or hunchback.

5. The vertical axis is present and the spine will ascend like a sunflower searching for the light.

Alignment is not compulsive (though it can be if you are a fundamentalist). Alignment saves energy. By adjusting the structure, the inner architecture of the pose, you allow the whole body to release and find a harmonious balance between agonist and antagonist muscles. This creates a healthy relationship.

There is no such thing as a straight back or a straight spine. The spine is more like a river or life or a snake, more like the sacred Gaṅgā than the Erie Canal. By letting go of unnecessary tensions, you allow yourself to be moved by the breath, and be vulnerable like leaves and branches of a tree are moved by the wind.

Again, as you sit, observe, feel, touch. Keep the back and front muscles soft. Don't become a statue. Touch the paraspinal muscles in the lower back. They should not be hard but have the texture of a perfectly ripe avocado. What we call abdominal breath is actually more diaphragmatic breath in a relaxed, meditative state. And finally, abdominal muscles should be available for laughing!

Make sure that spinal processes of the lumbar vertebrae are in, creating a nice little groove. This ensures a healthy lordosis. Bones are in, muscles are out. Release facial muscles and sensory organs. Pacify the brain, then descend into the cave of the heart. Settle down, literally, further into the diaphragm, into the belly, into the bowl of the pelvis at the bottom of the well. Feel the breath expand and release. Identify with the diaphragm. You are the diaphragm; it is not a foreign object! It is like sailing on the internal sea.

Everything has a sitting quality in sitting meditation. It is like a holotropic pattern or fractals. Sitting is everywhere. The brain sits inside the head, the lungs and the heart rest on the thoracic diaphragm. The abdominal organs sit on the pelvic floor and the legs on the earth. (The only troubling thing is that the earth itself is suspended in space!) It is normal to feel lightness, effortlessness, suspension, levitation, spaciousness at times, and other times groundedness, being rooted, anchored in Mother

Earth. Sometimes I experience both simultaneously. Experiment with those sensations after ten or fifteen minutes of sitting, when the mind begins to settle into silence.

Because of illusions or distortions of perception, it is helpful to get feedback from a teacher or a friend. I have seen people with very rounded backs or flat lumbar spines thinking they were too arched. It is always relative. For example, lying down on your back in Śavāsana can feel like a back-bend for a person with a collapsed spine, because relatively speaking lying down will unfold and open the front of the body and extend the spine more than sitting or standing.

Of course, the way you stand affects the way you sit and vice versa. And they both affect the way you breathe, and to a certain extent your emotional state. It is too simplistic and naive to think you can change your mind state only by changing your posture, but it definitely has an impact. An open chest with a radiant solar plexus and a wide diaphragm is a plus to face the challenges and intensity of life. Similarly, any form of trauma will tend to increase density of muscles, freeze the connective tissues, disturb the nervous system, and increase flexion of the spine.

So, readjusting the sitting body—fine tuning the release and comfort level of the pose—make the pose less physical. Feeling the energy of the subtle body can be the focus of the meditation itself—being in the moment, observing, witnessing. The seated āsana becomes an archetype, a symbol of a centered human being deeply connected to the spirit of the breath.

I would like to end this with two quotes, one from a visionary Rolfer, also a meditator, and one from my teacher, who has explored so deeply the subtle aspect of breath and posture so that separation between Haṭha Yoga and Rāja Yoga no longer exists:

The posture of meditation itself may appear as a kind of somatic koan . . . The koan may be simply stated: In a sitting or standing position surrender the entire weight of the body to gravity, and yet remain as tall as you possibly can be.

—Will Johnson, *The Posture of Meditation*

The spine in man can be compared to an Indian lute or vina. The gourd is the head from which sound is produced. The nose is the bridge which controls the sound vibrations caused by inhalation and exhalation. The resonance depends upon the tautness of the strings. If they are too loose no sound is produced; if they are too tight there is no vibration and they may even snap. String tension is adjusted to produce the required resonance, intensity and pitch. In the same way, the nāḍīs and nerves in the spinal column have to be positioned so that the breath can move with rhythm and harmony.

—B.K.S. Iyengar, *Light on Prāṇāyāma*

SIT!

Sit! This is not about dog obedience class but human mindfulness training.

Find a seat high enough for you to maintain the vertical axis of your spine. This maintains the natural forward angle of the sacrum, the sacred bone. Leg positions don't matter as much; how the spine grows out of the base, the altar, is more important. Sit in Vīrāsana, Sukhāsana, Ardha Padmāsana, Siddhāsana—as you like, as long as your knees are lower than your hips. The exception is Padmāsana, but that is another story.

The sternum is high, poised, elevated, like the one of a bird or of a small child. They are not the only beings who could have a noble pose. Every human being deserves space for the heart to pulse and the lungs to breathe.

First observe how you sit. Let the structure of your āsana, the ethos of sitting, be the center of your attention. Every school, every spiritual current or tradition may have a different proposition of focus: the heart, the hara, the navel, the Suṣumṇā Nāḍī, the whole āsana, the breath, the present moment, the infinite, the emptiness, the fullness. In sitting we have a double winner: the body is sitting, so we feel the spine, the balance between front and back body. We create ease without collapse and vigilance without rigidity. That means observing without being frozen. Be a live breathing statue.

Check when you sit if you are ahead of yourself. Is your head ahead? Are you using your back muscles as emergency breaks? Are you behind yourself? Are your shoulders posterior to the pelvis while there is tension in the hip flexors—especially the fourth head of the quadriceps, bypassing the hip joint? Are you in sync with yourself? That means that you finally are integrated on the vertical axis! You are yourself! No projections, a direct perception, no distance between subject and object. A perfect blend!

Tune in a subtle way the posture itself. This requires receptivity. Pratyāhāra, turning senses inwards, should be a prerequisite to all Yoga. It is a form of positive sensory deprivation, a selective focus.

Wherever the mind goes, the breath goes. And wherever the breath goes, the mind goes. If the center is undisturbed, it is like sitting in the eye of the storm. Even if the weather outside is erratic, agitated, changing, the inner weather is stable, quiet, silent, warm. There is only the wind of breath ascending and descending. The inner Gulf Stream of the vāyus, the natural irrigation system, is reaching each and every cell. That is now the center of attention. See how we go from external to internal, toward deeper layers of the same entity, the sitting āsana.

In winter the organism needs to adapt to external weather, sudden changes or intense conditions by practicing Bhastrikā, Prāṇāyāma and warming āsanas. But most importantly, you have to find refuge in your own cave, protected from physical and emotional bad weather. It is a low form of hibernation.

Just sit, with a high standard of physical and physiological adjustment. The guidelines are not a distraction; it is the meditation itself. Those micro pendulum-like movements, rocking the body from its base, spiraling out, oscillating. Those are signs of surrender. You cannot make IT happen; IT happens. (That could be another bumper sticker without the "Sh"!) You may think you are the pilot, but you are just the flight attendant; the flight is the sitting meditation, the Āsana or the Prāṇāyāma. Then all instructions are no longer instructions—they are descriptions, signs, metaphors, validations of your state of being. Like the softness of the eyes, the release of the corners of the lips in an unintentional half smile, the release of the forehead. Young from inside. Ageless. Timeless. Genderless. Then it is truly rewarding. Contentment. Bliss. Here there are no strict defined lines; it's more like watercolors. Laser-sharp concentration but softness of skin. All pores open like receptive eyes. Your face is like a full moon with a halo, a diffused light, soothed and soothing.

SATELLITE DISH

Āsana is the Seat. Ās- means seat. Building a seat for Prāṇāyāma and Dhyāna is a ritual. With a seat, you can appreciate the lordosis. "Topsacrumin!" would have shouted Mister Iyengar! Feel the open Tāḍāsana chest . . . the sacrum-sternum connection . . . the ascending energy of the spine and the psychic protection of Ananta's seven-headed hood, which I call the satellite dish. This is why the jaw has to relax, why Jālandhara Bandha is special, why the cervical flexion reflex has to be promoted versus the startle reflex. So, the reptilian brain is protected and open as a Source of Mystery.

STALACTITES & STALAGMITES

In deep caves stalactites meet stalagmites, sometimes forming a column. Similarly, Prāṇavāyu meets Apānavāyu in sitting meditation or in Tāḍāsana. In French we memorize the difference between the two by saying: "Les stalactites tombent (fall) et les stalagmites montent (ascend)."

WHATEVERĀSANA

SĀLAMBA TOWEROFPISĀSANA

In Head Balance with all the weight on the elbows, whole body slanted like the leaning Tower of Pisa.

SĀLAMBA BANANĀSANA

In Head Balance, feet hanging behind the head like a vertical Śalabhāsana.

CHARLESTONADHOMUKHAŚVĀNĀSANA

Bending the knees sideways in Downward Facing Dog and moving them like a Charleston pattern from side to side to test the release of the hip joint.

ŪRDHVA ŚĪRṢĀSANA as Tāḍāsana

ŪRDHVA TĀḌĀSANA as Śīrṣāsana

TIPYĀSANA
Downward Facing Dog with uplifted sitting bones. Prolongation of spine and legs crossing in space like the poles of a tipi.

SUPTAPĀDAṄGUṢṬHACOUCHĀSANA
Suptapādāṅguṣṭhāsana with one bent leg on a couch.

BAMYANĀSANA
Half-moon Pose in lateral flexion like Parighāsana, top arm over the ear and with all fingertips touching the floor.

PARIPŪRNAMACARENAVĀSANA
Dancing the Macarena in Full Boat Pose.

HOMAGE TO STEPHEN HAWKING

We have to remember the passing of noted physicist Stephen Hawking who died recently in England. Born on the 300th anniversary of Galileo's birthday, he died on Einstein's birthday—Pi Day, 3.14! For whatever reason I cried when I heard the news. Glenn Gould, Ramana Maharshi and Michel Petrucciani came spontaneously to my mind by association. No great Tāḍāsana for them in their tortured embodiment but it did not matter for those four extra-ordinary human beings, channeling, fully alive and receptive with a cosmic dimension. Maybe a much-needed reminder not to be a Tāḍāsana fundamentalist or have an Iyengar Tāḍāsana complex of superiority?

TUNING

Yoga practice is reversed psychosomatics. That is why it takes time—there are no 100 percent guarantees and it's not easy! The same āsana can be modified, adjusted to generate different side effects. It is nice to be able to tune an āsana, like a flute, but it is even better if the tuning holds. This is also why in any pose we need space to "tune" towards sharp or flat as needed.

ANA-TUMMY

How much momentum has your omentum!? Celebrating the 89th organ!

The omentum has three basic functions: it stores fat deposits; it contains milky spots that contain white blood cells, which boost immunity by getting rid of cellular debris; and it isolates wounds and infections by wrapping itself around infected areas. Omentum, peritoneum and mesentery are yoked! The mesentery is now officially an organ. One more reason to worship and respect adipose tissue. A protective layer for the organs. So, don't get too dry, we need juice/rasa and fat. Don't run too many marathons in a row or repeat too many Caturaṅgas sweating in overheated rooms . . . addiction and depletion are often good friends. Quite a number of yoginis and yogis I met over the years in Yoga conferences are undernourished at a deeper level, Vāta aggravated, too thin and chiseled, but they think they look young and healthy.

One more reason to retreat in Śavāsana and let Mother Nature heal. Let Vyāna Vāyu expand in all cosmic directions.... and be in sync with the Kaphaness and Inertia of Mother Earth.

ANATOMI-FA-SOL

A little Om work and research for you, the reader:

Rectus capitis posterior minor: its connection to the dura mater.

Nuchal ligament: its history in comparative anatomy.

Sesamoid bones: compare them in horses and humans.

Sella turcica: why is she so special?

Psoas minor, sternalis, pyramidalis, peroneus tertius, plantaris, palmaris longus:
Why are they on their way out?

Notochord: prehistory of the spine.

Recti abdominis of the turtle: Where are they located? Do they have a six-pack?

Adductor of the scallop: See why life is simple for them.

Quadrate bone, articular bone, and columella: follow the migration of reptiles' jaw bones, which became later our middle ear bones. That will be a great way to travel through time.

Have fun!

LORD OSIS

Most people with lower back pain blame the "sway back" or too much lordosis, but my clinical observation is that it's most often the other way around. The back is too flat. Paraspinal muscles are undertoned in the back and abdominal muscles are overtoned in the front, perpetuating flexion. The chest is depressed as a side effect. But in some people's minds they believe or maybe somebody told them that they were too "arched" (whatever that means). Often the hip joint is anterior to the ankle joint so it is not really hyperlordotic but may feel and/or look like it. We need stability between S1 and L5 and residual tone in the lumbar paraspinal muscles.

Of course, hyperlordosis or hyperkyphosis do exist. But actually, the second one is more commonly of a problem and probably the most important to counter as it accelerates the aging process and bone mass loss, and it creates pressure on heart and lungs. Hyperlordosis is usually occasional in extreme movement like deep spinal extension for those with loose ligaments, contortionists who sometimes have six lumbar vertebrae.

Now, to minimize kyphosis it's best to do supported backbends for the thoracic spine, Setubandha Sarvāṇgāsana with shoulder support to maximize the lift of the sternum and backbends on chairs, railings, back rollers, etc.

In Yoga we need counterposes to stay mobile and adaptable. Any abdominal toner will be an antidote to hyperlordosis, especially half boat and full boat, assuming the lumbar spine can/will truly flex (some Tāḍāsana fundamentalists think lordosis should be maintained in Navāsana). Ūrdhva Prasarita Pādāsana is also great. Abdominal muscles are flexors and in this context it is welcome.

Lordosis (neither hypo nor hyper) and laughing are proper to humans and need to be invited and cultivated or reset if needed. That is why Śalabhāsana, Supta Vīrāsana and Piñcha Mayūrāsana are important āsanas. They feed Tāḍāsana. Please, forget navel to spine, belly in, zipping your lower belly up and tucking heavily the tailbone. Liberate Tāḍāsana! Learn from traditional cultures where deep lordosis and natural postural integrity is the norm. Tone what needs to be toned or reeducated in appropriate āsanas and leave Tāḍāsana blossoming alone. Tāḍāsana needs to have a life on its own.

For a homework assignment I gave during a Teacher Training, one participant wrote (as a joke) a Prayer to Lord Osis! Another one a few years back spelled it "lower dosis" to which I answered in my feedback that if there is a lower dosis, there must be also a higher dosis.

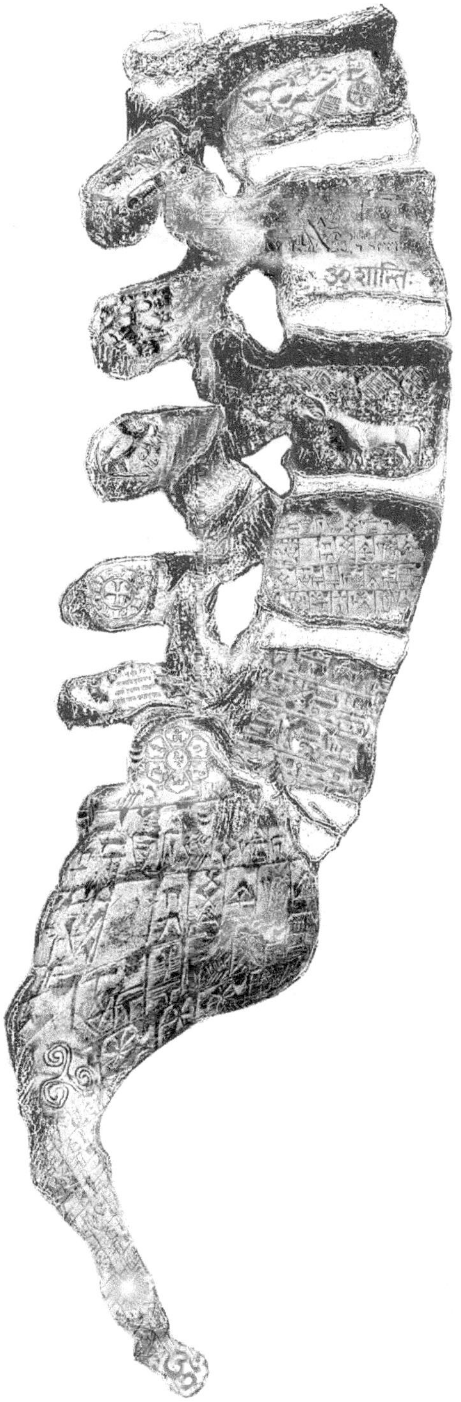
ॐ शान्तिः

SPINAL WAVES

If we had stayed on all our fours
Would tails have stayed on too?
Or does Time just claim certain things
No matter what we do?
—RICHARD ROSEN

Spinal waves—or cat/cow as it is known in the cultures of fitness, physical therapy and Western adaptation of Yoga—have been taught everywhere as a warm-up or part of back rehabilitation. I see the cat, never really saw the cow. We don't really know when they appear for the first time; they are not part of traditional classical Yoga, even less from the Krishnamacharya/Iyengar side of the spectrum. In early days I disregarded them as a cliché and something inauthentic. It is true that if they are presented as a mechanical exercise without consciousness, they are not very interesting. But in recent years I have learned to appreciate what spinal waves have to offer, and now I teach them consistently. They give the practitioner a way to mobilize the spine and explore the polarity of flexion and extension with the various curves of the spine, even though hamstrings, deep rotators or shoulder muscles might be tight. They also give a chance to reconnect with early patterns of life. When they are practiced mindfully, the spine moves with fluid undulations—hence the name "spinal waves."

From a teacher's point of view, reading the spinal movement will allow you to see the general fluidity or the quasi-paralysis of certain students' bodies. Observe how the freedom of being or the rigidity of blocks is revealed by these simple, primitive and playful patterns. The inability to let go or the absence of connection with body sensations can be side effects of cultural inhibition as well as the results of a sedentary lifestyle when sitting, driving, etc. are prominent.

Spinal waves also reveal which segments of the spine are hyper-mobile and which ones are overly rigid. Spinal waves have variations that can offer the student spatial exploration in the various planes of movement. They bring us in touch with primary and secondary curves of the spine and with essential patterns of development both ontogenetic and philogenetic. Through the practice you can evaluate how lifestyle and habits have minimized or exaggerated the curves of the spine, very often the cause of back problems.

The synchronization of the breath, though optional, can also test the ability of the student to focus and connect movement and breath harmoniously. Some people will show extreme confusion, reverse the patterns or create tension in facial muscles. It means they will reproduce those patterns in many other contexts. Spinal waves give an opportunity to promote and appreciate the value of deep relaxation, freedom of breathing and playfulness of movement.

We can also see that almost everybody tends to lead with the head (chin, eyes, frontal brain). Instead, initiate action from the tailbone, which sometimes we call the small brain.

Let's focus now on the most common one in the sagittal plane then we will look at the lateral and transversal waves.

SPINAL WAVE 1:
SAGITTAL FLEXION AND EXTENSION
alias cat/cow alias the Dolphin alias Adho and Ūrdhva Mukha

You're playing with the following pairs of opposites: mountain /valley; back muscles stretch/tone; abdominal tone/release; pelvic floor open/contract; and inhalation/exhalation.

Here's how to do it: Position yourself on your hands and knees, with a blanket under your knees (kneecaps are floating in synovial fluid and need protection). Keep your hands and fingers on the Yoga mat for a better connection with the floor, hands slightly ahead of shoulders. Spread your fingers as wide as possible, thumbs stretched toward each other to distribute weight equally and circularly on all knuckles. This minimizes pressure on your wrists. Compare how this feels with how it feels to keep your hands passive and your hands directly under your shoulders. That setup increases stress on the wrist joint. (The same is true in Adho Mukha Śvanāsana—downward-facing dog—and hand balances.) Press forward and down with exhalation. Vacuum the floor with inhalation, so the palms of the hands become like suction cups. Pressing your hands into the earth increases range of flexion and helps you project into your kidneys. Adjust the distance between your hands and knees to have enough space to move the spine. Keep hip-space apart between the knees. (Tight and/or inhibited students will sometimes keep their knees together or not release the ankles. They could also be scared or in pain.)

If your wrists are vulnerable, go on your forearms. You can also rest in Child's Pose at any time if needed.

Let's begin with the movement of the spine from tail to head:

Start with letting go of the spine, like a loose string. Neutral is when you let go, not when you are flat (a flat back is already flexion).

If your spine doesn't let go, the arch is not created by gravity. This could be due to fear or lack of mobility (in cases of osteoporosis, fibromyalgia or multiple sclerosis, for example). Or, it might be the product of a belief system that says the abdominal wall should be tight at all times or that a flat lumbar spine is good. Everybody needs more release and letting go. Without release, nothing will move naturally. The spine has to be available to be moved by consciousness and by breath. Saint Augustine said that Action follows Being. Or to use a musical analogy, silence is the cause of all sounds.

Begin exhaling and initiate the flexion of the spine from the tailbone, the coccyx, pointing it toward the floor. Let the lumbar spine follow, then upper back and finally the neck, by moving the chin toward the chest. Create a dome by moving both extremities of the spine away from each other. Engage abdominal muscles and draw them toward the spine as you exhale fully. For those familiar with Mūla Bandha, note that it is triggered spontaneously at the end of exhalation.

Reverse everything with the inhalation. Un-tuck the tailbone, release abdominal muscles and open the pelvic floor in order to inhale freely and let the back bending move through the spine toward the neck as a wave. Bring shoulder blades down and in, to lift the sternum forward and up as in Ūrdhva Mukha Śvanāsana (Upward-facing Dog) or Piñcha Mayūrāsana (Arm Balance), then point the top of the head forward and up. See that the cervical spine doesn't hyper-extend (no whiplash!) and so the craniosacral pattern is integrated.

Arms will spontaneously turn medially with the flexion (forward bending of the spine) and laterally rotate with the extension (backbending).

Adjust your center of gravity. Move slightly forward in backbending and back toward the heels with flexion. Be sure not to exaggerate, especially in extension to avoid compression. Also, stay in touch with the traction between tail and head at any given time.

Explore breathing options. If you know it, try Ujjāyi breath for slow movements. Bhrāmarī Prāṇāyāma (humming with exhalation) can also be great for releasing tension. Your natural state of breath is fine just to explore patterns. Just let the breath be. You can also stay in one of the final positions and breathe several cycles, as you would do in a classical āsana. Observe where the breath is resonating in your body.

As you reach empty lungs retention, Bahya Kumbhaka, you have the opportunity to practice the three Bandha (Jālandhara Bandha is there as neck is in deep flexion, Mūla Bandha is a natural and healthy addition to deep exhalation and Uḍḍīyāna Bandha may happen spontaneously as the lungs are empty.) If you are really adventurous and you pull with your hands, like vacuuming the floor (but still pushing simultaneously), you will enjoy a convincing Madhya Nauli, sealing the linea alba. Release them all to welcome the next inhalation. For me it counts as a lovely morning ritual.

You can also explore micro-flexion and -extension, localized into a specific segment of the spine.

If practicing with sound, choose music with loops or wavelike patterns. *Facades* by Philip Glass, *I Will Not Be Sad in This World* by Djivan Gasparian, or even David Darling's *Minor Blue* are good pieces for five or seven minutes of dolphin-esque play.

Enjoy surfing the spinal waves!

SPINAL WAVE 2: LATERAL FLEXION AND EXTENSION

alias the Trout alias Parśva

The waves we are exploring and practicing now involve lateral flexion and extension. Lateral movement is present in fishes of all kinds, in snakes and in salamanders. These creatures undulate with grace. Rotation is more of the spiraling movement, a vortex, moving like a slow-motion propeller. Those patterns are found in the animal kingdom as well as in plant life. Classical Haṭha Yoga āsanas, postures, also include some of those, very often in combination with each other. Flexion is found in most forward bends, and extension is found in all backbends. Lateral flexion is harder to find. Look at Parighāsana (Gate Pose) and Parivṛtta Jānu Sīrṣāsana (Revolved Seated Forward Bend) as the best examples. For rotation, look for examples with Parivṛtta Trikoṇānasa (Revolved Ttriangle) and Bhāradvājāsana (Seated Rotation).

This is an important one because human life is mostly sagittal, so moving laterally is underestimated and unexplored territory. Although you have to be a skilled Yoga practitioner to access some of the previous āsanas, you can practice spinal waves on all fours in your first session! So, spinal waves allow beginner students to explore the lateral plane. They bring the student in touch with the subtle undulations of the spine, with a great sensation of release in the kidney area and in the quadratus lumborum muscle of the extended side. The waves cannot be done without awareness or in a mechanical way like sit-ups or push-ups. They are not about "reps" or exercise but about awakening the spine. Mindfulness is required!

To practice lateral flexion and extension, place hands on the floor just a little ahead of the shoulders or forearms if the wrist is vulnerable. Bring the spine into moderate forward flexion so that the lower back looks almost like Child's Pose, then exhale and bring the tailbone toward one side—let's say right—and let the crown of the head move toward the same side of the mat to create a moon crescent shape. Then inhale moving back to the mid-line and exhale to the other side.

Several mistakes should be avoided:

1. The head will tend to rotate instead of moving laterally. You have to face the floor at all times; don't try to see your tail with your eyes. See how a crocodile moves his head and where his eyes are. Or imagine you are a cyclops with the fontanelle as your only eye!

2. If the hips move in the opposite direction to the shoulders, no flexion is created—just a swing like Chubby Checker!

3. The head might tend to lead instead of the tail, or it might move faster than the tailbone. It will help to keep the lower back in forward flexion and not to make the movements too big or too fast.

In addition to mistakes to avoid there are some options for exploring the pose's possibilities:

1. Spread the floating ribs away from the pelvis to create space on the expanded side.

2. If you like you may sustain the pose on one side and breathe into it. This is great for asthma as it opens and releases intercostal muscles.

3. You can combine lateral and sagittal movement in a slow aquatic dance, a play between the Dolphin and the Trout.

SPINAL WAVE 3:
ROTATION IN THE TRANSVERSAL PLANE
alias the Otter alias Parivṛtta

This is a contralateral pattern that you find in early development of the child.

Again, confusion can be present, since a lot of primary reflexes have been overruled by intellect or by stress. (The same confusion may occur in students who cannot differentiate Trikoṇānasa and Parivṛtta Trikoṇānasa.) So be particularly attentive to the placement of hands and knees.

On all fours, leave the right hand on the mat and the left knee ahead of the right knee (by 1/2 foot to a foot, since too much distance between the knees will induce hyperlordosis and will not allow the tailbone to release away from the head).

The left hand can rest on the left hip, or the left arm can be stretched overhead as in Utthita Parśvakoṇāsana, Extended Side Angle Pose. (This latter arm position is too stressful for students with rotator cuff injuries.) Exhale and rotate around the central axis. Then you can stay in the rotated position and breathe, rotating deeper with the out breath. Or change sides with the inhalation. Keep the chin released inward and bring the tailbone slightly under. These adjustments will help elongate the spine. This practice will be a great reference for Revolved Triangle later on in the Yoga practice. Now you can move around your flippers like a sea otter.

Do a few cycles of each spinal wave. Dolphin, trout and sea otter. A few minutes will do. Synchronize the breath with the movement or simply let the breath be.

All spinal waves can be practiced by everyone as a way to open the spine in all directions at the beginning of a Yoga or movement practice. I have found them very helpful to minimize or eradicate back pain. I also enjoy the fluidity and the nonlinear quality of the patterns.

We can also see as soon as we move to classical standing poses that the torso compensates for the lack of flexibility of hamstrings, deep rotators, etc. This gives strong motivation for practicing Supta Pādāṅguṣṭhāsana (Supine Big Toe Pose), Adho Mukha Śvānāsana (Downward Facing Dog Pose) and all hip openers. It will also show that most people have a healthy spine in a context where the limbs are out of the picture! Most back problems are in part due to tight hamstrings and rotators, which are not a limiting factor in spinal waves. That is true democracy—tight and flexible people in the same boat!

Also remember that Yoga is quality oriented. This means that awareness, mindfulness, how you move, how you are, and how you feel are more important than how far you can go. In terms of healing or even progressing, the patterning and the quality of your practice are—most of the time—more important than how much you can do in terms of range of motion, timing, or repetitions.

Contentment will come practicing simple spinal waves daily or when you have a call to be moved by your spine or to become again a fish or an aquatic mammal, our common ancestors.

SPINAL CURVES

We all turn into dried shitake as we age. In the Middle Ages people were barely making it to their mid-forties so gravity didn't put pressure on those joints and fluids for as long. Mozart died at thirty -five. Pergolesi at twenty-eight. Nowadays we have to prepare for at least twice more time standing, sitting and walking so let's have a Yoga practice that minimizes the aging process by respecting, cultivating, and elongating the natural curves of the spine; by repatterning the angle of the sacrum, which is one of the barometers of the aging process. When the sacrum bone is in a posterior tilt, it means it is vertical in Tāḍāsana, you will look older than your biological age. This is also why counternutation is a real problem. Take, for example, the implications of shifting the top of the sacrum backwards in deep forward bends.

In the '70s in Normandy, I had a student who started Yoga classes at age seventy-two. She was a seamstress, had terrible posture, hypolordotic, hyperkyphotic, and with a heavy compression of the cervical spine. She sewed all her clothes, skirts and robes herself. In two years, she gained three-quarters of an inch from practicing consistently a simple āsana prescription I suggested. She got taller so her front line grew, as a result the fabric line was above the knee and not level all around! For her generation and age, above the knee was too adventurous. She had to remake all her clothes. In addition, she had to get new shoes as her toes got un-hammered, wider apart and longer. Another magical benefit of Yoga.

Every Yoga student should be deeply in tune with the spine, create space to decompress the discs and the joints through mindful extension and flexion. This is at the core of the teachings. Decompression from longer, more sedentary lives is a priority. Decompression both mental and physical is needed since our bodies are often com-pressed, de-pressed and op-pressed. Play on the Yoga ropes and flying trapezes, hanging, floating, suspended like bats. Follow the spine in all Āsanas and Prāṇāyāmas. Massage it from inside like an underground living river.

Primary curves were present in utero and at birth. So, the back of the skull, the thoracic spine, the sacrum/coccyx unit/the back of the calcaneum were convex already. Only the thoracic spine can really move later in extension, not much but very precious. The thoracic curve can be aggravated by poor posture, driving, slouching, depression, aging, more so than any other curve. Cultures still carrying on the head avoid that compression and will not look at the floor when aging. We think they will compress the cervical spine but that is an ethnocentric projection. Similarly, African tribal cultures with strong lordosis have fewer back problems than we do.

NOTOCHORD

We always forget the spine was fluid at the origin, and has a soft notochord, like seaweed in the water. The vertebrae, which appeared much later, make us believe that the spine is solid. But in the spinal canal the cerebrospinal fluid flows like a little mountain stream, most precious and well protected. Fluidity of movement is needed and that is why spinal wave-like movements—undulations—are so important. It stimulates the cerebrospinal fluid (CSF), not to be confused with CCF (coriander, cumin, fennel) used in Ayurvedic cooking to facilitate digestion. This fluid is a little slow and stagnant by nature. With a little kick and especially deep breathing, the craniosacral pump is activated, releasing endorphins and making us feel less blue. The fluid system absorbs and transmits frequencies and sound waves well. It makes music a deep healer and Goddess only knows what it really does to the spinal fluid by sympathetic resonance! Mysterious chords of the spinal cord.

The sea squirt (didemnum vexillum), one of the closest living relatives to vertebrate, lives in the coral reefs and has a notochord. The lancelet, known as Amphiosus, has no brain or skeleton. It is a worm with gill slits, an invertebrate, that shares many features with backboned animals. It has a nerve cord that runs along its back and a rod running parallel to it. The human embryo has one too, but it breaks up and becomes part of the intervertebral discs. When we rupture a disc, the jelly-like substance that comes out tells a very old story. Is it not exciting that we coexist with some of our most ancient invertebrate ancestors? Prāṇāyāma and Āsana certainly have a word to contribute to this story.

VERTEBRA BY VERTEBRA?

Coming back from Uttānāsana, curling, rolling up one vertebra at a time *(teacher speaks with a soft poetic lyrical voice)* is a myth beginning in the idealized dance world probably and exported to fitness practices and Haṭha Yoga. What I have witnessed in traditional cultures, India or Africa, is that the hip joint is used perfectly like a hinge and the lower back does not change or lose its lordosis. It is a virtuous circle, creating more toning in paraspinal muscles that further protect the lumbar spine itself. The pose would be Pādāṅguṣṭhāsana halfway with fingertips touching the floor and a Tāḍāsana/Śalabhāsana-like spine with a concave back.

Beyond that range, if the palms are on the floor or the hands under the feet in Pādahastāsana, there will be lumbar flexion of course. In tribal or rural cultures, you have to see it to believe it. The hip socket is the hub of the movement. Coming back up vertebra by vertebra sounds like a pleasant journey, but it still creates weightbearing flexion—especially in S1–L5. It is romantic not functional. Even if a little rigid conceptually, we have to function like LEGO/Playmobil people. And of course, we need to create fluidity and mobility in the spine as well; like a snake or seaweed in water, but not standing—more in quadrupedal mode or on the floor. So, flexion is welcome in the proper context.

If you dream of isolating the vertebrae successfully, come down from Setubandha Sarvāṅgāsana gradually, keeping the knee in flexion, soles of the feet on the ground and towards the end to get L3, L4, L5, S1 (in that order) on the floor, raise your heels and engage the lower abdominals with a deep exhalation. L3 or L4, being the keystone of the arch, will be more difficult to move independently. With Gravity on your side and floor feedback, literally, in this case, it is possible and safe to unfold your spine one vertebra at a time. Blissful before Śavāsana.

QUADRATUS

Quadratus Lumborum tends to be too zealous attaching the ribs to the pelvis. We are grateful for its presence, but it can be tense and hard like stone. Rolfers know this well and use the elbow to reach deep into it. You can release the Quadratus Lumborum with the lateral spinal wave (lateral flexion on all fours), Parighāsana, Parivṛtta Jānu Śīrṣāsana, Uḍḍīyāna Bandha, Bamyanāsana (Ardha Candra with lateral flexion and top arm taking roots over the head).

One day a Yoga teacher came to me for a private session, with intense pain in the QL area. He thought he had kidney stones with the sharp pain associated with it. But in fact, he just had a spastic Quadratus. So, I tried the prescription list above. He could do everything very well, especially Uḍḍīyāna Bandha with the whole spine in flexion. And pain vanished by the end of the session.

Laughing, Bhastrikā, any backbend would have aggravated the pain by contracting that squared muscle. Toning on tension creates a spastic condition. This gave me the idea to teach a future workshop exploring the three Quadrati muscles in the body . . . Quadratus Lumborum, Quadratus Plantaris and Quadratus Femoris. Stay tuned.

KOŚA

In the last few years I have experienced the subtle layers of the Kośas. A psychic armor or a lightness of being is felt around the whole body. So, it gives a preview of how accessible the next āsana will be or if negotiation and more mindfulness is needed, instead of diving into it. Especially true of Uttānāsana but could also be for Padmāsana or for the length of time staying in Śīrṣāsana. There is something un-physical about it, instinct-based. The aura of the āsana can be thick or thin. Similarly, at times Śavāsana is glowing in the dark, like a solar garden lamp recharged during the day and softly shining at night.

HALĀSANAPHOBIA

When we open our eyes in Śīrṣāsana, Head Balance, we are gazing at the infinite. In Halāsana, the Plow, we just see ourselves and not far at all so halāsanaphobia is possible. For some the feeling of being trapped in a deep flexion, creates an anxiety attack . . . so, begin with Ardha Halāsana with legs on a chair or practice chest openers before.

NEW ROADS

Sometimes in life you have to regress to progress. You need to find the old crossing roads way back in time and take a new one. Same in āsana, go back to a clear early stage of the pose, maybe change your relation to Gravity with supports or seats and rebuild. Walk on a clear Path instead of burying yourself in old habits, compensations, dead ends and illusions of completion. Then the āsana will truly become your teacher.

In postures where we can stay, repose, meditate, be centered, we have a chance to reconnect with the pre-symbolic level of the āsana. Figure out the mystery of its creation. Why, when, for what purpose? Who was the first one in Śīrṣāsana?! What a strange idea! Same with Padmāsana. If it is a symbolic ritual, can we find its original purpose or meaning?

If we practice the āsana for the sake of it, we have a chance to feel what it has to offer. It becomes a spontaneous gift with no name, no label. The health and therapeutic positive side effects or the pathologies if any, from misalignment, overdoing or a tamasic agenda, will come later!

The Alpha and Omega of āsana, Tāḍa and Śava, as a secret code, are interwoven in every pose. There is no sense of aesthetic in Yoga āsana. It is beautiful or harmonious because IT is functional like Bauhaus furniture. Harmony includes vertical axis, natural shape, 3D abdominal cavity, soft belly with residual tone, ribs uncaged, wide spectrum of facial expressions, true voice, cosmic integration. IT is a side effect of being in the right place at the right time and IT becomes timeless, effortless and sustainable.

VIRTUOSITY OF PRESENCE?

2004. Workshop in Louisville, Kentucky. I taught an "intermediate, /advanced" āsana class with variations in Head Balance and connections between standing poses and arm balances. This reminded students and teachers that what really matters is the mindfulness, the presence, the consciousness, the internal feedback—seeing self in the internal mirror. The important thing is not so much the difficulty or the intensity of the āsana, per se, which is always somewhat subjective and could transform the class into Cirque-du-Soleil mode, where safety is sometimes questionable. Great musicians are charismatic by their sound and presence, not only by the degree of virtuosity. Is there a virtuosity of Presence!? A Vinyāsa of Being!?

ŚĪRṢĀSANATHON

Be bold, be cautious.

You must keep balance by the intelligence of the body (instinct, balance feeling or ability)
and not by strength. When you keep balance by strength, it is physical;
when by intelligence of the body, it is relaxation in action.

Yehudi Menuhin plays music on the violin;
it is with his violin that he expresses the divinity which is in him.
I play Yoga-āsana on my body. What is the difference?
How can we say playing the violin is spiritual work and performance of āsana is merely physical?

—B.K.S. IYENGAR

On May 15, 2005, Director François Raoult of Open Sky Yoga Center participated in the much-anticipated Yogathon at the Iyengar Yoga Institute in New York City. The event, organized to raise funds for Śrī B.K.S. Iyengar's October visit to the United States, gathered Yoga teachers from around the country to demonstrate Yoga poses for pledged dollars-per-minute. François chose the pose Śīrṣāsana, Head Balance. He held the pose for a personal best time of 52 minutes and raised $5,800. Below are his reflections on this experience:

Just when I was searching for inspiration to write the newsletter, the New York City adventure started! After several phone calls—the last one from Mary Dunn, one of the most senior and respected Iyengar teachers in the country—I finally gave up and agreed to participate in the Yogathon. The word "Yogathon" at first reminded me of the Yoga Olympics or the American Idol of Yoga. Some of my French Yoga friends made fun of it, asking, "What kind of fish is that?" ("Thon" means "tuna" in French.)

But after realizing it would be a fundraiser exclusively designed to organize and honor Śrī B.K.S. Iyengar's visit to the United States, I thought it would be a great opportunity to give back a little.

Mr. Iyengar has given us so much all these years, not just as a teacher in India but even from a distance when his presence is felt in the air. All the students and teachers who study at Open Sky Yoga in Rochester or in the various centers around the country with me benefit indirectly as well—sometimes unaware that Mr. Iyengar is still alive, alert, creative and practicing, even at eighty-seven!

Some Yoga "stars" or "hip" teachers who owe a lot to him are actually more known to the American public. Mr. Iyengar was named one of the 100 most influential people in the world by Time magazine in 2004, so at least we can give him credit for contributing to our success. Parents, grandparents, ancestors and great teachers—popular or not, we still owe them life no matter what!

So, I had to fly to New York City just to stand on my head, and then fly back home!

I prepared by building tapas, inner fire. Since people would be pledging per minute, I had to think about how long might be too long. Would extended Head Balance aggravate Pitta, the fire element? In recent years I had toned down Head Balance and backbends, being prone to nose bleeds since early childhood. I had to find a way to make a heating pose cooling—to make the effort effortless, as the great philosopher Patañjali said.

Beyond thirty minutes, Head Balance is somewhat unpredictable; you actually are not gaining much more benefit, and in fact it could be unhealthy, like running an ultra-marathon. You enter a zone where rationality and safety no longer exist, a sort of Shamanic quest, alone in the deep forest of your mind.

I used to practice relatively long inversion timings in the '80s. I worked then with Dona Holleman, a legendary teacher residing now in Italy, also on my own and of course in India's intensive training. Later as I studied more Ayurvedic science, I shifted toward forward bends and more sophisticated Prāṇāyāma (yogic breathing) as well as deeper Śavāsana (relaxation).

For the Yogathon, I knew the practice territory; I just didn't know how the context would affect things. I had already practiced Śavāsana in Victoria Station in Mumbai, one of the busiest places on earth—so the noise, even the show business aspect, did not phase me much. At one point I had three kids and two dogs around, so I like to think I have a high threshold for chaos. In fact, it is a good practice to find refuge in the eye of the storm!

There is the external form of practice—the āsana, the way they look, their external architecture, their esthetic. And there is the internal experience—the inner Maṇḍala, the state of Yoga being. In the best scenario they reflect and feed each other. Most often they are on separate channels, or maybe only one channel is present.

Nowadays external form is big, as various forms of power Yoga have taken the front stage and blended with cutting-edge fitness like Pilates. From that point of view if you have core strength and flexibility you are a better yogi or yogini, even better if you can do more spectacular poses. But I

believe it's more important how you experience the practice internally, your emotional balance, how you live your life as a human being. To love and to be loved are far more essential than the level of performance in āsana. Of course, there is a bottom line. But the best musicians are not always the virtuosi; they may be the tuners of the instruments or the sound engineers! Maybe even the drunken accordion player in the subway touching your soul is the real thing, not the PhD at Eastman School of Music. On PBS Ellen Koskoff has a great show called "What in the world is music?" We could ask similarly: What in this culture is Yoga?

Back to New York. The new Iyengar Institute is located in Chelsea. After a long elevator ride, you enter a large, beautiful space that offers views of the Hudson Valley. The Yogathon was planned for three hours, from 1–4 P.M. The headstanders started at two o'clock. There were only four of us. Other teachers involved in the fundraising chose backbends or sun salutations. Some meditated, chanted, or chose introverted poses like Śīrṣāsana or Sarvāṇgāsana requiring great concentration. Some tried to perform as many āsana from *Light on Yoga* as they could in two hours, starting on page one with a page-turner assisting. Others did Śavāsana with a hundred pounds of sandbags on their bodies. I thought about Śavāsana instead of Śīrṣāsana, but it might have been a bit of an escape!

The Yogathon was something of a three-ring circus, a combination of standup comedy and profound homage. I was truly in a relaxed, noncompetitive mode, not knowing—a good place to start. My partner was at my side. I had no idea how long I would stay, really. I had recently done twenty-to-thirty minutes at home without much of a sweat, almost daily, so I had a feeling I could go thirty minutes. But you never know!

It turned out to be more a devotional experience and meditation than a physical challenge. Of course, everything is a mind game. And you need the physical stamina to support it. Without the daily practice, forget it—at D Day, you cannot deliver!

I could feel the tremendous presence of Guruji, as most of us call Mr. Iyengar. Over the past several months he had appeared in several of my dreams, laughing like a little kid, with compassionate eyes. He had one arm around my shoulders, protecting. I also could feel the presence of all the students and teachers I had ever taught, several thousand probably, and all were contained as a cluster of psychic energy in one pose, one meaningful āsana, one moment.

By minute thirty my arms went numb. I didn't know if I was pushing the floor or not. Then I knew I had to rely on instinct of balancing and let go of fear. Even if my body was deeply involved, sweating, almost saturated by long toning, I had to be detached (Aparigraha) and surrender to Gravity (Īśvara Praṇidhāna). Then there is no time, no weight, and yet there is connection. The energy of Suṣumnā—a subtle channel of energy along the spine—may hold the pose for me.

At times I was extraverted, seeing the environment, responding to other people. Around minute thirty-five or forty, the crowd of two hundred or so was clapping for the two of us still in the pose. I clapped with my feet in Baddha Koṇāsana—where the feet are joined in prayer like hands—and we all laughed together. That was actually relaxing and gave me a second, or I should say a third or fourth wind! It goes by waves—you want to quit, you are scared, then again you fly, float suspended "by a thin line of awareness," to use Mr. Iyengar's language! After that I don't remember the other practitioner stopping. I was in some kind of a trance. I was alone but not lonely.

B.K.S. said that Yoga should make an extravert an introvert and vice versa. I completely agree. In fact, you have to learn to be on both sides of the coin and be able to switch quickly from laughing like crazy to being centered in deep silence. Those two opposites feed each other. That reminds me of John Lennon, who became a great meditator after a few years of primal screaming therapy. I could not resist practicing Head Balance in Central Park on the center of the Maṇḍala designed by Yoko Ono for John at Strawberry Fields, a wonderful garden near 72nd Street (don't miss it next time you are in Manhattan).

After fifty-two minutes, I released the pose, landing slowly. I had just turned fifty-two, so I thought it would be an auspicious number to stop at. I stayed in Child's Pose and could not move for a few minutes. Then life came back. In long practice you have to function like a diver coming back to the surface gradually, mindfully. In fact, a lot of skilled divers are interested in Yoga, especially Prāṇāyāma breathing.

Let me highlight the benefits of Śīrṣāsana. According to *Light on Yoga*, it cures almost anything! It aids concentration, memory and clear vision. Yehudi Menuhin practiced long Head Balances backstage before important concerts. Both Menuhin and Krishnamurti were students of B.K.S. in the '60s.

Śīrṣāsana, was given to me, with Padmāsana variations, by Guruji in 1989, when I got hepatitis in India. It accelerated the healing by a few weeks as well as alleviating my liver pain in an amazing way. The pose is a "boon," as they say in India, for the liver and for the digestive organs, especially with the rotations. It is also a great pose to rejuvenate the reproductive organs and the endocrine system if legs are in Baddha Koṇāsana or Upaviṣṭa Koṇāsana (legs extended and wide open).

Here is what B.K.S. Iyengar says about Head Balance:

- "In Śīrṣāsana, one has to watch from moment to moment and find out the subtle adjustments."
- "The time limit for Śīrṣāsana depends upon individual capacity and the time at one's disposal."
- "In Śīrṣāsana your body feels completely stretched and at the same time you experience complete relaxation."
- "People suffering from loss of sleep, memory and vitality have recovered by the regular and correct practice of this āsana and have become fountains of energy."

Śīrṣāsana is a physically challenging pose in the beginning, when you have to use arm and back strength. Then it becomes more of a psychological pose, if not a spiritual one. Should not all āsanas be like that? You have to combine Jñāna Yoga (the knowledge of Yoga technology and philosophy) and Karma Yoga (the intensity and drama of the action) to create the form of the āsana itself, building the architecture of the pose. In addition, Bhakti, the devotional current, carries you in the pose and allows you to sustain the state of Yoga.

You have to be embodied to go beyond the body. You have to find in āsana (and it shows more on long timings) the balance between doing and letting go, between yielding and pushing, between inhaling and exhaling, between pose and repose.

Of course, the emotional layer is huge. That is why tennis players often win the tournament in their own country or city. Remember Yannick Noah at the French Open? To be supported emotionally by the indirect presence of your teacher or guru, by all the student body and by family members (my kids and my parents all pledged something) and also feeling the presence in the room of my partner, that was the best feeling in the world. And also feeling other practitioners focused in their practice. Zen practitioners know that well from sesshins.

Of course, the idea of timing in Yoga has to be transcended, yet in this case the longer the more money for a good cause. You see the paradox! I had no interest in being in the *Guinness Book of World Records* for the longer Śīrṣāsana.

Timing and numbers, burning calories, have nothing to do with the real thing, per se. Health is not about numbers but about the clarity and embodiment of your life mission statement! A two-hour meditation is not better than a ten-minute one. It depends. You could be asleep for a long time or you could have a spiritual awakening in a flash! You can have a meaningful, efficient short practice or a longer one that is more mechanical or a sign of addiction to intensity that goes with pseudo anorexic/bulimic patterns. In Yoga we are quality-oriented first, repatterning the whole system.

Yoga bridges the physical and the spiritual.

So again, I thank you from the bottom of my heart, everybody, for your unconditional and loving support. That is the ultimate reward for a teacher and a human being. Namaste to all of you who organized, supported and pledged in New York City for what turned to be a successful fundraising event and a great internal experience, both at the personal level and for the Iyengar community at large. It was a great way to let the world of Yoga know that Śrī Bellur Krishnamacharya Sundaraja Iyengar, at the young age of eighty-seven, is coming soon to the United States (of Yoga!).

Postscript

Some friends who had pledged five dollars per minute were surprised and even angry when they had to sign a check for the fundraiser. They had no idea somebody could be in Śirṣāsana that long.

MŪRDHNI MARMA

Stromboli Island, first day of the retreat before the participants' arrival, practicing Śīrṣāsana like every day but with the ocean on my back and the volcano on my front, erupting and smoking every twenty minutes, a cosmic magma clock! By the way, a major eruption with evacuation of the island, happened few weeks after our Yoga retreat. We were almost the last ones allowed to climb to the top of the volcano at night and witness its power.

In Śīrṣāsana, I have three ongoing actions:

First, I am pressing the floor above the wrist just where my Sūtra bracelets from Thanjavur and Madurai are still having a life of their own, to bring mid-upper thoracic spine inwards and up.

Second, I am adding Mūla Bandha with a little abduction of the femurs and keeping it sealed, bringing legs back together as one, inner knees, inner malleoli and inner big toes all fused towards the midline, madhya.

Third, I bring active pronation in the feet with toes extended, what we call a Yoga foot and was taught very well by Dona Holleman in Boston at Patricia Walden's invitation in the mid-80s.

I rotate those three actions in a loop until they become one. By then, they become less physical, more subtle, like a memory print, the filigree of the pose. No more weight left on the forearms. Arms become the hulls of an imaginary catamaran (kattumaram in Tamil).

Now, I am balancing only on the back rim of the fontanelle which looks like the crater of an old volcano. It is the vertex of the head, the Śirṣā which gives its name to the āsana. It is close to Mūrdhni Marma, in the middle between Śivarandhra and Brahmarandhra. Viṣṇu, associated with Mūrdhni is always sustaining the world between the creator Brahma and the destroyer Śiva.

Marmas are power points, similar to those mapped on the meridians of Chinese medicine. According to Dr. Lad, "they are junctions between consciousness and physiology and provide a window into the interchangeability of energy and matter." It is said that Mūrdhni is the meeting point of a thousand Nāḍīs. It is associated with the pineal gland and therefore regulates melatonin. It may be why Śīrṣāsana is a mood enhancer! My name is François and I am addicted to Śīrṣāsana.

TO CORE OR NOT TO CORE

The relationship between each psoas and each dome of the diaphragm is like a cobra. The tail arises from the distal end of the psoas, the lesser trochanter, curls up over the front of the pelvis, rears up behind the peritoneum to the lumbars, and the hood of the "cobra" is the dome of the diaphragm. The psoas can support the front of the spine so that the abdominals are free to breathe and be breathed.

—THOMAS MYERS

Abdominal muscles, all of them, are primarily exhalers allowing laughing, speaking, chanting, elimination, birth: all ruled by apāna or udāna vāyu. If the psoas major and the lumbar paraspinal muscles stabilize the spine, they become available for breathing.

I believe stronger lower back paraspinal muscles, to maintain a healthy lordosis, are needed more than strong abdominals. Both for posture and breathing benefits. Abdominals are also flexors of the spine.

Usually, global flexion of the spine is a reflex of fear, a protective shield, a sign of aging or of a poor environment including sustained working positions. Flexion in the right context, at the right time, place, and dose, can also be a positive thing. It can help to release back tension or make you feel secure, for example, if you sleep in a regressive fetal position or curl up on your side at the end of a long Śavāsana.

Ideally the abdominal wall with proper residual tone is creating a container for the organs, with just the right presence to not compress them. They have to be adaptable for multitasking. Core strength is fashionable, and various schools argue about what it really is, how much is needed, often reducing it to the front body, more exposed and visible. It was not part of Yoga until a decade ago when Core Power and Core Whatever became marketable and therefore took over the Yoga world (well, one world). From the rectus abdominis, including the pyramidalis, if you still have them both, to the transverse abdominal, we need core release, core expansion, core meditation as well, not just core strength, so we can actually live and breathe safely at the center of the human Maṇḍala.

For me, the real core is made of the small intrinsic muscles of the spine, rotatores, multifidus, etc. They are toned when we carry on the head, reacting to Gravity and developed in Śīrṣāsana variations. They are the deepest, anchored on and between the spinal processes. They are the Source of movement.

EXTERNAL ROTATION

Turning out is actually quite natural as the feet prove it in Śavāsana. Look at babies on their back with legs in Baddha Koṇāsana and later in life crawling like salamanders. But in bipedal station it could create problems if kneecaps are not moving in the same direction as the midline of the foot. In a static Tāḍāsana, turning out is fine but may induce a hyperlordotic spine. This may be why in ballet they tuck the tailbone as an antidote to deep lateral rotation. When walking, better to be closer to parallel tracks as if you were skiing. A homeopathic dose of external rotation is natural. In fact, even if in your mind your feet are completely parallel, your prints in the snow will tell you that you are still turning out. I have had the experience many times.

External rotation in walking or running will trigger pathologies by inviting an excess of pronation and sometimes will invite the navicular bone to slide out of the bony structure of the medial arch. The navicular can come out easily because it is a little narrower at the top. It was designed for a vertical foot. Dramatization: if you turn out, let's say fifty degrees, with each foot and follow simultaneously the direction of each foot, how far will you go? It will be a short trip!

INTERNAL PILGRIMAGE

To see we must forget the name of the things we are looking at.
—CLAUDE MONET

A map of El Camino trails in the South of France, a map of the moon, a cosmic map of the universe, a subtle map of the energy body. See, all those trails and lines have names. Intersections of the Śrī Yantra triangles have names: "bedhana," "sandhi" and "marma," peaks and valleys on the moon, inner avenues. Naming them, drawing them, finding them, traveling in or on them may be helpful, may bring the unconscious conscious. And then we forget the names and just feel, see, experience the beauty, the vibration. Feeling the feet on the earth, the body in space or water, the winds of Prāṇa blowing in those channels. Āsana and Prāṇāyāma are defined. They have names like you have a name, a Mantra with sound and meaning. Alignment matters in a cosmic, sacred architecture sense to create a specific map of the āsana. We become, because we already are, the āsana. Then nothing else, nothing, it just is.

May your practice, as inner pilgrimage, lead you on those inner trails, rims of canyons, top of mountains, feet of glaciers, surfing the waves of the internal sea and diving in the underground rivers of Prāṇa. Śavāsana after Prāṇāyāma and deep listening in the silent tail of resonance after chanting are ways to enter the gates of the inner Maṇḍala. Of course, you will encounter also rajasic zones of turbulence in the mind—and no seat belts are provided! But then again, you have the opportunity, like the salt child, of a deep merging. Read the following story out loud as poetry for the imaginary audience of all your cells. You may experience sympathetic resonance and haṃsa bumps . . .

"There was a child made all of salt who very much wanted to know where he had come from. So, he set out on a long journey and traveled to many lands in pursuit of this understanding. Finally, he came to the shore of the great ocean. "How marvelous," he cried, and stuck one foot in the water. The Ocean beckoned him in further saying, "If you wish to know who you are, do not be afraid." The salt child walked further and further into the water dissolving with each step, and at last then exclaimed, "Ah, now I know who I am."

PRONE AND SUPINE

"The more dorsiflexion, the less supination. The more plantar flexion the more supination." Pronation is a natural movement of the foot that occurs during foot landing while running or walking. Composed of three cardinal plane components: subtalar eversion, ankle dorsiflexion, and forefoot abduction, these three distinct motions of the foot occur simultaneously during the pronation phase.

During supination, a combination of plantarflexion, inversion and adduction causes the sole to face medially and it makes you lean towards the outer edges of the foot. Supination exacerbates the weakness and natural laxity of the ankle. As in ballet, standing on the distal phalanges of the toes in plantar flexion will tend to destabilize the ankle and of course will shorten the Achilles tendon and the deep layers of the calf muscle.

If you stand up on your toes or on the ball of the foot, the antidote to supination will be to move the inner maleoli towards each other as if they were attracted by a magnet in the midline.

Supination is especially unhealthy in all Yoga crossed-legged position like Sukhāsana and Padmāsana. In Sukhāsana lateral arches and fifth metatarsals have to be parallel to each other and of course hip joints have to be "open" to allow external rotation of the femurs or release the knees towards the floor. A good Baddhakoṇāsana is always helpful. If nothing works, sit higher and support knees and the crossing of the tibias or sit on a chair. The negative karma you build over the years and decades of sitting on the floor is not always obvious. Patañjali suggests detecting impulses in early stages when it is still subliminal and is not a labeled pathology yet. In this case, it could create instability in walking or running overtime by a passive aggressive stretching of the outer ankle ligaments. It becomes especially obvious in Padmāsana, the Lotus, which most Westerners will tie too wide, convenient but dysfunctional, with the illusion of symmetry. A good Padmāsana is asymmetrical, both knees will not touch the ground. Just because some Buddha statues have the knees touching the earth and the soles of the feet facing the sky, in such a way that we can appreciate the sculpted cakras, does not mean it's a good idea. Finally, a warning for Zen practitioners: Padmāsana on the zafu makes it worse and may give you a scoliosis!

Say, "No to pronation!" if it is weightbearing, like in Tāḍāsana, walking, Vṛkṣāsana, any Āsana balancing on one foot. And say, "Yes to pronation!" in all other Āsana, especially in inverted poses to create an extension and prolongation of the spine on the vertical axis, in Śīrṣāsana and Sarvāṇgāsana, pointing the ball of the big toe with the foot slightly pointed. I call it flextension. It helps the whole leg to receive traction, a tridimensional release creating space in the ankle, knee and hip joints. Pointing the foot only as in gymnastics, ballet, synchronize swimming and Pilates will only release the front leg and contract the back line as well. It may be only an aesthetic statement, pleasing to the eye like an arrowhead or a Gothic cathedral roof point, but with no meaning and less function. Sometimes a symbolic gesture or an artistic representation transcends functional movement, but in this case the pointed foot mudra is not even interesting. Pointing at what? At the jury for more points?

So, here is the prescription for life: pronate actively in space by toning the peroneal muscles and don't supinate unless you have no choice. Nature already provides supination as a poisoned gift.

WEIGHT BEARING OR WEIGHT LIFTING?

Heaviness is the root of lightness.
—TAO TE CHING

By practicing Saṃyama on the relationship between body and Ākāśa and by concentrating on the lightness of cotton wool, passage through the sky can be secured.
—HARIHARANANDA ARANYA, PATAÑJALI III, 43

By knowing the relationship between the body and ether, the yogi transforms his body and mind so that they become as light as cotton fibre. He can then levitate in space. This is the conquest of ether.
—B.K.S IYENGAR, PATAÑJALI III, 43

Years ago, for my birthday, I decided to treat myself with a set of Olympic weight plates. In Iyengar Yoga, we place weights on specific places to further ground the body in restorative poses. On the sacrum in Child's Pose, on the groin in Supta Baddha Koṇāsana, on the upper femur bones in Setubandha Sarvāṇgāsana and on the thighs in Supta Vīrāsana. It looks intense to an outside witness, but it actually feels really good, even blissful, if the pose is well adjusted and supported. It is the opposite of weight lifting.

Most of the time we use eight-to-ten-pound sandbags. When traveling or teaching abroad, I sneak in the kitchen of retreat centers and "borrow" bags of rice or lentils. Should we call this weight bearing or weight yielding? The extra weight amplifies the force of the gravity field and is deeply Vāta pacifying. Vāta doṣa is light to not say virtual and appreciates the comforting presence of weight. Think comforter and hot chocolate in a Swiss chalet or the pressure of loving hands on your skull when you have a headache. In a strange way, the sensation of heaviness involving our own body mass creates a sense of weightlessness or levitation. Levitas does mean lightness.

Going back to my birthday gift story, I arrived at a well-known sporting goods store at the mall and asked for the manager of the free-weights section. I found the perfect fifty-pound plate and asked him if I could try it. He said, "Of course, go ahead." I placed myself in Supta Vīrāsana on the floor and I guided him to adjust the weight on my quadriceps. He tried to stay cool and understand my purpose but looking at his facial mask, I could see he was thinking that I should be institutionalized.

I said with a big smile, "Perfect, exactly what I need, I will buy two." Not sure he got it, but he got the commission. To end on a heavy (but not sad) note: in Śavāsana, would it not be great if our brain was just one more sandbag?

The Brain is just the weight of God—
For—Heft them—Pound for Pound—
And they will differ—if they do—
As Syllable from Sound—
—EMILY DICKINSON

MOBILE & STABILE

I have always been a big fan of Calder, for Stabiles are like āsanas. Mobiles create a perfect equilibrium, transcending pairs of opposites as Patañjali would say (II, 48). They are crystalized movements, standing waves. Some major works are at the Guggenheim in New York City and also at the Soulages museum in Rodez, France.

Change "art" into "āsana" in the following text written by Calder:

> "How can art be realized?"
>
> Out of volumes, motion, spaces bounded by the great space, the universe.
>
> Out of different masses, tight, heavy, middling—indicated by variations of size or color—directional line—vectors which represent speeds, velocities, accelerations, forces, etc.—these directions making between them meaningful angles, and senses, together defining one big conclusion or many.
>
> Spaces, volumes, suggested by the smallest means in contrast to their mass, or even including them, juxtaposed, pierced by vectors, crossed by speeds.
>
> Nothing at all of this is fixed.
>
> Each element able to move, to stir, to oscillate, to come and go in its relationships with the other elements in its universe.
>
> It must not be just a fleeting moment but a physical bond between the varying events in life.
>
> Not extractions, but abstractions.

– *From Abstraction-Création, Art Non Figuratif, No. 1, 1932.*

HIMSA

Save the most and kill the least.
—DR. TIWARI

"I learned so much from my injuries," students or teachers will say.

It may be true, but I'd rather expand the range of consciousness to have previews of troubles at their latent unmanifested stage, then teach and learn what to do and what not to do for prevention.

Yoga and injury are not meant to be associated. "Yoga injury" is like saying ahimsa-himsa! It would be betraying ahimsa. Repetitive injury is incompatible with mindful practice, the ability to anticipate one's needs and the use of Yoga to prevent future pain. Too often Yoga therapy is about fixing Yoga injuries. Like sports therapy does for sports. In sports it is part of the deal, you come back after surgery or rehabilitation like a hero. I give private sessions for students injured during Yoga practice or classes (not at Open Sky Yoga of course!). But teachers are at the least co-responsible. In over forty years of teaching I have thankfully had only a few incidents in my classes! One teenager broke his big toe coming down from handstand at the wall, an experienced student early morning before class took the wrong set of ropes to hang; but overall, I can say I have a good record. I've injured myself a couple times, showing what not to do in Padmāsana or while moving a heavy gong in a squatting position.

Each style of Yoga has its own pathology and its shadow. This is well presented in Jack Kornfield's seminal book, A Path with Heart. Take, for instance: "Just as every community has a shadow, every set of teachings will also have an area of shadow, aspects of life that they do not illuminate wisely." In fact, every āsana can have its own specific pathology if you overdo it, don't pay attention or don't respect what I call the cosmic law of the joints. The pose can be too passive, too aggressive, too yin or too yang. Students can have preexisting pathologies aggravated by a certain āsana. It also depends on the context, which belongs in the psychotherapy department. You have to work on yourself in other ways than Downward Dog or Sun-Salutation-until-you-drop. Be aware of your tendencies and low-level addictions. If you sweat too much, you may deplete other systems. And there is only so much you can drink to make it up; it will flood your cells!

Weak links in the body exist where there are only fascia and bones or vulnerable junctions: wrist, inner knee, sacrum-fifth lumbar disc, atlas-axis, sacro-iliac ligaments, etc.... In anatomy books those will be white areas, red being muscle tissues. Those places should not be overstretched, overused, or receive too much weight, nor should muscle attachments like upper hamstrings in Hanumānāsana or front leg of Trikoṇāsana, for example. Therefore, props are needed. The spirit of the practice is more important than the āsana. How you enter and touch the practice, how you project yourself into it. It's the same with massage.

In Ayurvedic terms, the doṣa is affected by the guna. A rajasic Pitta can be a dictator and practice neo-fascist Yoga. A sattvic Kapha would be a saint and meditate or chant Bhajans all night. A forward bend can be heating if done aggressively, clenching your teeth trying to nail the pose. Head Balance can be cooling if done in a sattvic, energy-saving, effortless way.

On the Yoga planet, to say nothing of the Yoga jungle or circus, āsana is overemphasized. Prāṇāyāma, Dhyāna, and Śavāsana are underrepresented. That is also part of the problem.

Strokes in Yoga are fairly rare and idiosyncratic so we can't generalize. To respond to William Broad, author of the controversial article, "How Yoga can Wreck your Body," Dr. Lou Papa, M.D. writes, "It is similar to warn people about the dangers of swimming in the ocean based on isolated shark attacks. In 2002, 4-5 million people in the United States were practicing Yoga and there were 46 visits to the emergency room for Yoga related injuries. But in the previous year those were the numbers for fitness and sports categories: Basketball: 512,213 Bicycling: 485,669 Football: 418,260 Soccer: 174,686

Baseball: 155,898 Skateboards: 112,544 Trampolines: 108,029 Golf: 47,360."

So, I am still happy to report—even though the words Yoga and injury should not coexist—Yoga is amazingly safe.

HUMAN DOG

Looking at dogs, lions, bears in downward dog, downward lion or downward bear—an elephant in sitting meditation, or, a marmot in Tāḍāsana, an owl in revolved neck pose—what can we learn? They obviously are natural-born yogis—no second thoughts.

After realizing that dog is god spelled backward, and that we, Iyengar students, have been made fun of as downward facing dogmatics, it is time to bring some clarity to the subject!

Can you see the common ground and the difference between Dog's dog pose and ours? Number one, look at their spines. Dogs don't have a lordosis (a concave arched lower back or lumbar spine). Therefore, they can stand in Tāḍāsana only for a short time, with support (unless they are trained at the circus professional level with a treat). In this position, they still have flexion in their back legs, along with a head-forward pattern. This is where we humans are going when we have "bad posture": short hamstrings, head zooming ahead of ourselves, flat lower back and hunched upper back. So, what is normal and good posture for a dog in Tāḍāsana is pathological and dysfunctional for us!

This should help you see lordosis as a good thing, something you should cultivate, even worship. Hyper-lordosis is the problem, not the proper amount of it. Of course, different schools have different points of view and sometimes distorted perceptions about what is the proper amount or what is too much. It is colored by belief systems.

So, our Adho Mukha Śvānāsana needs to maintain extension and traction in the spine. Our lordosis is precious; it allows us to stand upright on the vertical axis. Therefore, in downward dog if the hamstrings are released properly (after a few years of alert consistent practice), the spinal processes will not protrude through the skin. The spine will be at its longest.

Our upper back, thoracic spine, can backbend about five degrees at least. We can promote that in Dog Pose and it becomes an anti-aging pose—or as some would say with a marketing edge, it promotes youthfulness!

If a human spine in downward dog looks like a dog's spine in downward dog, we have several problems. We restrict breath in the belly, tighten the hip flexors, keep the hamstrings tight and either don't inform the upper spine at all or overuse the shoulder joints. (That is why so many students complain of pain in the upper arms or saturation in the rotator cuff—deltoid-upper trapezius area.)

As soon as we bend forward with straight legs, that story is magnified. This is now a true hazard for the sacrum-fifth lumbar disc. This is why the intermediate stage of Pādāṅguṣṭhāsana with concave back is a key pose and an initiation to all forward bends. This is one of the only poses where you can see your lower back, facing a mirror, over your head!

TO PLACE IN A SPECIAL WAY (VINYĀSA)

Vinyāsa means to place (nyasa) in a special way (vi). The reference to a style of Yoga is just a late spin in history. Of course, the art of sequencing is essential. In art, in music, inside one inhalation or exhalation, within a breath cycle, there is a Vinyāsa, a progression, a rhythm, a beginning, an end and a story line in the middle. Great songs have an underlying structure, a harmonic Vinyāsa of chords. If you travel from India to Tibet, you will cross the small Himalayas then the big ones; that is a Vinyāsa of travel. There is definitely a possible Vinyāsa of restorative poses. Maybe even a Śavāsana Vinyāsa, deeper and deeper layers of yielding, release, dissolution and inner silence.

KNOTS

Every knot is like a letter of an alphabet.

—WENDY CHIEN

Have you ever asked yourself: Who was the first yogi or yogini crossing her or his legs in full lotus, Padmāsana? For what purpose? Well, tying knots is a very ancient practice. Before yogis were tying knots with their legs or their whole body, knots were made with plant fibers and vines. Knots pre-date writing. We found them with cave dwellers before the Bronze Age. 3000 BCE Sumerians were intertwining serpents. So were the Assyrians, who had connections with the Indus Valley civilization.

Incas used quipu, a complex knots system to keep track of transactions but also for telling stories and myths. Native Indian and ancient Hebrew tribes and of course all sailors, especially Egyptians, were familiar with the art of knotting. We found them also in pre-Christian Celtic art.

"When the yogin stretches and relaxes his body and entwines his limbs in his āsana, isn't he also practicing those knots, both malicious and benevolent, expiatory and propitiatory?" asks the great historian of religion Paul Lévy.

Ligio, in religion means to link, knot and attach. Knots were used for communication between people and as part of their relationship with the sacred.

Mircea Eliade mentions in his book, Images and Symbols, the existence of beneficial knots and bonds in early religions. Cutting the bonds appears in the *Atharva Veda*. Knots, strings and cords protect oneself against illness and evil spirit.

In the courtyards of the great Indian temples, the trees are covered with thread, amulets of all shapes and colors, often related to fertility wishes. The same knots could protect you or help you realize your wishes but could also be used to have a malefic effect. In pre-Vedic times, forces of good and evil were playing a giant cosmic game. In Borneo aboriginal culture, the husband of a pregnant women was not allowed to cross his legs or wear knots. Some people were condemned in France, Scotland and Salem for bewitching others with the use of magic knots.

So, what about Padmāsana? Predating Haṭha Yoga, we find it everywhere in early Buddhist and Jain sculptures. But before that era, it remains a knot-related story and mystery.

STICK FIGURES

All āsanas compose the alphabet of a secret language, runic, primordial shapes and symbols. My students know how much and how fast I like to write āsana sentences at the end of a session, drawing "stick figures" as if they were Egyptian hieroglyphs or Anasazi Indian petroglyphs.

If you have the famous giant āsana poster in your studio or Yoga space, look at it with eyes half closed from a distance and you will have the revelation of an ancient language. In Crete, the script known as Linear B found in Minoan palaces looks like āsana figures. Imagine if we were hiding my drawings in a treasure box, and archeologists found them in a thousand years and tried to decrypt them!

It is actually part of the teacher training to draw stick figures. Some students, at first, don't see the point but everyone eventually does. You cannot go wrong drawing with the mind of a child. It can be sophisticated, artistic, naive, brut, minimalist, realist, surrealist, out of proportion, messy, compulsive—but it remains the symbol of the āsana! The style of the drawing, like graphology, reveals your doṣa, your profile. So next time you see stick figures in a book or you draw them in your notes, don't be shy, be in awe!

SUSTAINABLE YOGA

Practice makes everything bigger than life and it goes back to Life.

Here are a few suggestions, a pool of possibilities for your daily practice. I wrote this in 2014 as my father was living his last days. So, it is essential.

We need āsana, yes, the minimal amount to be functional, cosmically integrated, and to prevent or minimize health issues and their negative side effects. It is not a Vinyāsa. It is for you to compose and write the music of your Sādhanā, to find the best transitions and sequences or to respond to the needs

of the moment. We're dealt a hand of cards and we have to invent a new game every day. Practice has to explore different relationships to gravity; upside down, sitting, standing, supine. And travel through all planes of movement; sagittal with flexion and extension, frontal with lateral poses and transversal with rotations.

TONING

Tone anything that looks like a diaphragm: the soles of the feet with deep plantar flexion, the pelvic diaphragm with Mūla Bandha, the thoracic diaphragm with deep inhalations (adding Antara Kumbhaka if you have a green light for it), the vocal diaphragm with chanting mantra, toning, overtoning and singing.

Tone the secondary curves, especially the back of the neck, lower back, and paraspinal muscles to maintain verticality and stability.

Tone the abdominal wall, a kind of vertical diaphragm, with the Navāsana family (Paripūrṇa Navāsana, Ardha Navāsana, Ūrdhva Prasārita Padāsana), with deep slow exhalations as well as Bhastrikā or Kapālabhāti. Tone, yes, but not at the expense of elasticity and adaptability.

Generate just the right amount of residual tone so as to not compress the vital organs. Add Mūla Bandha and Aśvinī Mudrā (I named it Mūlaśvinī Bandha) for residual tone in all sphincters to prevent or minimize incontinence.

FLUIDITY

The spine needs to be adaptable and fluid. Explore spinal waves (cat, cow, snake, dolphin, the whole zoo). Invite traction whenever possible, hanging from branches, ropes or by moving in two opposite directions with equal energy. Roll on back rollers and variously sized inflatable balloons.

VERTICAL AXIS

Reclaim Tāḍāsana by adjusting the subtle relationship between sternum and sacrum. Balance on the Śirśa of the head in Śīrṣāsana. Explore all standing poses if you are a newcomer, fewer if you are more experienced. Ardha Candrāsana are great to play with. Create and cultivate extension of the spine in Adho Mukha Śvanāsana, Śalabhāsana, Adho Mukha Vṛkṣāsana, Piñcha Mayūrāsana, and Vīrabhadra extended family to name a few.

STRETCHING

Hamstrings and calf muscles: make sure they are upgraded and long enough to improve and master Supta and Utthita Hasta Pādāṅguṣṭhāsana. Taking the big toe with your fingers or, more accurately, big toe taking your fingers or using a belt. Avoid losing the natural lordosis. Āsana, of course, can be modified to keep integrity regardless of your range of motion or abilities.

Elongate the psoas major with preparation to Vīrabhadrāsana I or any nameless lunge. Early stage of Eka Pada Rājakapotāsana and Supta Vīrāsana are great if your knees are not talking back at you.

KYPHOSIS

Kyphosis tends to increase with poor posture and aging. Do one āsana, such as a supported backbend like restorative Setubandha Sarvāṇgāsana or Purvottanāsana modified on various supports. There are endless variations on tables, shelves, grand piano, backroller, sandbags, tennis balls, railings or even the front of your car.

LOWER BACK

Release tension in your lower back with supported Child's Pose, Adho Mukha Vajrāsana with the arms in front, Adho Mukha Sukhāsana, squatting with the back against the wall. Resting for ten-to-fifteen minutes with calf muscles on a chair and a small pillow is divine.

INVERSIONS

Effortless Śīrṣāsana and Sarvāṇgāsana with any variations. Viparīta Karaṇi Mudrā will reverse the gravity field for a moment on this planet.

Anti-gravity = anti-compression = anti-depression = anti-aging.

Tune the timing and spirit of the āsana according to your doṣa.

ORGANS

To enhance circulation, digestion and elimination some basic rotations like Marīcyāsana III will help, even early stages. Uḍḍīyāna Bandha along with Dakṣiṇā, Vāma, Madhya Nauli and Nauli, per se, will release the diaphragm, massage all abdominal organs and improve metabolic function.

DEEP RELAXATION

Śavāsana: more than ever, lose yourself to find yourself in Śavāsana. Come back to Śavāsana as the source of all actions. See Śavāsana underlying everything like the empty screen and the blank tape behind the images and sounds of your life's screenplay. Keep Śavāsana as a watermark everywhere you go.

Relaxation balances the nervous system, minimizes anxiety. It facilitates all natural functions: breath, sleep, homeostasis, and releases the heart which really needs a good vacation from time to time as it works non-stop day and night. An oasis of peace and silence in the eye of the existential storm.

BIGGER PICTURE

Pacifying Vāta: no matter who and where you are, minimize Vāta doṣa as the culture is highly vatagenic, traveling fast across the globe or surfing the internet. Keeping your lungs and your heart healthy with the slow inner massage of pranayamic breath. Cultivate good residual tone in key places and keep overtoning in the sound department.

SOUND

Music is essential to life and to humans. Listen to a wide range of music in deep meditative mode to nourish the cells and the heart. Listen to Ahāta and Anāhata Nāda, the struck and unstruck Sound. Play or replay a musical instrument if you have one around. If not, choose and find one. It is never too late to start the Journey. Or just sing. Tibetan monks are trained to play all ritual instruments in a few months. No need to be a virtuoso or be concerned with aesthetics. Just play like a wild child. It will change your life and keep your brain ahead of the game. Laughing and smiling are optional but strongly recommended by the house whenever the opportunity presents itself.

PART THREE

Teaching

LETTER TO A NEW STUDENT

Creating sparks in your eyes again
Seeing the full moon as your face in Śavāsana
Beyond age and gender
Witnessing the lightness of your steps after practice
Seeing the introvert becoming extravert
And the extravert an introvert
Moving from one to the other with ease, mindfulness and humor
And beyond the occasional frustration, sleepiness or boredom
Seeing life at its best
Vibrant, essential
From deep inertia to full engaged action
Coming out, waking up, letting go
Illusions of perception fading
Fog of Vṛttis dissipating
From your third eye, reclaiming the Halo
Letting your solar plexus finally shine
Finding your own voice, true resonance of your being
What a blessing to teach you
To teach you how to teach
For you to be a bead on the mala of transmission
Following the spiral of transformation, the gradual awakening
Walking a path of no return and yet returning to the Source
Giving you the signs
Being absorbed in the vortex of the moment
Channeling, improvising
Guiding, sharing, confronting, caring
Doubting, believing
Having faith in doubt
Learning to be present
Teaching you

DRINKING FROM THE SOURCE

I keep the Faith. I keep the doubts. More and more questions, fewer answers—about music, art, origins, Yoga, lineage, transmission. But I cannot help it . . . When somebody asked Marie Madeleine Davy, a great Christian mystic, whom I had as a teacher at the Ecole Nationale de Yoga in Paris in my early twenties, "What message do you think you are bringing to people?"

She answered: From time to time, something is filtered through me and I am not responsible for it . . . when the water tank is full, it must overflow . . . and she quoted Saint Irénée of Lyon, "The Source thirsts to be consumed and so, if we are called to drink it, it is impossible not to find it."

ADVANCED

If there is such a thing as an "advanced" teacher training, being parachuted into India by yourself for a few months without a compass would be it! Traveling with no agenda will teach you a lot of things. Mental flexibility and range of consciousness would count far more for graduating cum laude than long hamstrings or flashy backbends!

THE SECRET SITS IN THE MIDDLE

Teaching is more about the process of building the foundation and the underlying invisible patterns, as well as showing the way to the pose than about achieving the pose as a finished product. In a group class, students have a wide spectrum of range of motion, kinesthetic awareness and previous life history. We have to find a common ground. Collective classes did not exist, even early in this century. Michelangelo did not have a group painting class on Tuesday night, only one-on-one instruction or assisting the teacher/guru/master for years, sometimes living in their house.

Anyway, what makes a posture more "advanced" is very subjective and also cultural. For example, Supta Vīrāsana or Mālāsana is a 2 on the scale of 1 to 60 in *Light on Yoga*, from India's point of view, it is almost like Śavāsana. For students in the West, who are not squatting while waiting for the bus or eating at floor level, it could be a quite hellish pose or not even possible, and would rank a 23 or 52 on the same scale. We have to start with a homeopathic dose, with the beginning tracks to go on the journey toward the final stage, extract and collect the various ingredients, decompose and recompose the pose. Experienced students know how to adapt in the moment without frustration and also have the ability to anticipate their needs, nothing to do with the ability to do or not. Otherwise, if we based levels of classes and students on physical ability alone, we are in the Yoga Olympics department or back to the competitive, self-destructive pseudo-military world of gymnastics. If you have the chance to be in the "final stage" of an āsana, have full awareness of the vāyus, the currents of energy in the pose. Turn it into a shamanic experience and a deep meditation, literally standing in the middle, medi-stare.

As Robert Frost experienced as well:

We dance around in a ring and suppose
But the Secret sits in the middle and knows.

Ask yourself: If the āsana were a human being, a living creature, how would it vibrate, resonate? If it were a chord, a sound or a note, what would it sound like?

I had a dream once, where āsanas and their variations were like musical chords with their inversions. In this context, inversions are not upside-down postures, but various combinations of the same notes in a musical chord.

SEE, THEN ACT

We need to SEE first. See with an eagle eye, penetrate reality with a laser beam. "See then act," said Doisneau, the great photographer. "Action follows being," wrote Saint Augustine. Quality of presence, life and travel journeys, clinical experience is what makes a good non-ethnocentric Yoga teacher.

SEE ME, FEEL ME, TOUCH ME, HEAL ME

Listen to this song again. After teaching another module on assisting Āsana and Prāṇāyāma in Brussels, these lyrics came back in my head like a mantra in a loop. See, feel, touch. Heal. Bonnie Bainbridge Cohen, visionary teacher and head of the Body Mind Centering School, used almost the same words in her book's title: *Sensing, Feeling and Action.* Touch, like music touches you, is a primary need of human beings.

Still, in group classes, it is better to use words and good semantics first, to place the student in a good structural and pranic alignment and then, if needed, do the fine tuning with a final touch or adjustment. Touching, of course, needs good intention and meaning, a clear mission, otherwise it is useless, could be disturbing, or turn into a form of abuse. For example, no need to do a radical manual adjustment if props are not well used to modify the pose first and adapt it to the needs of the student. Address the obvious and the essential first, then go to details.

If the subject of touch resonates with you, read Ashley Montagu's revolutionary book *Touching* again, perhaps a little outdated but still a powerful reference and for francophiles, Noëlle Perez's mystical book on the Hand, *La main, agent d'unité* is stunning. Take, for instance:

> *" Le travail de la main, la sensation que passera la main, doit absolument venir du Centre, pas de la surface. Elle doit transmettre l'expérienc synthétisée dans le Centre, le Coeur, Hṛdaya. "*

> *"The work of the hand, the sensation transmitted by the hand, should absolutely come from the*

Center, not from the surface. It must convey the experience synthesized in the Center, the Heart, Hṛdaya."

The skin is a fantastic organ of perception— receptive, sensitive. It feels itself and will tell you everything. Under stress or after trauma the skin and the connective tissues become like a wall or the defensive moats of a fortress so nobody can "touch you" or you cannot be touched, in all the meanings of the word. One prescription is to have breath or sound move and touch you from inside. Caressing your heart, massaging the spinal cord. For some wounded souls, it may be the beginning of a long Journey.

TEACHING IN THE MOMENT

(Note: the remaining sections in this chapter were part of a keynote address to Teacher Trainees.)

Often when I teach, I feel that I am channeling all the teachers I've had, and their own teachers. Also, all my life experiences are incorporated with my needs of the moment, needs for safety, for clarity of purpose, for recognizing my energy level; and the student needs or abilities, range of motion, repetitive injuries, fatigue, enthusiasm. Very often the minority wins; somebody coming to class with a broken pelvis, or chronic fatigue, or in grief over the loss of a family member, cannot be ignored. You can suggest private instruction but sometimes you just have to face the picture, you cannot send the student back home! So, the whole class may have to shift, unless that student knows enough to be guided in a separate sequence of āsana. With skill, you may be able to care for the individual without losing the group's attention.

To improvise on a theme is a trademark of an experienced teacher—to follow a philosophical concept, a metaphor or a technical point through the various āsana and practices. It weaves a thread through the practice or the class. And it helps to focus the attention of the practitioner. Any theme can generate teaching—the vastness of the sky, the shape of the spine, the internal feeling of the pranic flow, the expression on a student's face in Śavāsana, the resistance or the surrender to practice, a quote from Patañjali's Yoga Sūtras or the Upaniṣads, the sound of a bell. Sometimes a specific predetermined agenda will serve, like minimizing pronation of the foot or easing anxiety. It is somewhat of an acting game, a jazz or classical improvisation. The structure is always present, underlying the instructions of the moment. That is also why the art of sequencing has to be developed in the future Yoga teacher.

CONFIDENCE

A Yoga teacher has to embody confidence and ease. Doubts are contagious. If the teacher shows hesitation the student will also be confused. However, up to a certain point you can have faith in doubts. By that I mean that a certain amount of questioning is healthy. To digest and assimilate the teachings, you have to ask yourself or your teacher(s) questions—why, how, in what context this instruction makes sense. Context—when and to whom you make a statement—is everything. One of the big differences between a beginner and a mature practitioner is that the second one understands the importance and the relativity of the context. Sometimes confusion or distortion occurs when you quote a teacher out of context; factional wars have started over this. Śrī B.K.S. Iyengar may have taught the same pose differently according to the person he was teaching, may have taught it differently the year before or in a different country where the culture was different. So, to turn an instruction into an absolute statement is a dangerous tendency. And overconfidence could be masking insecurity.

You may have doubts at time, if you are having a difficult day or if you experience a setback in your practice. But also, you will have tremendous faith in your work when you see it as a gift and a service to people or society. Sometimes you may feel like you're falling into a dark hole. You may feel that what you teach has lost its purpose. Or you deal with the, "I know nothing syndrome," after taking a seminar or a retreat. You may feel like one of your students knows more than you do, and they might. Sometimes I blank out in the middle of a class for a few seconds and it feels like eternity because I doubt my own teaching skills. Or I feel like a fraud because my practice should be stronger or my life more harmonious. In the earliest years of my teaching, I used to teach Śavāsana, deep relaxation, lying down and more than once I fell asleep. Students didn't notice. They thought it was deeper because of the long silence! Then you have to remind yourself of your mission and be vigilant.

Recognize your strengths and share your struggles and weaknesses, so students will not see you for more than you are. It's easy to build up stories, but deep inside you know where you are at. Be real, yet maintain an appropriate distance. Share only what is relevant to inspire practice or help the student resolve obstacles. The student may think he or she is the only one to deal with certain issues—pain, emotional release, the need to cry, darker impulses of the unconscious. By sharing your own experience, you may validate the student and minimize anxiety. Find a balance between acceptance and change. Make a list of what is non-changeable, less changeable, and changeable—in you and in the world. In Ayurveda, you certainly have to accept your constitution. You may not like it, but you can work to minimize its negative effects. The teacher is a facilitator and can also be a cathartic presence for the student unfolding life's potential.

In a teacher role you have to magnify everything, almost like in a commercial, to get a message across. You have to project your voice bigger than life. You are acting and living your own class. Find metaphors if simple explanations are not working. If one metaphor proves ineffective, find another one, rephrase it. Talk about your own experience so students can relate. But don't put yourself down. Just do your best, and if you are teaching from your experience and your heart, everything will be fine.

ETHICS

In a situation of power—teacher, parent, physician, etc.—you have to be continuously and acutely aware of how you relate to the student: your tone of voice, your quality of touch, and eventually the projections, the transference and counter-transference patterns (especially if you are in a vulnerable place yourself like after a loss of a family member or any big shift in your personal life).

Clear boundaries are essential to a good learning environment. In a position of power there is always a risk of potential abuse as well as the opportunity for healing old wounds. Verbal and sexual projection, if not abuse, are present to various degrees in every part of society. Your responsibility is to see as clearly as possible the patterns you re-create unconsciously—from your culture, your education, your family—and to transcend or at least minimize them so you can see people for who they are not what you think they are or what they appear to be. I remember in a leadership seminar a few years ago having judged too quickly another participant, a fundamentalist Christian who simultaneously labeled me as an old hippie. It took us about four days to see that we had a lot in common, that we were concerned with the same essential issues. Then we exchanged poems and gave each other a long hug that I can still feel in my heart. Strive to connect from Ātman to Ātman, instead of being entangled in a web of projections.

India says, "All credit goes to my teachers; all the mistakes are mine." This may be great for technical knowledge, but teaching always involves the personality, the psychological profile, the doṣa of the teacher. So be aware that if the doṣa is exacerbated by a certain type of practice, a behavioral pattern may be created that could be unhealthy or excessive. You have to see if your teachers have dysfunctional patterns; you don't want to reproduce them unconsciously. It is frightening to know that like attracts like, for the best and the worst.

So please be mindful. For example, I talk sometimes too much when I teach, or I might use a sense of humor with a sarcastic edge that is very french. You don't have to identify with that and copy it. You can still appreciate and be grateful for the skills or gifts of your teachers or leaders. You can still love and appreciate your parents, for example, and not reproduce some of their patterns—especially if they were alcoholic, violent, or victims of some other addiction.

Take the best and cut the rest. As a role model for your students, it is your responsibility to do your best to be mentally and emotionally healthy, as well as be a technical expert in the subject of Yoga.

Being a Yoga teacher is a cross between being a priest, a physical therapist, a psychotherapist, a teacher, a physician, a spiritual guide, and a fitness instructor. For example, the back-care class sometimes works more as a group support than an āsana class. The spirit of the group, the energy of the teacher may have a great impact in healing back pain, as well as the practices taught at the so-called physical level.

It is a tremendous responsibility for me to share what I have learned. It is also a huge responsibility for you to transmit the flame of Yoga, Yoga Dīpikā, to your future students. Teach from your heart and disregard what is hip or fashionable. Let your teaching evolve from your practice and from your relationship with your students. That way it will keep its essence.

GROUP DYNAMICS

Some of you have practiced and even taught Yoga for some time; others are less experienced. The group is eclectic. Some of you have studied anatomy in medical school, movement language in modern dance, Sanskrit or Indian philosophy. I selected the group by various criteria: previous experience, motivation or potential. All of you are passionately dedicated to learning. I appreciate the depth of your commitment and I know it represents a financial sacrifice as well as devotion of time. I thank you for that.

Don't assume you know more or less than others—a comparative mind will not help. So please, empty your cup, be humble and welcome the teachers of this program with a fresh mind. There is a tendency for clans to develop inside a group or to be annoyed, consciously or not, by some individual personalities, questions or comments. Be aware that has usually to do with your own history and not with the person who attracts your attention. And remember, such reactions will occur as well with your own students.

Here is an illustration of that group dynamic. It reminds me not to judge too quickly:

"In the spiritual community that G. I. Gurdjieff led in France, an old man lived there who was the personification of difficult—irritable, messy, fighting with everyone, and unwilling to clean up or help at all. No one got along with him. Finally, after many frustrating months of trying to stay with the group, the old man left for Paris. Gurdjieff followed him and tried to convince him to return, but it had been too hard, and the man said no. At last Gurdjieff offered the man a very big monthly stipend if he returned. How could he refuse. When he returned everyone was aghast, and on hearing that he was being paid (while they were charged a lot to be there), the community was up in arms. Gurdjieff called them together and after hearing their complaints laughed and explained, 'This man is like yeast for bread.' He said, 'Without him here you will never really learn about anger, irritability, patience, and compassion. That is why you pay me, and why I hire him.'"

Similarly, minimize criticism toward other styles of Yoga even if you have your opinions, which may be valid. This is always a work in progress for this Pitta mind! Teach only what you know well. Explain why you teach it that way. And welcome students from other traditions. Sometimes belief systems, including your own, can obscure vision. This chilling Sufi story addresses that issue:

"A prophet once came to a city to convert its inhabitants. At first the people listened to his sermons, but they gradually drifted away till there was not a single soul to hear the prophet when he spoke. One day, a traveler said to him, 'Why do you go on preaching?' Said the prophet, 'In the beginning I hoped to change these people. If I still shout it is only to prevent them from changing me.'"

Remember the obstacles listed by Patañjali: disease, mental laziness, indecision, carelessness, idleness, lacking in moderation, living under illusion, missing the point, inability to maintain the achieved progress, scattered mind (Chapter 1, Sūtra 30-31). Remember also the causes of suffering: ignorance, egoism, attachment, repulsion, and fear of death (Chapter 2, Sūtra 3). Let's work together to ease these obstacles so we can embody with our lives the teachings of Yoga and keep the tradition alive. As Mahler writes, "Tradition is not the worship of ashes, but the preservation of fire."

THE SEED

The seed of Yoga was planted in your heart by your first teacher, all the way back to the very First Teacher. Some other event or karmic sign may have influenced your Path. For me, it was meeting those two hippies in Beirut, Lebanon. I was on my way back from Egypt and Sudan and they were on their way to India. Waking up at 4:00 A.M., practicing Yoga. I was sleeping until 10:00 as I was not yet a yogi, but I could see them when opening an eye. First time I witnessed Yoga āsana practice. When I left that Jesuit youth hostel, I had a few words with them. And one showed me his pocket watch. A photo of his guru was pasted inside the cover. This image had a profound influence on me, a mini samādhi moment. And as soon as I got back to Normandy, after hitchhiking through Syria, Turkey, Greece, Bulgaria, Yugoslavia, Austria, and Germany, I signed up for Yoga classes at the local cultural Center. My first teacher was Jean Claude Garnier who introduced me to Jean Bernard Rishi and Karin Stephan, who cofounded the Cambridge Iyengar Center with Patricia Walden, as well as Noëlle Perez, who introduced me directly to Iyengar . . . Karma.

DOWNWARD FACING DOGMA

Too much personal input or improvisation can dilute, if not pollute, the teachings, and generate confusion. Yet too much rigidity or dogma can destroy them or attract only compulsive fanatics. Our style is sometimes called downward facing dogma, for the acute precision of the technique and relative obsession with Adho Mukha Śvānāsana!

CORRESPONDANCES

Teachers have to channel and listen to searchers, pandits, intellectuals, and share what they received in accessible terms to fellow human beings. In French, the word for teaching is "enseigner," to give the signs, to show the way, to guide on a path with symbols. Like in Baudelaire's poem, *Correspondances*:

La Nature est un temple où de vivants piliers
Laissent parfois sortir de confuses paroles;
L'homme y passe à travers des forêts de symboles
Qui l'observent avec des regards familiers.

Nature's a temple where each living column,
At times, gives forth vague words. There Man advances
Through forest-groves of symbols, strange and solemn,
Who follow him with their familiar glances.

(translation Roy Campbell)

So, study anatomy, psychology, astronomy, music theory, art history, anthropology, history of religion, archeology, semiology, etc. Read the book of Life, yes, but how does the reality of the experience resonate in you? Does it affect the life force, are you touched and moved by It? Does it refine and clarify your life mission? Do your teaching and/or practice benefit?

PART FOUR

Miscellany

NAṬARĀJA-RAP

Is it to redefine your butts, that you dance for us, Naṭarāja?
To flatten your guts, that you dance for us, Naṭarāja?
No if no buts, if you flatten your tummy, you'll feel like a mommy!
Is it to trim your waistline or to be vertically-aligned
That you dance for us, Naṭarāja?
Is the fitness bootcamp to prepare for war
To sweat and be tough, to be all that you can be
To die of exercise, worrying about your size
Tell me, Naṭarāja
You're no buns of steel, you're here for the feel
To be in trance is your cosmic dance
Hey Naṭarāja, are you proud of your descendance?
You had passion, it turned into obsession
Did you dance, dance to be fit?
Or did you dance to dance, for the sake of it?
O Naṭarāja, you have the power of the belly
So far from anorexis, dancing with elegance on the central axis
Silencing the lake of the mind into eternal bliss
Dance, dance for us
Free of form, free of time, free from the weight of the world
Free to open the gates of the maṇḍala, free to be ourselves, free to be free!
Is it not time to send an alarm
Et laisser couler nos larmes?
So, I am begging you, Naṭarāja, Lord of Dance, Grandfather of Yoga,
Dance, dance, dance, dance for us!

(To be rapped with a beatbox or a drum machine)

OLYMPICS

All human beings tend to be competitive, if not with others then with themselves, sometimes for survival needs. Pitta doṣa fueled by Vāta frenzy rules the world! But in Yoga or art, it is not relevant. Identifying, anticipating and responding to your needs is what makes a practitioner more mature and promotes a good practice and a good life. It is hard to be competitive in a resting or creative mode! If you rest deeper and longer than somebody else, what kind of medal would you win? A gold consciousness award? If I ever participate in a Yoga Olympics, I would compete in the extreme Śavāsana category. I would rather die virtually in Śavāsana than for real in a marathon or an acrobatic āsana.

The only sport that I ever practiced was fencing between the ages of nine and twelve. My teacher was Sir James, an English aristocrat. I ended up participating in the regional championship of Normandy in the foil category. I placed second to last and my opponent was only five years old. So, I made the wise decision to quit! But fencing karma came back forty years later in Rochester, New York. I got an offer to teach Yoga to the fencing team as part of the preparation for the 2004 Athens Games. Rochester Fencing Center had an international reputation at the time, with a few potential Olympic medalists. In fact, they won a few medals in Beijing four years later. I became friends with one of the senior coaches, also a Yoga student. Twice a week, I would see young athletes. Some were already injured, bandages on knee and wrist. I was thinking that their chances of medals were thin. Two or three of them got really into Yoga and would come to the studio to relax. Foilists and épéeists are in Vīrabhadrāsana II forever on only one side. Saberists are more in an early stage of Vīrabhadrāsana I, more sagitally oriented. It was easy to find a practice to create balance: refining alignment of Vīrabhadrāsana II, practicing the other side, counterposes for front leg always in flexion and back leg always in extension.

I taught breathing practices and relaxation to be able to face a high-level competition without stress and improve mental clarity, as fencing is a little bit like chess. Well, they loved restorative so much, they got so relaxed and self-aware, reflecting on life's mission, that they lost their motivation to compete and decided not to go the games. They were too stressed and damaged already by years of abusive coaching and aggressive training. One senior coach actually got fired. The other coach (who had invited me) was not thrilled as you can guess, as I was paid well to train them. But years later, two of those young women thanked me for having brought balance back into their lives. This made my day. They kept fencing, low key for the love of it, instead of competing at a high level. They had children and harmonious lives. No Olympics. Yoga won the medal. Fairy tale.

NATURE AND CULTURE

Where the whole man is involved, there is no work. Work begins with division of labor.
—MARSHALL MCLUHAN

The sacred and profane had no separation originally. Then symbolism came and created a gap so we need to go back to the pre-symbolic level to have a direct experience. Paul Ricoeur, the French philosopher, claims, “We are those who have not finished killing our idols and who have finally only begun to listen to symbols.”

I saw a documentary on a tribe of Amazonian Indians, who live in complete autarky and don’t have to “work.” Almost a utopian harmony. The elders were saying: “Even when we do nothing, we are never bored!” Obviously Amazonian Indians or South Indian farmers do not have Spinyasa class on Sunday, Pilates on Tuesday and cakra balancing on Wednesday. So how do they stay functional in posture, stamina, etc.?

If we are too sedentary, driving, using computer with TMSD (too much sitting disease), what do we really need and how much of it, to stay fully alive and moving, breathing freely like most animals on the planet? How much is too much (running ultramarathon fueled by multivitamin pills and powders) or too little (watching golf tournaments 24/7 on the golf channel munching on cheap guacamole and pints of ice cream with giant sodas)?

One answer is Yoga, practicing all aspects of it. Culture and Nature co-existing harmoniously. Re-uniting labor and play.

TO BE, TO FEEL, TO ACT

As a joke on my computer desk, I have an icon for, “to do list,” actually two icons, one related to personal life, one for business and I also have an icon, “to be.” As you can guess, the “to do” lists are long and procrastination is often an issue—even for a Yoga teacher! The “to be” list is short: “Be!” In fact, it should be empty. It’s the same kind of paradox as talking or writing about Silence.

When we practice Yoga, there is often confusion about the agenda. Is it for the journey or for the goal, or both? Is it a physical, psychological or spiritual exploration? I like to remember the words of science fiction writer Ursula LeGuin: “It is good to have an end to journey toward; but it is the journey that matters, in the end.”

When we create an āsana, we play a position like we play a composition of music. First, we have to build the underlying structure, the sacred architecture. In doing so we follow the cosmic and esoteric rules of nature. We also seek to expend minimal energy, to be as functional as possible. This is like establishing the foundation or creating the skeleton of beams when building a house. We have to create the optimal conditions so life can happen inside—so breath can breathe, heart can pulse with contentment, and fluids can flow and nourish the tissues.

For example, in sitting meditation the seat is essential, and how you sit on it. The rest might not be up to us. In a good practice, as in good travel, you are always surprised. How fascinating that “āsana,” the Sanskrit word for Yoga posture, originally meant, "seat, to sit." It also refers to the low platform on which the yogi did his practice.

We say, in Iyengar Yoga, that the place where the body touches the ground is the brain of the pose. In standing, that would be the feet; in sitting, the sitting bones and the legs; in Head Balance, the Śirṡā (crown) of the head, in Shoulderstand, the shoulders, and so on. First, observe the base, the seat. It is like setting up your altar for the ritual to take place. Then you realize there is somebody living in there.

In Yoga we have an inward experience of that living space as well as an awareness of the structure; they mutually influence each other. Each āsana has a different breath, as people have. One quest could be: What is the breath of this pose, where does it live, how does it resonate? So, Prāṇāyāma, yogic breathing, is already there; it has nothing to do with breathing exercises and everything to do with awareness of what is.

Form and content: that is a polarity you cannot ignore in movement, in fitness or even in advertising! How can the external image reflect the inner substance? Look at cosmetic surgery; it reflects suffering, inner drama, frustration about aging—not contentment. A depressed front spine will compress the heart and the digestive organs, creating even more depression and disturbing natural functions.

So, we adjust the living sculpture of the body from gross to subtle levels. Then, attention goes with the pulses of life, the underground river of Prāṇa. Many Yoga practitioners, blinded by the fact that it takes physical energy and stamina to align and sustain a pose, fail to experience the ethos, the field, the ecology of the pose. Yoga can be sold as a form of fitness, stretching and intelligent toning, with little or no processing of internal life or connections with a bigger picture. Ironically, that is often what people mean when they ask, "Do you teach Haṭha?" It means they are not interested in Yoga's spiritual overtones. They might already be content with their religious orientation. Or, they just want to exercise—not sign up for another belief system, reevaluate how they inhabit their bodies, or think about their life mission. Many don't want to think or question, just do and sweat! And please, make the cool-down or the relaxation short; we didn't pay a class fee to lie down or sit!

I said "ironically," because in India, Haṭha Yoga, referring to the text *Haṭha Yoga Pradīkipā*, is a very esoteric set of practices, certainly way beyond physical planes. It plays with the polarity of the sun and moon energies, the solar and lunar plexuses.

The "fitness" industry, seeing which way the wind blows, certainly has adopted yogic concepts like inner strength, inner peace and body-mind connection. How many health clubs have added the word "mind" to "body" to better sell the same old things revamped with a pseudo-spiritual glow? It's becoming a common way to market weight loss or a flat tummy. Of course, you have to meet people where they are. But, still, at some point it should not be called Yoga anymore. There is a lot of bad spiritual Yoga out there—and also, to be fair, great, sound fitness classes.

Is Yoga—or any practice—based on form or content? As in music, we cannot separate the technique from the interpretation and the emotional content. In music, you have to learn to play an instrument or sing, so there is a physical component. But really, would music qualify as fitness? It would be like playing the cello to burn calories, the saxophone to lose weight, or playing the piano to sleep better and give flexibility to the finger joints!

Traditionally, Yoga practice is more about being in a pose and discovering ways to sustain it. The fast-paced, sun-salutation based Yoga that we see developing with various denominations (Power, Vinyāsa, etc.) is quite recent in history. Westerners have endorsed it more than the meditative forms because the culture itself is fast, with an obsessive-compulsive edge. Consider that anorexia or anorexia-like patterns such as never enough, low self-esteem and substance abuse are quite common. And since like attracts like, as we say in Ayurveda, the choices people make in their lives tend to magnify the issues. Of course, there is an obesity problem, so people have to move and break the sedentary ce; but what I see is that the already-thin people over-exercise—often plagued by sports injuries—while some of the overweight crowd just watches abs-machine commercials and dines at all- you- can-eat buffets, which the American culture promotes at the same time as diet pills.

What really matters is the emotional balance, the equilibrium of the nervous system, the contentment of living a meaningful life, the ability to sleep well and have a rich dream life. To have no regrets when you finally dissolve at the end. I remember the words of John Lennon: "Life is what happens when you're busy making other plans."

If you feel oppressed or ill at ease with yourself, open from inside. Learn to breathe freely, practice a receptive passive backbend and see that your ribcage may be too much of a cage. See what will come out of the cage and see how the cage transforms itself into an adaptable woven basket! Open the doors of the inner kingdom and the windows of the brain, the sensory organs. Soften the skin so the life force can flow everywhere and irrigate the vessel. The breath then will reclaim its full territory. Then you can simply be.

STRAIGHT!

Straight is a word I do not like in the orientation field, for it implies that the non-straight are crooked or defective; life itself and of course the spine have curves. Rivers bend, waves are spiraling. Life is a vortex, a maelstrom, not a straight line. Same when we say it is right, where does that put the left? Symmetry is overrated. Life can be organized around a vertical pole or a vector of energy as a reference, like sunflowers are toward the sun. It is never a straight line. Look at DNA.

Some still have a belief in their mind that a straight spine or straight, flat back is "good" posture as if lordosis was evil or an insult: *Hey, you lordotic!* That is why, "tuck the tail," and "navel to spine," are popular instructions or why some meditation students retract their chin to have a straight neck. The teacher may have in mind verticality, uprightness, poise, etc., but the word straight would be misleading. It is repressive and creates tension, restriction in the throat and in the front body. The front of the neck and front of the spine, especially in lower trunk, are vulnerable places and should stay soft. In some ways, we need more front care than back care. The back needs strength and residual tone in the secondary curves to allow the freedom, vulnerability and safety of the front.

Straight, right, symmetrical . . . potential trouble of imposing and controlling too much to get the perfect shape. It's a "long and winding road," sings Paul McCartney. If we had a street demonstration the slogan for all curves of the spine would be: Elongate, don't negate! Traction, yes, Retraction, no! Follow the curves, don't flatten them!

DAYDREAM

I was trying to daydream, but my mind wouldn't wander.
—STEVEN WRIGHT

Daydreaming is essential to humans. According to *Psychology Today*, daydreams help define our sense of self, improve social skills, develop creativity and make us be more engaged with life.

"Daydream" is also the title of a song from Wallace Collection, a Belgian "Moody Blues" pop group who flirted with classical music.

Daydreaming in underrated.

MASK & VEIL

Prāṇāyāma removes the veil covering the inner light.
—PATAÑJALI SŪTRA 2.52, TRANSLATION BY B.K.S. IYENGAR

The virtual veil can be past karma, education, conforming to social norms or being nice all the time. In Venice during Carnival, you intentionally wear a mask and then remove it. Easy to remove the veil! In plastic surgery or with Botox injections, it's also a choice but not reversible. How do you unveil if you change your mind? Bringing back the original woodwork in your old house is a lot more work than painting one more coat over it before you sell it. People who have had Botox injections cannot mimic emotions of others. They cannot mirror the faces of those they are watching or talking with and it could alter their ability to understand what people are feeling.

In India and most traditional cultures, the faces are very expressive and spontaneous; joy, sadness, anger, we see them all everywhere. Pilgrims and their extended families on the grounds of Thanjavur or Madurai temples offer full colorful expression of life, unlike Paris or New York City subways that feel, by comparison, like a depressing black and white wax museum.

In Kathakalī, traditional South Indian theater, there are nine expressions called bhāvas and in psychology there are six to nine. They overlap. The nine emotions in Kathakalī are: Śṛṅgāra (love/beauty), Hāsya (laughter), Karuṇā (sorrow), Raudra (anger), Vīra (heroism/courage), Bhayānaka (terror/fear), Bībhatsya (disgust), Adbutha (surprise/wonder), and Śānta (peace or tranquility).

In classical Psychology, we find anger, contempt, disgust, fear, joy, sadness, and surprise. It is important that you are able to actually play or simulate those expressions. In real life.

I remember giving a private Yoga session to a student who used to be a drag queen and could not sing a song with his real voice as he was used to lip-synching perfectly. His facial expression was fixed, geisha-like. I taught him two simple bhāvas of Kathakalī, joy and anger. I was taught the basics in a small village by my friend Pradeep Kumar. He won Best Actor award in Kerala for his role as a vampire in the *Mahābhārata*. After a decade of practice and receiving various teachings, taking voice lessons, that devoted student, originally on the dark side, began to see a sattvic light. He is now chanting mantra with an affirmed beautiful voice accompanied by the drone of his śruti box and enjoys the direct connection with Nāda and Life.

One way to release the mask(s) is deep in Śavāsana. Peeling layers and layers like an onion, until naked. It will dissolve under the force of gravity and the deep relaxation response. But the unconscious resistances may not melt that easily.

I had several experiences of removing an actual mask. I did a few years of foil in my early teens, wearing a fencing mask. I went to Venice Carnival a few times. The tradition of the mask started in the thirteenth century when Venetians would hold celebrations and parties from December 26 until the start of Lent. And wore elaborate masks to conceal their identity, mixing lower and upper class. The Carnival masks originated during the great pest epidemic, early seventeenth century. The epidemic ravaged Venice many times, and a beaked mask was used as a sanitary precaution by actual doctors. The long nose would hold herbs and flowers that would filter the air and cover up the horrible smells of plague victims.

For several days, I put the mask on when I woke up to go outside, and I kept it on all day long, if I had the discipline, walking in the cold fog of February. I ended up forgetting I was wearing one. In some parts of the cities, they gather by families of masks. All Renaissance types meet on a certain plaza at 8:00 P.M. The skeletons may gather on another one at midnight (I was in that group!) and those wearing masks made out of painted pasta somewhere else. When I took if off at night, it was quite strange and liberating.

I also played the role of a bird, wearing a mask, touring Europe theater festivals. Sweating and moving at the speed of a bird during the show and taking it off at the end. This created that same liberating experience, being yourself again. Showing your true and real face. I am not a bird.

Note: The irony is I'm writing this text during the coronavirus pandemic, when wearing a mask is widespread.

TURN OUT

In 1661 King Louis XIV founded a ballet school, l'Académie Royale de Danse. In this school, Mr. Beauchamp, first ballet master of the Academy, named the five positions of the feet and began to develop the ballet technique as we know it today.

The legs were slightly turned out as a result of the fashion in France of gentlemen wearing wide-topped bucket boots which forced them to swing their legs as they walked so that their toes turned outwards as the feet touched the ground.

As ballet became more popular and women started participating, turnout disappeared. It was not until ballet was performed on a stage with the audience along one side only that turnout was re-introduced. It was required because the King and his family decided they did not want people to face their backs to them. The only way the dancers could move backwards and to the side with no effort was to turn the legs out. Later, Carlo Blasis, director of the Academy of Dancing at Milan, established the concept of rotating the legs ninety degrees from a forward-facing line.

Is it not interesting that, because of a king's wish, generations of dancers, children and adults, have destroyed their big toes in hallux valgus, lost arch support and also often compressed sacro-iliac joints, inducing painful sciatica. It is not about function, not even aesthetics. A sad story. Thank God for modern dance. Martha Graham, Twyla Tharp, Merce Cunningham, Pina Baush, Anna Teresa de Keersmaeker, to name a few, went barefoot and dropped the turnout (well, not always) for parallel feet. African dance, along with drumming, came back in the picture, rooted in the heels like flamenco.

Tāḍāsana is closer to the African tribal way of standing, like Masai warriors, than French aristocrats dancing ballet for the King in the seventeenth century.

Coxa vara or valga, the angle of the neck of the femur, is a genetic pattern and will determine genu valgum or varum as well as a different potential of external leg rotation for everyone. In Yoga, this plays in Vīrāsana, Padmāsana. And especially in Baddha Koṇāsana. If your knees don't touch the floor, they don't touch the floor. We have to be wise and accept that our potential is unique. Sure, you can progress with practice, but it is exponential with a ceiling. This story sends many yogis and yoginis for hip replacement later in life, after years of overplaying Upaviṣṭa Koṇāsana and Samāsana. Be careful if you feel like Hanumān (āsana) when you wake up!

THE EIFFEL TOWER

Noëlle Perez had a samādhi-like vision one day looking deeply at the Eiffel Tower, as she was walking her beloved dog Pañtā. A perfect symbol for the eight limbs of Yoga. The four pillars (Yama, Niyama, Āsana and Prāṇāyāma) still going all the way to the top, supporting as a foundation the more subtle añgas and the levels, first, second floor and third floor, Pratyāhāra, Dhāraṇā and Dhyāna. Finally, the antennas and satellite dishes at the top, neo-gothic cathedral arrowhead, cosmic emitter-receiver of Samādhi!

BLIND FAITH

Certainly, body image matters to many. And in our culture, it matters usually way too much. But what if you are blind? Would you have plastic surgery if you could not see yourself in the mirror? What matters then? I remember downhill skiing with a completely blind friend, way back in the late sixties, in the French Alps. I was constantly shouting numbers to give directions so he could follow You can imagine the level of trust it required from him. Stunning and scary. He had to surrender completely, fearless. We also went with him, climbing on glaciers, roped together. He was in the middle. But what moved me the most was to see him touch everything, how he liked to be in contact with his wife.

Love at first sight can be a problem, especially for Pitta type! Love at first touch? Love at first sound like in Supervielle's novel, *The Girl with a Violin's Voice*? Love at first smell, yes. We know that is primary and what rules the world. A reason why the perfume industry is not going away, even in times of crisis.

Yoga involves all senses. Perception is crucial. The whole body is the sensory organ, it leads to synesthetic experiences. Everything is an opportunity to learn about life and its mysteries, about the secret language of the universe. I learned a lot from my blind friend and later it helped me when I had the opportunity to teach a few visually impaired organists and composers in Paris. I also learned later that my friend's second wife was blind as well. When they wanted to have children, doctors warned them that they would not likely see. But against all odds, they did.

FATHERS

In 2014, I saw my father of incarnation and my father of transmission leave the front stage of the cosmic theater . . . the wheel is turning . . . feeling sad, yes, but also something beautiful, liberating and meaningful about it. A form of realization. Now flying with my own unclipped wings.

FREE SPIRIT

Do you have the discipline to be a free spirit?
—GABRIELLE ROTH

The more constraints one imposes, the more one frees one's self of the chains that shackle the spirit.
—STRAVINSKY

Both Roth and Stravinsky were experiencing the most freedom when improvising on a given theme.

How do I practice? Whom do I learn from? Why and what do I play on my own? There is discipline and freedom.

Playing music does not make you necessarily a musician. Similarly, chanting spiritual formula or Bhajans does not make you more spiritual. Kabir was already warning us:

Are you looking for me? I am in the next seat.
My shoulder is against yours.
You will not find me in stupas, not in Indian shrine rooms,
Nor in synagogues, nor in cathedrals:
Not in masses, nor kirtans, not in legs winding around your own neck,
Nor in eating nothing but vegetables.
When you really look for me, you will see me instantly.
You will find me in the tiniest house of time.
Kabir says: Student, tell me, what is God?
He is the breath inside the breath.

What are my deep aspirations, my obstacles, my limitations?

Can I self-prescribe Āsanas, Prāṇāyāmas and Śavāsana the same way a musician plans a daily practice or rehearses for a concert? Like figure skating, you have compulsary figures and free dance! Well, the only difference is that Yoga is not a performance art. It could be strange and disturbing in Yoga conferences to clap after an āsana show.

Find the balance between mandatory practice, fixed curriculum and improvisation, channeling, free practices, between action and relaxation, between acceptance and change. Then contentment, Saṇtoṣa, may appear out of the deep blue!

Balance between a guided tour following your teacher, a book or a video and immersion on your own with no agenda. Sometimes you need to have an organized tour to break the initial fear of being on your own. Or to be sure you don't miss certain important milestones. For example, the first time I was in Egypt, I was seventeen, on my way to Nubia to follow Rimbaud's steps and I missed the pyramids!

When visiting at the museum, same thing, it is nice to have a good knowledgeable guide once and then you can come back alone and improvise. A few years ago, I went to all museums and churches in Italy in search of all angels playing music in the paintings of the masters, using binoculars. I learned a great deal.

You can follow the foot patterns in every āsana; you can become the foot and take yourself for a ride though all āsanas. Or identify with a certain organ and travel the poses as if you were that organ. In your practice, you can focus on things close to your heart.

Become a free electron in the Yogātom.

HIGH HEELS, SHOULDER REST, FORKS AND OBSTETRICS

Not long ago in India, eating with my hands directly touching and almost kneading the food, gathering little mountains of rice and dal on a banana leaf gave me this impulse to write more about it. Most of the Yoga group traveling with us was also using fingers by the third or fourth day. Some were still using a fork after a couple weeks. Even the Mahārājas, or the kings in France in the Middle Ages were eating with their hands. No forks, no distance. At Ramana Maharshi Ashram, eating with all the pilgrims on the floor is always a very powerful experience—ancestral, timeless. No table, no chair, no plate, no spoon, no fork, no shoes. Just the Presence.

Modern romantic violin has a shoulder rest between the instrument and the shoulder. Baroque violin does not. Indian and folk violin is played like a cello with direct contact with the heart and the belly. No distance again between subject and object. The instrument is part of the body and resonates in it. Look at how babies are carried in Africa or Native American tribes, where the baby is in direct contact with the mother and can hear her heartbeat. In a car seat there is more distantiation and anxiety. To be a yogi is to be more primal, organic, connected, wild, not so neo-romantic. It has shamanic roots. But we also have to be civilized to live in society.

High heels, like forks, create distantiation. Catherine de Medici was fond of both. In the same period, Louis XIV decided to witness his mistress giving birth lying down, like a show. To this day, obstetrics follow that ignoble path where the field of gravity is no longer an ally. At the other extreme women can give birth by themselves standing or squatting in the Amazonian forest.

LIGHTS & YOGA

JYOTI & DĪPIKA

Viśhoka vā jyotiṣmatī I, 36
Inner stability is gained by contemplating a luminous, sorrowless, effulgent light.

Tataḥ Kṣīyate Prakāśāvaraṇam II, 52
Prāṇāyāma removes the veil covering the light of knowledge.
—PATAÑJALI SŪTRA, TRANSLATION BY B.K.S. IYENGAR

Jyoti is a sweet first name for Indian children and could be any kind of light, a lamp, the sun, inner or outer. Prakāśa means illumination, the emanation of light, light coming from a source before reflection. Dīpa is a lamp light, pradīpa is the lamp light having come forward to illuminate a space or a room. Jyoti relates primarily to celestial light and how celestial bodies shine while Prakāśa is a more general term.

Inner light appears in Ājñā cakra region after chanting, Prāṇāyāma or Trāṭak.

Dīpika has been lit by the teacher or guru, is rekindled by practice, by meeting with remarkable men and women and is burning in all of us with a soft glow. *Light on Yoga*, Yoga Dīpika, a seminal book written by Śrī B.K.S. Iyengar is referring in a subtle way to *Haṭha Yoga Pradīkipa*. But it also evokes the flames of the beautiful little oil lamps released at night during the Puja in the Gaṅgā by the pilgrims, from Haridwar to Varanasi.

LIGHT & DARK

With the solstices past and my Thanksgiving nights earlier in the deep canyons of Utah, I am particularly aware of the light and darkness polarity. This plays in Yoga quite a bit as well. The shining quality of the inner dome of the head after Kapālabhāti, the soft luminosity of Jyoti in deep meditation or Śavāsana, the piercing light of the bindu in Ājñā cakra after chanting OM. All of these emerge from the darkness of the inner body. Similarly, we see the stars better in complete darkness away from the lights of civilization. Places where we can see the night sky clearly are less and less common. Look at the *Black Marble Map*.

Go camping in those dark holes, there are still a few, like the black triangle of Quercy, not too far from where I live. Of all pollutions we face, light pollution is perhaps the most easily remedied. So hopefully, away from the crazy luminous Vṛttis of Las Vegas, the desert can be a place of contemplation again.

PAVAMĀNA MANTRA

Om asatomā sadgamaya
Tamaso mā jyotirgamaya
Mṛtyormāmṛtaṃ gamaya
Om śāntiḥ, śāntiḥ, śāntiḥ!
Bṛhadāraṇyaka Upaniṣad 1.3.28

From Tamas to Sattva, from darkness to light, from ignorance to consciousness. Awareness is a path of no return, the same with any education. By the time you know how to read and write, you cannot ignore what is in the document you are going to sign or that a scribe is signing for you. You cannot pretend you don't know if you know. Sometimes it is painful, that is why ignorance is so convenient.

The good news is that guna is easier to change than doṣa. It can evolve. Your primary doṣa may be in excess now—you can minimize it but you will die with it! On the other hand, if you are tamasic or rajasic today you still have a chance to die in a sattvic luminous state. Good luck and Courage!

Lose yourself.

Find yourself again.

Then leave yourself alone!

Don't interfere, make yourself invisible, wear spiritual camouflage, blend in.

Take yourself out of the equation.

Prāṇa will flow freely in your Nāḍīs.

MIGRANTS

Half of the matter forming the Milky Way probably came from far away galaxies, says the Royal Astronomical Society. So, each of us could be in part made of extragalactic matter Our origin is much less local than we believe.

Daniel Anglés-Alcázar adds: We, human beings, could consider ourselves like space travelers or extragalactical migrants. Key word is migrant! Where were French people 5,000 years ago or Americans 1,000 years ago? Where were the prehistoric yogis 10,000 years ago? Where did the Aryan people come from before invading North India? We were all nomads not so long ago and must not forget that borders used to follow natural barriers, mountains, oceans, shores, and rivers or there were none. Nationalist-based wars, slavery, drought, quest for an Eldorado, desire for adventure, call of the Unknown, moved hordes of people, made them travel in exile by fear, from hell to idealized paradise . . . and it is still relevant today. Lesbos and Lampedusa islands are real. So be kind. Your ancestors may have been on one of those precarious boats. You could be on one of them in the future.

We were all migrants.

MOST COMMONLY ASKED QUESTION BY MY STUDENTS:

I don't see myself. I don't have a mirror! How do I know what I am doing?

Possible Answers:

1. Welcome to Yoga.
2. Find the inner mirror.
3. The mind's eye can see. If the mind is clear of vṛttis. The mind reflects like the moon.
4. Over time you develop X-Ray vision, clairvoyant abilities.
5. Just as sound waves reverberate through a room or a cave, so do breath waves inside us to provide in-formation about the shape, volume and texture of the inner body cavities.
6. If you walk around a stupa, you will identify gradually with its center.
7. Trust direct experience. Can the body feel itself? No duality between object and subject.
8. The guru, teacher, assistant, coach gives feedback with words, touch and visual demonstrations. Teaching shows the Signs. Over the years, you will gather more and more clues and by deduction, my dear Watson, you will know where you are and see yourself!
9. Illuminate the blind spots with luminous consciousness!
10. Keep practicing. Stop and observe.
11. Develop kinesthetic awareness gradually by repeating the experience like Japa-ajapa for āsana: Āsana-anāsana.

POST-WORKSHOP SYNDROME

This goes for all Mondays after weekend Yoga seminars or the week after a longer retreat or Journey. Handle with grace what I call the post-workshop syndrome. Your perception has been sharpened, there is a certain intensity and also a churning of emotions and past karmas that make you more vulnerable. Take it easy, settle down, give yourself time for transition toward what we call real life. This applies both to the students and the teacher. If you are a teacher, digest and absorb the weekend or retreat materials before sharing them with your students. Iyengar used to say that one day in a Pune Yoga Intensive would take at least a year to be integrated. After most workshops or some cathartic classes, you will experience aftershocks, the internal ocean receding after a psychological and physical tsunami. But near the Shore Temple in Mahābalipuram, the receding sea after the tsunami revealed what may be one of the seven lost Pagodas of the Myth, which archeologists knew existed but could not find. So, there is positive transformation as well. Ideally, take a day off or even a week if it is a longer retreat to rest and absorb the teachings. The return to work and family spheres could be a shock, like a spaceship or meteor entry into the atmosphere.

RUNNING TO DEATH

To my students who are long distance runners, forgive me!

2009. Three more people died in the Detroit Marathon, and one in New York City. The New York Times and the Democrat and Chronicle placed a couple of lines in the sports ticker, while the winner got a full page naming the sponsors. That is not about health, of course. Remember the world champion in the Athens Olympics throwing up, dazed, running into the crowd and backwards away from the finish line!? And as I got a reminder through the words of Matthew Hall: "Death will always be part of long-distance running. The marathon owes its name and a lot of its mystique, after all, to the mythical Athenian who collapsed and died after a breathless declaration of victory following a 25 mile run from a battleground in Marathon." Yes, human beings may be born to run and still do in some tribal cultures. No doubt. Still, the central character of the book *Born to Run* died while running.

The real question is: Where is the middle way between overexercising (including death) and doing nothing, like watching the Weather Channel 24/7!? How much is too much and how little is too little to be functional, physically and emotionally?

Of course, being completely biased toward Yoga, as I never practiced any sports or placed one foot in a health club, I believe a good, balanced, consistent, moderate Yoga practice touching all facets of the diamond (strength/stamina-oriented āsanas including core toning and releasing; āsanas increasing range of motion in every possible joint; restorative āsanas; Prāṇāyāma from Bhastrikā to Bhrāmarī; Yoga of sound/mantra; and Śavāsana) is enough to answer the needs of the modern human being. My teacher and his teacher before him had long, healthy lives (ninety-six and one hundred, respectively) and they "only" practiced Yoga. Add a good sleeping pattern to it, immersion in nature's elements a few times a year—at the foot of the glaciers or deep in the ocean—and moderate intake of organic, sattvic, healthy food. Let's not go too much into details in this category, as everybody is trying to sell their soup, from raw food to overcooked khichadis and it can be confusing!

So, going back to the running to death topic: I had this idea to organize a Śavāsanathon™®—that is, virtual not real death. A day of deep relaxation where teachers and students could just lie down like corpses for as long as they like. They would come and go quietly, and people would pledge a few dollars for a minute of deep rest instead of a mile of running. Less casualty, raising money while relaxing, a sattvic Pitta fundraising!

SHOPPING FOR RELIGION

Your daily life is your temple and your religion.
—KAHLIL GIBRAN

Oh, and if you are shopping for a religion or a belief system, here is a suggestion: travel back around 30,000 BCE, cave painting era, pre-everything, less confusing and closer to Nature, a time when music and language were one! There were human beings then. No separation between labor and play yet, or between sacred and profane. Not too many religions or diets to choose from, simple. (Well, it was not a stress-free or golden era either.)

ASANISM

Life experiences influence and nourish the practice and the teachings of Yoga. Anatomy, philosophy, psychology, travels in other cultures, anthropology, art, poetry, etc . . . educate and change perception. Ethnocentric views are minimized. Subtle differentiation between things or people who appear to look alike superficially or at first glance, will be possible. Racism, sexism, ethnocentrism and asanism will be minimized. Asanism is like thinking that all the standing poses look alike or not see the point to have so many seated forward bend variations! Advanced practitioners are more refined in perception. Continuing education is needed to differentiate. I am not an asanist.

BEYOND YOGA

In ancient times, pupils went in search of guru.
Today guru go in search of pupils, that's why spirituality looses its fragrance .
—B.K.S. IYENGAR 1968

Over the years and decades of teaching around the world, I figured out that if you add the words "potent," "beyond," "mind & spirit," "inner," "flow," "deep," "new paradigm," "core," "power" or "advanced" to anything, it works better! You can also use fake Sanskrit, connecting all letters at the top with the same bar, on your advertising: that will attract a few people.

Often, not always, if you see this, you should be suspicious and run away! Yes, there are exceptions. What about "Deep Inner Core, Flow Beyond Yoga World Tour with Swāmi Raoultānanda?" Okay, I am a little sarcastic, French and arrogant. Sarcastics are disillusioned romantics and Pitta types are more judgmental than average. If that is the case, mea culpa, mea maxima culpa.

YOGA IS

Live your questions now and perhaps even without knowing it,
you will live along some distant answers.

Be patient toward all that is unsolved in your heart and try to love the questions themselves.
—RAINER MARIA RILKE

Whenever students or teachers ask me a question in classes or Yoga retreats, my first answer is always, "It depends." That follows an Ayurvedic principle that you have to adapt the suggestions and prescriptions to each person's genetic set-up, psychological profile and health history. Some people need strength, some flexibility, some both. Some people need to let go of their belief system if it's too fundamentalist or ethnocentric, others need to go deeper in the roots of their religion or culture. Some people need warmth, some a cooling environment. Some need to sustain Yoga poses for long timings, others may need to flow from one to the next, some need abdominal strength, some need deep release and softness in their belly. Some students need to move or sweat, if truly overweight; some need to rest or meditate; some have no more to sweat or are pseudo anorexic.

How do we know what we need? Does what we need correspond to what we want or what we choose to do? Are we aware of the side effects of our actions or of the long-term resonance of our health practices or lifestyle habits or exercise routines?

Yoga is a science, an art, a philosophy, a life-style, a fitness practice. Side effects of Yoga practice include clarity of perception, better range of motion and flexibility, stamina and strength.

Eliminate confusion and complication. Welcome complexity! For most, āsana is for fitness, philosophy is for intellect and religion for the spirit or the soul. Let's attempt to unify them in the United States of Yoga!

FOR THE SAKE OF IT

Yoga is the journey and the destination. Traveling to India, Africa or anywhere in the world gives us a chance for great meetings with people, landscapes, situations and events that can be life and consciousness-altering. Similarly, you can travel inside yourself! You have to take the dive, the risk and prepare yourself. The mind has to be open like the sky. No need to do Yoga for this or that.

On a Denver flyer, years ago, the title of my seminar was "Yoga for the sake of it." One student thought that it was about sake, the drink! And strange coincidence, we went for dinner to a Japanese restaurant! I am not yoking.

SCRIPT FOR STAND UP COMEDY: YOYOGAGA™

Q: How many Iyengar teachers does it take to screw in a light bulb?
A: Three. One to put a block under the bulb, one to wrap a strap around the bulb and one to talk about their personal experience with Mr. Iyengar.

—ANONYMOUS

Since we already have Brew-ga (beer and Yoga), Doga (Yoga with and for your dog), Broga (only men), Chocoga (chocolate happy hours Yoga), Yogacappuccinopilates, Spinga and Spinyasa (spinning and Yoga), Woga (Yoga in water), Snowga (skiing and Yoga), what about Icyvinyāsa (moon salutation in a giant freezer) or Brryoga, in a really cold room, Spindoga (spinning with your dog), Brrrewbroga (beer and Yoga for men in icy water). Ladygagayoga and Yoginimartini are self-explanatory. Some of the previous names are actually for real. What the hell is going on in the Yoga World?

I just invented a new style of Yoga called Yoregami™. Organic Ramen, Machalatte and Yoregami would be a perfect match for the Manhattan Yoga jetset. To take a posture, just fold the body like we fold Origami paper, along the dotted lines. Actually, anatomic names are clear: popliteal fold, gluteal fold, inguinal fold, presplenic fold or even median glossoepiglottic fold. Fold mindfully in the right places otherwise you may reach a high degree of frustration or pain.

Cigaryama, pairing cigars and Prāṇāyāma, is my favorite. For example, smoking an oversized Cuban cigar coupled with Bhastrikā or a small, vanilla-flavored one with Bhramarī, etc. Alternate smoking is more advanced: let smoke come out through alternate nostrils.

What about pairing French cheeses and restorative poses like Roquefort with Supta Baddha Koṇāsana and Marolles in Viparīta Karaṇi Mudrā? Chewing Laughing Cow during laughing Yoga? Yogababa: using rumbaba for eye bags in Śavāsana along with groovy Reggae music. Safari Yoga: more romantic, ending with Savannāsana, Śavāsana in the savanna among wild animals, testing fight or flight versus relaxation response.

Even more advanced, Yoyoyoga, playing with a yoyo in Naṭarājāsana. Not to be confused with Yoyomayoga, cello music during practice. Yogaga means just going crazy doing Yoga. But let's be serious: reading *Yoga Journal's* advertising pages in full boat, Paripūrṇa Nāvāsana, for twenty minutes would be a great way to tone, strengthen, firm, petrify or freeze your abdominal wall and be educated at the same time. Special option for twelve-hour certified master online teachers: synchronizing Bhastrikā with Aśvinī Mudrā and playing overtones in a didgeridoo. That will rock the boat.

All these practices are patented, were tested by seven generations over a few weeks and are a 10,000-year-old proven methodology leading toward enlightenment, mental and metaphysical health. The line of transmission from the akashic records has been uninterrupted and flawless until today. They all originated in India, actually 40,000 years ago and were practiced all over the world along with Sanskrit and a proto-paleo-diet. They are also mentioned in an ancient sacred text, unfortunately eaten by glacier termites near Mount Kailash. Careful: Kuṇḍalinī will be rising so fast you will need an advanced snake charmer handy to be safe. Ask your doctor and your guru to ask your fitness insurance if those Yoga styles are appropriate and safe for you.

By the way, if you are wondering, Open Sky Yoga's real name is: Anthropologically Based Alignment, Laughing for no Reason Influenced, Normal Temperature Yoga (ABALRINTY). That is actually the Truth! But it would not be marketable.

— Soi-me Françoiraoultānanda, ADDPHD, @, ABALRINTYT, C30000HLACAYT
(Certified 30,000 Hours Laughing and Crying Advanced Yoga Teacher).

AYURVEDIC RAMBLINGS

Better to live with reality, otherwise reality is going to come live with you!
—ROBERT SVOBODA

Tamoguna makes alcoholics, rajoguna workaholics and Sattvoguna Yogaholics!
—GEETA IYENGAR

Once upon a time there were five Bhūtas: Ether, Air, Fire, Water and Earth, three Doṣas: Pitta (Fire and Water), Vāta (Ether and Air), Kapha (Water and Earth) and three Gunas (Sattva, Rajas and Tamas) and they all decided to create the Universe. They are still alive and well today.

Some people think, if not familiar with Ayurveda, that having three equal parts of Pitta, Vāta and Kapha is heavenly like it will be perfectly balanced and even. In fact, that is a definition of hell because if you're not doing well, you would not know which doṣa to take care of or antidote. Knowing the dote is essential. Being self-aware of the dote is what Yoga practice offers. It reveals your Ayurvedic constitution, like in a mystery novel where you are the main character. When the primary doṣa is way ahead of the two others, life is a no brainer, you just minimize it!

When first confronted with their doṣa numbers of the Prakṛti, after a test, some are excited, amazed and recognize themselves, but others feel trapped, boxed in and lose a sense of freedom. Actually, your Ayurvedic constitution is just describing your natural genetic tendencies with a list of adjectives.

You can have a Yoga practice and a lifestyle management to minimize or prevent inherited weak links from your ancestors. Use some of your free will that way. Make the best out of it. Happiness is the balance between acceptance and change. Be sure you know what is changeable, less changeable, not changeable at all. Make three lists and don't mix them up; you would be miserable and frustrated if you do so.

For gunas, there is always hope that you can become a better person over the course of your life. It is work-in-progress. Some call for a therapist on their deathbed. You can begin in a very dark place, selfish, self-destructive, asocial, ultra-orthodox, mafia-like and later in life be radiant, adaptable, tolerant, content and be of service. Spiral your way from Tamas towards Sattva, from darkness to light, as the Bṛhadāraṇyaka Upaniṣad teaches us. Yoga, psychotherapy, personal development, immersions in other cultures assist us to evolve on the spiral of Life. Welcoming new and old paths, becoming less ethnocentric, phobic, racist or sexist … Easier said than done!

But doṣa will be doṣa, sorry.

I always had nosebleeds. I had nose surgery as a child in Venice. Like in a James Bond movie, I was carried first like a young king in a sedan chair across Piazza San Marco then placed into a speedboat ambulance on the Grand Canal directly into the basement of the hospital. They cauterized my nostrils poorly. Then altitude, heat, dryness, spices, handstand would trigger bleeding again. So, I applied the antidotes of a yogic Pitta-pacifying prescription: more Sarvāṇgāsana and less Śīrṣāsana, more forward bends and less backbends, no Bhastrikā and more Śitalī Prāṇāyāma in the Summer, oiling inner nostrils with Nasya oil, less coffee, more rose water and cucumbers, less sun salutations and more Śavāsana. Goodbye, nosebleeds. Thank you, Ayurveda.

Knowing your Prakṛti and primary doṣa helps to have compassion for yourself and even laugh at yourself. Others, friends or family, if realizing your primary doṣa is acting out, may forgive you or be more indulgent. A doṣa shows more in your initial reaction to anything. As a teacher, if you can guess the doṣa of your students, it will contribute to making them feel welcome, to have a better understanding of their patterns and to anticipate their needs.

As a student, as far as the doṣa of your Yoga teacher goes, be aware that "like attracts like" for better or worse. We are attracted by somebody or something with similar interests but therefore have less chances to change. Bikers hang out with bikers, teachers marry teachers, asocial people drift with nobodies or other asocial types. Addicts are addicted to other addicts' company. Fire attracts fire. For example, if we look at the doṣa of the Iyengar school, it has a majority of Pitta Vāta members and those few Kapha types may have Pitta secondary. In the Aṣṭāṅga Mysore school, more Vāta Pitta overall and at Kripalu, and Kuṇḍalinī ashrams, more often Kapha Pitta or Kapha Vāta . . . scary?

The Medicine Buddha in those magical Tibetan thangkas holds a plant, Haritaki, one of the three fruits found in Triphala (the two others are Amalaki and Bibitaki).

Strategic toxicity or wise indulgence will give you a long life with less frustration. If you are too pure or obsessed with purity, you may swing the pendulum the other way at one point and relapse. "Everything in moderation, including moderation," has been one of my mottos. It does not mean to be following the middle way 24/7.

If you are orthorexic or compulsive and fanatic about Ayurveda, which is preaching moderation, not sure it will work!

A sattvic Vāta person would be clear, creative, brilliant, joyful, inquisitive, flexible, mobile. A tamasic one would be incoherent, fragmented, fearful, anxious, insecure, erratic.

A sattvic Pitta would be direct, inspiring, encouraging, enthusiastic, motivated. A Tamasic one would be controlling, critical, judgmental, impatient, irritable, angry.

A sattvic Kapha would be cheerful, amiable, kind, compassionate, committed, steady. A Tamasic one would be confused, dull, attached, greedy, lethargic.

Sometimes teachers have to teach the opposite of what they need to practice from a doṣa point of view. And we hope they are already sattvic with enough rajas along to have the drive to teach!

The dose is the medicine. That is true also for Āsana and Prāṇāyāma. The timings and the intensity. How you project yourself in the pose matters more than the pose itself. For example, books may tell you that forward bends are cooling and pacifying but if you practice them clinging your teeth and goal-oriented, they will aggravate Pitta and Vāta. Similarly, if you can almost rest in deep backbends or invite Śavāsana in Śīrṣāsana, you will make it Pitta-pacifying whereas in theory they generate heat.

Once upon a time, I gave a workshop on Ayurveda and Yoga in Rochester, New York, and decided to have snacks suitable for each doṣa at the intermission. I consulted with Dr. Robert Svoboda and for Kapha type we got ginger tea, buckwheat toast, shredded carrots and apples with cinnamon. For Pitta type, cucumber raita, rice pudding with rose water, lychees, grapes and coriander cumin fennel tea. For Vāta type, medjool dates, soaked almonds, guacamole, warm spice soya drink and peppermint tea. All snacks were labeled to avoid confusion and for educational purposes. Well, Pitta people (some had already noticed the snacks on the way in) and those still not familiar with Ayurveda left the classroom to get downstairs first, ate most of the snacks, regardless of the signs. Kapha people were still upstairs asking questions to the teacher. The Vātas remembered eventually that we had snacks and ate the Kapha ones. Kapha type ate the Vāta snacks, well, what was left of them. "Like attracts like" was confirmed one more time. The story is slightly exaggerated, influenced by the Pitta side of the writer.

Ayurveda is a lifetime game you can play at any level. And your health will likely improve. I am the living proof.

YOGA FOR DEPRESSION

It's such a great feeling to know you're alive.
—MISTER ROGERS

A few years ago, I was on my way to teach a workshop in Montreal called, "Yoga for Depression." It was a misleading title on the flyer; I should have been more aware of it. So, I arrived at the Canadian border after a depressing few hours drive through Upstate New York. The officers asked me what I was going to do in Canada. I only had a Green Card at the time. I answered that I was going to visit friends, a half-truth. Got scared of saying I was going to teach, as in theory I needed a work permit. I gave countless workshops in Canada before without any trouble, so I felt confident. For whatever reason, they decided to search my car and found the famous printed flyers, "Yoga for Depression," so they sent me back home with a warning that I could have gone to jail for a few days or could have paid a huge fine. I had to cancel at noon the seminar which started at 5:00 P.M. So now every time I pass the border I am stopped because I am flagged in the system for lying to an immigration officer. I do have the permits, so I am fine. The worst part of that story was that thirty students and teachers were waiting for me, some actually suffering from depression, wishing to learn how Yoga could help. So, I am sure some of them got more depressed with that cancellation just a few hours before. This happened unfortunately before I was certified in Laughing Yoga, otherwise it would have been a great opportunity to practice. It was really depressing for me as well to cancel last minute a seminar on depression. Next time I will title it "Yoga to Minimize Depression," not "Yoga FOR depression !"

THE FOAM OF THE DAYS

悶

Men (muh-un) is a Chinese character for depression. One explanation is it represents an airless room that depresses the heart/mind.

This character is in the Shuowen dictionary, compiled in the second century CE, where it is defined in terms of a synonym: mournful, sorrowful, melancholy, depressed, to be sick at heart, sad. Also, in the *Daodejing (Tao Te Ching)* as "dull and afraid."

Is it not fascinating that compression, inner pressure with no breathing space, would be related to depression? Active and supported backbends open the lungs, liberate the diaphragm, expand the whole chest cavity from floating ribs to collarbones, promote deeper inhalation and may act as anti-depressant, literally. The ribcage is no longer a cage with trapped birds inside but an open space like the sky we see in Magritte's painting, *The Therapist*.

In the novel, *L'Écume des Jours (The Foam of the Days)*, by the French surrealist writer Boris Vian, one of the characters, Chloe, is depressed and very ill: she has a water lily in her right lung. The volume of her apartment changes according to her moods and to the kind of music playing. The corners of the rooms change shapes and the ceiling goes down as depicted in the Chinese ideogram. "Lamps are dying," said Chloe. "Walls are shrinking. And the window, here, as well as the ceiling is substantially lower. The rug is much thicker."

How we feel affects the inner caves of the body but also our perception of the external environment. As Eric Franklin mentions in *Dynamic Alignment Through Imagery*: "Breathing, alignment and psychological factors are interdependent."

The abdominal cavity changes shape but not volume, much like a water balloon. Thoracic cavity changes both shape and volume like an accordion bellow. Form and content influence each other mutually.

All members of a big extended family in traditional cultures live all in one small yurt or tipi but have good relationships and could be in a good space, sukha. Some modern families with an only child have huge houses in wealthy suburbs looking like neo-Greek temples with refrigerators and freezers the size of a truck, a walkie-talkie system to connect with the child in his far-away bedroom or playroom stuffed with video games and they could be in a bad space, duḥkha. I have witnessed both firsthand. I gave private Yoga sessions in upper-class neighborhood mansions for jetsetters who were on anti-depressants. And for a few days, I slept on the floor of a small palm leaf hut hosted by a poor farming family, lined up with their six or seven children, in Śrī Lanka. They were in a good mood. I remember giving them just a postcard of Paris when I left, I did not have much. And they cried.

Inner meteorology matters. This is why in all Yoga, Art and Music are needed to let the Sun in.

HĀSYA

Laughing Yoga existed way before Dr. Kataria "invented" it. In his Ashram of Pune, the controversial Rajneesh had created in the seventies, a laughing meditation as part of a three-day program: one day of crying, one day of laughing, one day of silence. Not a bad idea. Crying and laughing, like the masks of tragedy and comedy, which we find in Commedia dell'arte and Kathakalī, are deeply connected. Children can go from one to another so fast or even can laugh and cry at the same time. Iyengar himself, on the other side of the great city of Pune, had actually a great sense of humor and loved to laugh with his pupils, but unfortunately, that part of the teachings did not get always transmitted to his most senior disciples. Sad omission in transmission.

Laugher epidemics are universal. Contagious laughter in some churches is a form of glossolalia, speaking in tongues like Bobby McFerrin's vocal improvisations. Laughing is primal as the first onomatopoeia.

For years, I laughed so much at Laughing Yoga, making fun of it. As an outsider it really appears stupid. But that is the funny point. Naturally karma came back at me and I got the call to be certified in it. That was a birthday present to myself. I was pleasantly surprised to meet wonderful, devoted people, nurses, therapists or various professionals who wanted to share Hāsya Yoga in hospitals, nursing homes etc. as a form of Karma and Bhakti Yoga. We never laughed at the expense of somebody or at racist or sexist jokes. We laughed because of the comedy of absurd situations or images. For no reason. It breaks the social mold and mask, tapping into a very primal response, liberating the diaphragm, generating tears of laugher. It allows you to experience the warmth, the tingling of blood circulation and feel yourself, to have sensations.

The "Laughing for no reason" of Dr. Kataria as well as the Mindfulness meditation of Thich Nhat Hanh are both great antidotes or complements to serious, dogmatic, judgmental, Pitta-dominant types of Yoga.

When you get certified in Laughing Yoga, a more challenging journey than you may think, after literally rolling on the floor for three days, you receive a little card, the size of a credit card, to put in your wallet. On it, you will find a printed list of a few laughing exercises to practice for when you are in trouble. For example, your flight at the airport got canceled and you are on your way to your honeymoon in Venice or to teach an important Yoga workshop. So, you can choose the cellphone laugh. I have done it a few times. Sometimes just for fun, with no reason, that is even more funny. Self-consciousness has to vanish.

First, you place the cellphone at your ear and pretend somebody is calling you, making jokes or whatever is supposed to make you laugh. It's all fake. Nobody is calling you. Then you start artificial forced laughing even though you really don't feel like it. Because of the absurdity of the situation, you begin to really laugh. There are people standing around you, in line or sitting. Some will laugh, seeing you laugh, likely they will go for smiling, yawning, sighing, a phenomenon known as echokinesis. It is so surreal that you are now laughing for good, more and more. It works.

Laughing generates a wave of dopamine, oxytocin, feel-good hormones from the opiates family and it will deflate right away your stress level. It generates tears of release. You feel alive. "Depression manifests as our inability to be present for the experience of life," writes Stephen Cope. That is why laughing is an anti-depressor.

When you have recovered from laughing, you will do what you have to do, rebook your flight, rent a car or go to another creative plan or accept the fatality and make the best out of it.

Along with lordosis, laughing defines us as human beings. Rabelais and Bergson noted that, "Laughing is specific to human." But actually, there are a few exceptions like the Kea Perrot of New Zealand who laughs while playing with friends.

Finally, I discover that if you cannot fake laugh at yourself as an exercise in laughing Yoga, you cannot laugh at yourself for real! Very profound. Try it. It is a practice and a blessing.

I recently found out there's a photo of me demonstrating the "diabolic laugh" in *Le Yoga du Rire*, a French-Canadian book from Linda Leclerc, a mentor of mine.

I was so wrong when, years ago, I was laughing at Laughing Yoga.

APHORISMS

ĀSANA

May you find in Taḍāsana the vertical axis of Life and in Śavāsana the ability to merge with the Infinite.

After Sādhanā, when your feet are released, longer and wider, un-hammered, you will have more square footage.

Flatten the learning curve but not your spine.

The āsana is playing you. How is she singing, what message is she sending? Are you available to receive it?

Could we sell relaxation figures as well as action figures?

Every pose should be named Sukhāsana. Adho Mukha Sukhasvanāsana, Bakasukhāsana, Etceterasukhāsana. And notice that no Āsana is named Duḥkhāsana.

Postures are sacred architectures and breath brings them to life.

The tuning ability is the yin in the yang of the āsana.

Search for the Ātman of the āsana, its essence, its archetype.

When you walk backwards, you cannot be ahead of yourself or fall forward.

Sternum lift better than facelift?

Every pose is in every pose.

How to reconcile and harmonize the functional and physical side with the symbolic and spiritual layers of the practice is part of the quest.

Sitting transcends the polarity of Taḍāsana and Śavāsana.

Āsana is overrated. Prāṇāyāma and Śavāsana are underrated.

All roads lead to the sac-Rome.

In Āsana and life, detect and minimize compensations of all kinds early to prevent troubles.

Maximize positive side effects and minimize negative side effects by raising the range of consciousness (ROC) first then the range of motion (ROM)!

If I were into politics, tucking the tailbone and navel to spine would not be on my program but Mūla Bandha and promoting continence would be. I am bi-continental myself. Actually tri-continental if I count Mother India.

All we need is Taḍāsana, Śavāsana and Lovāsana.

MISCELLANEOUS

Yoga is included in V-oyag-e!

What is the content of shape?

The more I am aging, the more new-agey I become.

What is a opposite of a headache? A headbliss?

Easier said than undone!

Visualization is halfway between thought and sensation.

Can you see a blind spot if you are color blind!?

Yoke & Roll™
Maybe I am an inner yogi and an outer bhogi?
Or I am just a Boogie-Yogi!

Pression /de-pression/com-pression/re-pression/op-pression /de-compression

Do you know your ABC?
Ahhhh, be and see!

Yoga is a no-brainer. Is everything else a brainer?

I am an impure purist and an orthodox dissident.

Finding the dote requires consciousness, vision, intuition, knowledge. Then you can apply the antidote prescription as your own yoga therapist.

Minimizing the gap between what we do and what we think we are doing. That is yoga

In a civilized Western world, where stress is high, perception of reality is clouded by various addictions, including yoga addiction.

Nothing has NO side effects. No thing has no side effects.

How clear is the mind of a cloud?

On my yogic passport it says USB, United States of Being?

Open Sky Yoga is an eye opener.

Yoga for the Sky of it.

Finding your true Path. Not easy. But never too late.

Better to draw petroglyphs than spread glyphosate.

Yoga. Yoked? Yes! YYY would make a nice logo. An antidote to KKK?

I am not joking. I'm just yoking.

If you are dis-orient-ed, you can always re-orient yourself.

Love is first, before air, water and food.
At the end of the day, at the end of life, Love is all that is left.

LOL: Light On Life.

Basic teacher training: upgrade your standards, learn the rules. Don't give up.
Advanced teacher training: lower your standards, transgress all rules. Always let go.

Orchestre is the anagram of Rochester.

Is underdoing laziness or wisdom?

Is overdoing sattvic passion or addiction?

Yoga will help you find yourself in the lost and found of Life.

Become a free electron in the Yogātom!

PRĀṆĀYĀMA

The breath is with you all the time, calling for your attention. Is the line busy?
What is the message on your answering machine?

Secondhand smoke
Secondhand perfume
Secondhand breath holding anxiety

The breath is none of your business.
What is your business anyway?

ŚAVĀSANA

Do all āsanas emerge from and merge back into Śavāsana, the cosmic sleep of Viṣṇu?

In Śavāsana, as a group, we find common ground.

Homage to Judith Hanson Lasater:
Be sure to lax and new before you can relax and renew.

Stress response is not controllable.
Relaxation response is and can be invited, practiced and good news, is also built in the system!

May your Śavāsana glow in the dark!

NĀDA

In art history, painting went from concrete to abstract and, in music, from abstract to concrete.

Listen to the soundtrack of a movie whose title could be, "Here and Now."
Hey, wait a minute! It is not a movie.

Prāṇāyāma, deep Śavāsana, restorative poses and chanting prepare for a different kind of listening, a direct perception, an immersion in the primordial Ocean of Sound, a state of absorption and being absorbed, a glimpse of Samādhi.

AUM, like a footprint in the sand, leaves an AUM print in Ājñā Cakra.

The yoga alphabet begins with A and ends with anusvāra, MMMM!
Both effortless sounds. Same in AUM…

Consonants are diving boards for the vowels to take off and have a good time to sing with them.

Oh My God! In Om-ing there is OMG. And OM in OMG !

Bow the strings of your hams.

The best way to advertise is by AUM of mouth.

PART FIVE

Breathing

To Be Inspired,
Exhale First

STEPWELLS

The wells predate everything but the streets. In South India it's the temple tanks, like the one in Chidambaram or next to Tillai Kali—both there before the temples, which were built around them. Water is the sacred Mother and She provides.
—DOUGLAS BROOKS

I always had a fascination for stepwells, water tanks and norias. Actually, my house is built on a land where a noria was still operating early in the century. Donkeys were helping to bring water out of the well. There is an old stone watertank buried deep in the ground like a sanctuary and a century-old fig tree still benefiting from the underground water streams.

Pauline Oliveros, a mystical contemporary composer, recorded a whole album, *Deep Listening*, in a giant underground watertank, creating natural reverberation and echoes.

Stepwells are different. We find them mostly in Northern India and even more in Rajasthan. The one near Amber Fort and Chand Baori are the most stunning. I think Escher may have used them as an inspiration for his drawings, *Cycle, Ascending and Descending, Relativity* . . .

The floor map looks like a Maṇḍala, a labyrinth, sacred geometry patterns you would encounter in a wild dream.

The connection with Yoga is found in Tāḍāgī Mudrā, a variation of Uḍḍīyana Bandha.Uḍḍīyana is described in the *Haṭha Yoga Pradīkipā*, around mid-fifteenth century. Tāḍāgī is found in the *Gheranda Samhita*, a late seventeenth century text.

In that practice the belly is hollowed, vacuumed by Uḍḍīyana Bandha in a supine position with arms extended over the head. The abdominal cavity is actually becoming a cave and looks like the bottom of an empty stepwell, a dry lake or pond, hence the name Tāḍāga.

It is helpful to practice it before the traditional Uḍḍīyana Bandha, where you stand with the spine in flexion. The full extension highlights and facilitates the widening and lifting of the false ribs while staying empty lungs in what we call a false deep inhalation. It increases the suction as deep exhalation usually creates flexion and is antagonist to spinal extension.

Try it as an appetizer!

ONE BREATH PER MINUTE

There is something special about a cycle of one minute or more . . . Adding inhalation, full lungs retention, exhalation and empty lungs retention, hence 4 numbers . . . 30/0/30/0, 20/10/25/5, 20/10/20/10, etc. Filter the air through the windpipes. We say it is like breathing with a thin straw, but it is more like osmosis. Sponge-like absorption. Make the commitment to be slow. Really slow. Like you decide to walk extremely slowly, barefoot in the woods or on the beach . . . it is a mind game as well as a practice. You build gradually over the years . . . and then you will be ready for the final open-ended exhalation!

VESICA PISCIS

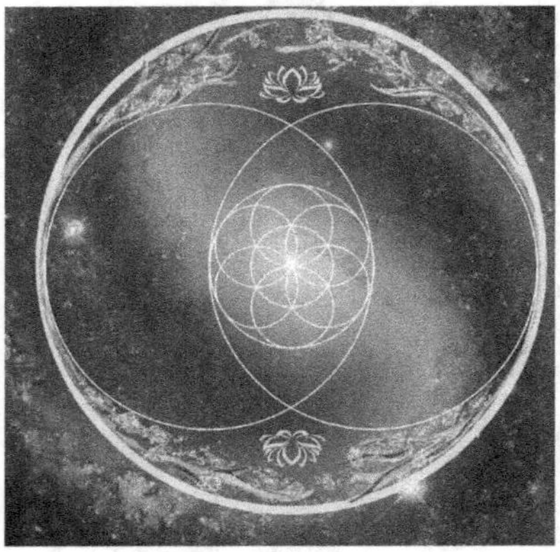

On the door of my parents' house there was a Flower of Life carved in the wood. The door was custom-made in Saint Véran, a small mountain village of the French Alps. I didn't realize it for years until I started to study sacred architecture and tree of life, seed of life, etc . . . Then I looked closer at the first two circles intersecting, creating a third entity in the middle, named Vesica Piscis. It has been a very essential image in early Christian esoterism. But it literally means fish bladder! It is an ancestor of the lungs and helps the fish to adapt to water pressure. There is a connection between the shape and the content. Same with breath in abdominal and thoracic cavities for humans . . . Container and content inter-are. Our lungs come from the evolution of Vesica Piscis! It reminds us that we once were diving and swimming. The abdominal cavity fluids are still called the internal sea . . . we are swimming inside ourselves because we are the diver and the ocean! Parents' house, wooden door, Flower of Life, Vesica Piscis, fish bladder, lungs, Prāṇāyāma, you see the thread?

THE BREATH CHANNEL

Observe your breath. It is strange, since we are our breath, we should be the first one to know it well. It is not like we are observing somebody else breathing . . . Actually, the breath is observing us. Or the breath is like a magnet calling for our attention. The problem is that we are not always present. Is there anybody in there . . . ? IN THERE . . . in there . . . in there . . . echoing like Pink Floyd in *The Wall*. We are so used to projecting our senses outwards that we are projecting them inwards the same way. We are already in, we are the in. So, no need to drive in. That is why so many are missing the connection. The same thing happens while observing the phosphenic activity in Ājñā Cakra. It is manifested. We just have to be on the right channel. But some of us have lost the remote control . . . or are just watching the Vṛttis channel. Ongoing erratic agitation 24/7, like the news channel or the cooking channel only have news or cooking. The breath channel is also there 24/7, we just have to find it!

BREATH ATTENDANT

In all classical Prāṇāyāmas, breath can be coached, monitored, assisted, manipulated, attended and directed. You can become a breath attendant. It is almost the same job as a flight attendant as both involve air element. Without deep connection or consciousness, it becomes mere exercise with no meaning, especially if counting. If you are counting, count as if you were reciting poetry or like in *Knee Play* of Philip Glass' opera, *Einstein on the Beach*, one, two, three . . . Count as if somebody else was counting for you! Now, how do you learn to feel, to see or listen? By being present, waiting for the doors and windows to open, by being patient. Open them by stretching your antennas in all directions. Be like a probe on a new planet recording all sounds and images . . . So, a certain form of channeling takes place and reveals the wild nature of breath—the primal, pre-verbal, pre-historic, pre-everything nature of Life.

IRRIGATION SCIENCE

Prāṇa has to be present, in the proper amount, in the organism. This means the bed of the river cannot be dry or flooded. In a healthy ecology, it flows naturally. Then you can play with resonance and irrigation. There is no point in placing dams on a river or playing/listening to music to activate the fluid system if the river is dry like in a desertic land. To bring juice, rasa, again and recharge the batteries (nervous system), deep rest, good sleep and also a good environment are needed. It has to rain to fill up the wells, the underground aquifers, the water tables. Underground rivers have to flow to feed the ground ones!

Rain is what we receive, any kind of nourishment, Īśvara Praṇidhāna—pure water of springs and mountain lakes, pure water of the cerebrospinal fluid, but also intellectual stimulation, great teachings, visual and auditory arts, touch. So, if the rivers of Prāṇa are abundant and flowing, then Bandha make sense to irrigate the system in a specific way. You have dams, locks on the canals to regulate the flow or divert the water where it is more needed. Prāṇāyāma is a science of irrigation. Ashoka, the great Buddhist emperor and Mauryan dynasty rulers applied that science to India and Śrī Lanka wonderfully. For a lot of human beings, the whole system is too dry (artificial tears, tight flat belly, lower abdominals zipped up, rock hard Recti Abdominis, buns of steel, etc.). If everything is already locked, no need to double lock. That will increase pressure on the heart and the sensory organs. And actually, often deep inside, induce organ prolapse and weak sphincters. Prāṇāyāma is not a military training to go to war . . . it is fluid freedom. A group of yoginis and yogis in Śavāsana create not a war field but a peace field.

INNER GEOGRAPHY

In every āsana I ask: what is the breath of this pose? Like every person has a different way of breathing. Sure, there is a universal aspect and a common ground, a common ocean, a common space but look at the breath and posture connection. In flexion, like Child's Pose, the backs of the lungs respond, in Setubandha the upper front is resonating. If you are collapsing and depressed, it will offer a really different space to breath than being, for example, in extension, in a receptive backbend. And if a deep breath cycle enters the body, it will inflate any available space. That is why, for example, in Child's Pose, kidneys, between floating ribs and posterior pelvic rim, feel like another pair of lungs . . . The spaces between the twelfth floating ribs and the posterior iliac crest, home of the Quadrati Lumborum, resembles the sound holes of Man Ray's famous photography, *Ingres' Violin*.

When you settle down, the breath settles down. When the body is in the background, the breath moves to the foreground, and you are able to witness it and then witness the witness and witness the witness of the witness . . . all the way back to the Source. Staying longer times in restorative poses, observing it in a warm welcoming environment . . . experiencing the āsana as a living entity. Are you able to yawn in the āsana as a liberation, not out of boredom or impatience, to repose in the pose?

NO RUNNING!

When I was ten, I ran around a pool, slid on wet tiles and fell heavily on my coccyx. From the shock, I could not speak for few minutes. Mute. I was articulating the words of the sentences, but no sound was coming out. A silent movie. Breath, voice and nervous system are deeply connected. I know.

NĀḌĪ ŚODHANA

After Nāḍī Śodhana, I feel lateralized. I see with a very wide angle. Hearing becomes peripheral. Prāṇāyāma Kośa is defined on the sides of the body like an unfolded Rorschach test or giant butterfly wings.

DAMARU

When we sit in meditation, we are transformed as the Damaru of Śiva . . . by the breath currents moving up from the base of the pelvic floor and down from the cranium, both converging towards the heart region.... The damaru, a small drum made of two human skulls, one man, one woman . . . became the mridangam and later the tabla. In 1981, in Lamayuru Gompa, Ladakh, I traded part of my camping equipment for a wonderful old damaru. I realized it was a mistake later, freezing while trekking . . .

In *The Laws of Manu* . . . the performance of Prāṇāyāma, accompanied by a mantra/japa will burn away impurities just as the defiling impurities of metal are burned away in the fire. Prāṇāyāma could be experienced as a high-efficiency furnace regulating internal heat, Agni and the Vāyus, the winds of the breath but also as an air conditioning system cooling the brain cells, the sensory organs, the central nervous system and the excess of Pitta doṣa, if needed. We can apply again the motto of François I, King of France, "*Nutrisco et Extinguo*!"

KAPĀLABHĀTI & BHASTRIKĀ

After Kapālabhāti and Bhastrikā, Kapāla is bathed by the inner light of Jyoti. It has an antidepressant effect. You just have to adapt the intensity and the number of cycles to your primary doṣa. You can practice it sitting, lying down, in some basic āsana and also while walking your dog in the park . . . My dog Tachi, an evolved Tibetan terrier from aristocratic lineage, used to practice his own version of Bhastrikā along with me, I am not joking. He had a strong murmur in his heart, was supposed to live only six months but died at almost eleven years. He did Restorative Yoga his whole life, like Anantāsana on a support to keep the heart spacious and had this kind of Bhastrikā panting breath as a survival instinct.

Bhastrikā is an old-fashioned bellows. I actually have one at home. You have to squeeze, contract to blow air on the fire but no need to spend energy on the way back. It is proactive only on the outbreath. In traditional cultures they can pound grains into flour with a heavy stick for hours. They use gravity to crush the grains without using force and it rebounds upwards with no action.

Similarly, inhalation is an unconscious spontaneous rebound, no need to think about inhaling or do anything about it. The boomerang will come back by itself. What is essential is that there is an underlying field of relaxation, Śavāsana-like behind it. Bhastrikā becomes sattvic.

Example of Practice:
EARLY A.M. SĀDHANĀ, March 2020

Bhastrikā in a light, non-Pitta-aggravating way, about three minutes then a few Viloma cycles, interrupted long Ujjāyi inhalations and deep slow exhalations with the glottic sound. Bhramarī drones with several fundamentals from low to high frequencies, creating overtones by sweeping through all the vowels internally, changing the position of the tongue. Facing the sun rising… clearing sinus labyrinthian caves and tunnels, generating a soft glowing luminosity inside the head cavity. Then a few minutes later, reading about the life and philosophy of Giordano Bruno. Anybody who was burnt alive by the Inquisition is worth reading and is probably closer to Yogic spirituality!

A PLAY IN FOUR ACTS (DEEP SLOW BREATH)

Pūraka (inhalation), Antara Kumbhaka (full lungs retention), Recaka (exhalation),
Bahya Kumbhaka (empty lungs retention)

Director: The Mind
Assistant director: Sensory Organs, especially Inner Nostrils and Skin
Background actors: Air, Gravity, Atmospheric Pressure

Leading role for Pūraka: Diaphragm
Best supporting actors: External Intercostals, External Obliques, and Recti Abdominis

Leading role for Recaka: Transverse Abdominal

Supporting Actors: all other abdominals, Internal Obliques, Recti Abdomini, Pyramidalis (if they still exist!), Internal Intercostals

Special effects: The Levator Labii Superioris Alaeque Nasi muscle (lifts the sides of the nostrils)

Figurants: Scalenes, Serratus Anterior, Pectoralis Major and Pectoralis Minor, Trapezius, Latissimus Dorsi, Erector Spinae, Iliocostalis, Quadratus Lumborum, Serratus Posterior Superior, Serratus Posterior Inferior, Levatores Costarum, Transversus Thoracis, Subclavius Sternocleidomastoid, etc . . .

Leave of absence
During Pūraka: all abdominal muscles
During Recaka: on vacation in the Bahamas, The Diaphragm

Soundtrack: Ocean and wind sound (by narrowing vocal cords), silence (deep and superficial)

Cameo appearances during retentions: Iliococcygeus, Puborectalis, Pubococcygeus Transversus Perinei Superficialis, Bulbospongiosus, Internal and External Anal Sphincters, Transversus Perinei Profundus, Sphincter Urethrae Membranaceae

BACKWARD GONG

The beginning of in and out breath is a soft attack like a bow on a string. Not a hard attack like a drum or a keyboard string hit by a stick or a hammer. A gong played backwards: imagine over few minutes from the silence, the resonance phase all the way back to the impact. That is how the beginning of Ujjāyi slow in breath should sound over the first five or ten seconds.

DIVING BOARD

Traveling from Prāṇāyāma to Dhāraṇā to Dhyāna is like learning to bike gradually without little wheels.

In Patañjali's Aphorisms, at the end of second chapter, the Prāṇāyāma Sūtras (II 52, 53) are a diving board into the Dhāraṇā and Dhyāna Sūtras (III 1, 2).

UNDERGROUND RIVER

After a long restorative Setubandha Sarvāṇgāsana (twenty-minutes, plus), take the support away with great care. Lie down directly on floor level, after rolling the spine from C7 to S1, and feel Ujjāyi breath up and down the spine: it is like an underground river. Maybe the mysterious watermark of Suṣumṇā Nāḍī? Trace it with the color powder of your mind and you may find the resurgence.

CLAY CUPS

Śvetaketu, his father said, you are conceited and arrogant and think yourself well read,
but did you ever ask for that knowledge by which one yearns for that which cannot be heard,
sees that which cannot be seen, and knows that which cannot be known?
Whatever is that teaching, sir? the son inquired.
Very well, my son, by knowing one lump of clay,
you know the essence of all things made of clay,
their differences being only in name and form.

—CHĀNDOGYA UPANIṢAD

Practicing Prāṇāyāma is about cooking the unbaked pot of the torso! A few decades ago in India, all cups for the traditional spiced tea, the chai, were made of uncooked clay by hand, the kulhad. Such a great feeling to hold it. Then we could throw them through the train windows and there would be giant piles of clay on each side of the tracks, when leaving or entering a train station. They would turn into earth element again and dissolve . . .

Nowadays the plastic cups will pile up for centuries on the side of train tracks. Sometimes, Yoga tradition has evolved the same way, from a natural primitive shamanic environment with a deep ecological vibration to an artificial urbanized fashion business with "Yoga music," rubber Yoga mats and fake waterfalls in the malls. A path of no return?

INNER TREKKING

If the chest is the mother and the air the child, at inhalation, the mother lets her child come to her, and at exhalation, she lets him go without following him but still protecting him.

—B.K.S. IYENGAR 1975

In Ujjayi Prāṇāyāma, the air, the mind and the sensory organs will be your Sherpas; Follow them!

The first base camp is in the valley of the pelvic basin, in front of the sacrum and coccyx. The sacral auricular surfaces are listening all around for secrets and sacred messages to be received. That is for the very beginning of the in-breath. It appears to originate at the bottom of the well, even if it is partially an illusion. The pelvic diaphragm and the thoracic diaphragm are in phase, they sculpt together the wave of the breath and have a good time riding along in parallel motion.

Then the breath moves in the front of the lower belly, behind and above the pubic bone climbing and expanding through the abdominal cave three-dimensionally . . . on the way towards the second base camp located along and below the twelfth ribs.

It travels to the back body just before opening and widening the floating ribs like a set of small wings. Filling up the space of the kidneys and adrenals, puffing the area of the Quadrati Lumborum as the gills of a fish, filling up the lower part of the inferior lobes of the lungs.

Then it moves again to the front of the torso in the lower ribcage, behind the xiphoid bone and clearly expands the ribcage, widening, deepening, blowing like balloons the middle lobes (assuming the lower chamber of the superior lobe of the left lung plays as a middle lobe).

From now on, the buoyancy of the lungs, like a hot air balloon, keeps lifting the sternum, spreading the rib basket until we finally reach the last base camp in the upper front, under the collarbones, at the apex of the upper lobes. Filling up the armpits, the space between the nipples and the pectoral area. It creates a vertical Setubandha Sarvāṅgāsana, living at the inner mountain top.

By then you can plant the tent for the night. Stay at the top. Enjoy the view. The Sherpas will prepare the chapati and the chai . . . the Kumbhaka begins… time is suspended. This is an inter-mission. Between inhaling and exhaling, high tide. A deep silence takes place when the clay pot—the whole torso—is full.

Stay at the top mentally a little longer with this memorable 360-degree view when beginning the downhill, the exhalation. Slowly descend, using your mental brakes. The sternum is still high . . . The abdominal belt, from the periphery to the core, begins its long and powerful compression, expelling the air gradually all the way to the end . . .

Arriving at the bottom, we stay with empty lungs, calling for Uḍḍīyana Bandha as a reflex. Mūla Bandha has already appeared during the last part of the outbreath . . . finally releasing slowly the contraction of the pelvic floor and abdominal muscles to open the door to the new inhalation, waiting to invade all that available space. A tsunami of air is pushed into us as we are the bottom feeders of the atmosphere. We just have to anticipate and slow it down so the whole team of Sherpa can ascend again the inner Mount Meru with the next group of climbers.

Note: During the ascension, the ribcage is always slightly ahead of the lungs, anticipating. During the downhill, the lungs are ahead, and ribcage is slightly left behind . . . they join each other during the retentions.

PIZZA THROWING

Letting go with exhalation first then fill up on the rebound . . . We need to create space, physical and emotional space, so there is room to receive breath or whatever else is there to be received, like music for example. Otherwise the incoming breath will hit a wall from inside, an inner armor, a shield. It may feel like the internal ceiling of the torso is low. We say in French, "le ciel est bas ou le ciel est lourd,": the sky is low and heavy. The ideogram for depression in Chinese represents an airless room that depresses the heart and mind.

Inversions help the diaphragm to release by gravity, as if you were exhaling in Tāḍāsana. Chanting, humming, exhaling, yawning, sighing, laughing, all release the diaphragm and Uḍḍīyana Bandha even better. Empty lungs, the diaphragm is NBU, not being used, is on vacation, vacant . . . it is antagonist to the abdominal wall. From that point of view, if you exhale efficiently, abdominal layers especially the transversus abdominis, contract and diaphragm releases. Some people contract the belly, but if it is not connected to breathing they would have an anxiety attack in Kapālabhāti or Bhastrikā. The widening and lifting of the ribs, similar to what we see in the ribcage in Ujjāyi or Viloma during the second phase of the in-breath, give the diaphragm a passive stretch . . . Just reminds me of witnessing the world champion of pizza throwing. It was in the Rochester, New York airport a few years ago at the inauguration of a new family pizzeria. The mayor cut the ribbon and then the world champion came along. Spinning pizza dough in the air, turning them into giant floppy frisbee. We could see through it like a thin layer of fascia and all around emerged a ring that would become the stuffed crust. Aka the circle of muscle fibers attaching all around at the base of the ribcage from the xiphoid to the last floating rib. It was stunning and I thought: "Wow, that looks like my diaphragm in Uḍḍīyana Bandha, Agni Kriyā, Agni Sāra etc . . . !" I did not share my discovery with the mayor of Rochester . . . but it made my day. Yoga is everywhere if/when you wear yogic lenses.

BUMBLE BEE BLISS

Bhramarī means bee. Bhramarī Devi is known as the Goddess of blackbees and Bhramarī Prāṇāyāma, the bumble bee breath. It is described in the *Haṭha Yoga Pradīkipā*, a fifteenth-century text compiled by Svatmarama. Inhaling rapidly, producing the sound of a male bee. Then exhaling with the sound of a female bee. A blissful experience, Ānanda, fills the mind of the yogi.

I am a big fan of humming. Humming, unlike Om-ing, is non-denominational. Everybody can hum. You can teach humming to children in a public-school Yoga class with no fear of parents' retaliation or being arrested by the Yoga police. But chanting Hare Kṛṣṇa or Om Mani Padme Hum may be asking for trouble.

There is some confusion about the sound of the inhalation. Some commentaries don't mention it at all, others refer to a snoring sound, others more to an Ujjāyi-like sound. I am opting for the last one. Inhaling with sound can be stressful, except Ujjāyi and windy vowels. What really matters is the long smooth exhalation. Humming on the exhalation is deeply calming and easier than Ujjāying.

We could say Bhramarī is a manifested Ujjāyi and an unmanifested AUM, somewhere in the middle. So, we can glide from one to the other two on the same exhalation. In the *American Journal of Respiratory Critical Care Medicine*, it is mentioned that humming helps sinus ventilation by increasing Nitric Oxide levels inside the nose. Humming would therefore prevent sinusitis.

Most NO is produced in the nasal cavities, paranasal ethnoid, maximallary and sphenoid sinuses. It accelerates the mucociliary escalator. During exhalation, the motility of the cilia is stimulated which improved immune function. Nitric Oxide dilates blood vessels and releases the smooth muscle cells in the arteries.

PRACTICE

Humming in your bathtub with ears underwater is intense and beautiful. Just plugging your ears with your fingers in Ṣanmukhī Mudrā will do. With a high frequency, it will resonate deep in your cranium. With a low frequency, like a Tibetan Lama, it will resonate in your chest. If you highlight the overtones by altering the volume of the mouth cavity and the placement of your tongue, inviting various vowels, you will have the best of both. To access the overtoning diphony, you can do the following exercises: the chewing gum and the chewing cow. Just hum with lips closed and pretend you are chewing gum or ruminating side-to-side like a cow. Exaggerate the jaw movements. Plug the ears again and listen to the sweeping rainbow of harmonics inside your head.

The level of intensity can vary. Medium is best. The sound needs enough life and power to resonate and be conducted by the bones of the skull. Too loud is aggressive and will disturb your neighbors. Not enough intensity would bring you back to the sound of Ujjāyi. Less intensity is energy saving, therefore allows a longer time of humming exhalation.

Practice a cappella with a group of friends or Yoga students. Or hum by yourself with the drone of a śruti box or a tambura. You will no longer hear your individual voice. The śruti or the tambura are humming in their own way and become one with your voice. Follow the fundamental frequency, the octave or the fifth above, climbing the first few steps of the natural harmonic scale.

It is said that humming helps insomnia. Hum yourself back to sleep. I have done it. Better than counting sheep forever. Humming clears your mind and induces moments of bliss. Hum your way to Samādhi?

Celestial humming can be found in the music repertoire:

Villa Lobos. *5th Bachianas Brasileiras for voice and six cellos.*

Sviridov, a Russian composer. *Reveille and Chorale concert in memory of Alexander Yurlov.*

Luzmila Carpio, charismatic Bolivian folk singer. *Lullaby to Mother Earth.*

Philip Glass and Paul Simon, *Songs of Liquid Days: Changing Opinion:*

Gradually
We became aware
Of a hum in the room
An electrical hum in the room
It went mmmmmm
Maybe it's the mantra
Of the walls and wiring
Deep breathing
In soft air
Mmmmmm

IT TAKES MY BREATH AWAY

It is breathtaking, we say, when something is so beautiful, we almost stop breathing. It is breath taking, "ça me coupe le souffle," in French, literally, it cuts my wind. If it takes my breath away, where is the breath going!? In the Yoga tradition, that suspended time is referred to as Kevala Kumbhaka. Mystics would say the breath is holding you. The subject becomes the object. But what is left of us in Bahya Kumbhaka? Retentions can be witnessed in the extraordinary rituals of the pearl divers of the Red Sea. Fewer and fewer are diving as the oil industry destroys the coast of Bahrein . . . They chant, scream, practice some kind of Bhastrikā, enter in a trance and dive for a few minutes. Still, be very careful and moderate with retentions in your Prāṇāyāma practice. They may have a special mystical status, awaken Kuṇḍalinī but can also be disturbing your health. Idealism and romanticism can be a poisoned gift. A fair amount of great apnea divers never came back alive to the surface. It took their breath away . . .

BANDHA & ABANDHA

Is there a word for the opposite of Bandha like A-bandha? Or a positive word for opening/expanding?

Here's Douglas Brooks' answer:

"The word "Bandha" itself rarely has a positive sense, philosophically. It's used almost exclusively to suggest bondage, constraint or limitation. Abandha is often the sense of its non-occurrence. For "freedom," which is the opposite of bondage, there are words from the /muc verb, like Mocana or Mukti or Mokṣa. In general, it is fair to say that Yoga language is more about control than about expansion."

Still better to translate Bandha as seal than lock. Like wax seals in medieval times or the one on that secret envelope in *The Three Musketeers*. Seals are beautiful and efficient. I have a few at home to seal my envelopes.

Often people are already locked up and they get addicted to the Bandhas because like attracts like, thinking they are more "advanced" and they end up double-locked. They would need to unlock first, let go of the mask, the passport photo, the armor, the carapace then they could decide and "control" how the Prāṇa should flow in a refined fluid system. If the river flows freely, we can place dams in strategic places for better irrigation. If the bed of the river is dry, no need.

HAṂSA

There is an Upaniṣad dedicated to Haṃsa and a Śrī Haṃsāvataram Gāyatrī:

Oṃ haṃsa hāṃsāya vidmahe
Parama haṃsāya dhīmahi
Tanno haṃsaḥ pracodayāt

The mantra So'ham Haṃsa is a classic. It could be a projection of the mind on the existing sound of Ujjāyi. India likes correspondences. Ssss and Hmmm are unmanifested consonants. The glottic sound is located in two different places in the back of your throat . . . as if the sounds Ham and Sa were manifested. In natural breathing, the mantra is sung subliminally So'ham . . . Haṃsa. It works both ways. So, on the in-breath, Ham on the out-breath, ongoing day and night, amplified in Ujjāyi with reverberation and maybe even further in Bhramarī with the humming drone.

When I Ujjāyi, I hear the inhalation sound more as a sibilant . . . And you could not have a sibilant on the exhalation, which is more like a foggy colored vowel, an unmanifested Bhramarī sound . . .

Even as silent internal mantra, still feels better to hum on the outbreath, hummmmm . . .

Haṃsa, like Garuḍa, is a mythical creature, a wild goose, maybe a swan. A Haṃsa may be a goose, gander, swan, flamingo, or another aquatic bird of passage. According to tradition, it is a migrating spirit. A whole Upaniṣad is dedicated to Haṃsa. A few years ago, when we visited the mystical Cathar castle, Peyrepertuse, not far from the Spanish border, we found ourselves in an authentic medieval market and festival, with jugglers, acrobats, early music, strange chimeras on stilts and this amazing flock of sacred geese parading around under the skilled guidance of Turquin the shepherd. And instantly I thought, those are the Haṃsas!

On a personal note, as far as I can remember when I was drawing as a child or a teenager, there was often a crested bird flying across the page, a migrating bird with a special status . . . Could be a Haṃsa . . . a precursor sign of my future Yoga life . . .

At a Yoga of Sound seminar in Paris in the fall a few years ago, at the very end of the workshop, in the silence following the last collective OM chanting, we heard wild geese flying above us and their nasal calls, distant relative of the seagull . . . Triggered an instant awakening. I played Michel Polnareff's song *Complainte à Michael*. It felt as if we had broken the bars of a virtual jail cell window and we were free to fly toward the Infinite. Complete liberation . . . Mokṣa!

PART SIX

Śavāsana

ODE TO ŚAVĀSANA

Lying down, seaweed on the sand waiting for the tide
Driftwood moved by the currents
Horseshoe crab peeling off layers for centuries . . .
Long deep smooth exhalations softening the internal domes.
Gol Gumbaz, Blue Mosque, Notre Dame, as expanded ceilings of the belly
Oh! that connection to the heart, caressing the inner walls
Of the ribcage, open, no longer a cage
Pericardium and diaphragm forever in love
And at the end of each cycle, diving deeper and deeper
No boundaries, no inner, no outer, a spiritual camouflage,
Making yourself invisible by becoming the same elements that bind the universe,
Earth with earth, a state of positive inertia, hibernation in all seasons . . .
Fluids merging into the primordial sea
Vāyus, winds of breath back into cosmic winds
Inner atomic space, ether, playing again the music of the spheres
Fire churning, central heating system
Finally, saying yes to gravity and repose in the pose . . .
Everything becomes quiet, silencing the mind
Prāṇa percolates the skin, absorbed by osmosis
Cooling the rays of the solar plexus
Brain cells reflect like full moons
Mirror in the mirror in the mirror in the mirror . . .
Lightness and heaviness, sedimentation process
Glowing in the dark, floating in bliss
Slowly descending towards the bottom of the Lake
No more gender, age, social mask, or role-playing, no expressions
Only imprints, watermarks, subtle traces left in the cosmic sleep of Viṣṇu
Life as the Source!

CLOUDS

Through clear waters range to the vast blue autumn sky,
How can they compare with the hazy moon on a spring night!
Most people want to have pure clarity,
But sweep as you will, you cannot empty the mind.
—KEIZAN ZENJI, CO-FOUNDER OF SOTO ZEN

During inhalation, the breath should move exactly like the clouds that are spreading in the sky.
—B.K.S. IYENGAR

People are like stained-glass windows. They sparkle and shine when the sun is out,
but when the darkness sets in, their true beauty is revealed only if there is a light from within.
—ELISABETH KÜBLER-ROSS

In one of our shadow-puppet shows, a member of the troupe created a moon like that, with light from within. The theater was in the dark, obviously for shadows, and my friend built a cubic box painted in black with a handle, a cutout of the moon crescent on one side and inside the box a flashlight. What gave the moon a halo effect was covering the cutout with an opaque kind of transparency paper. Then we could move the box slowly as the moon migrated in the night sky with that soft glow. Simple, but astute!

Back to Yoga. In Śavāsana or in sitting meditation, observe the luminosity. The head cavity, does it glow in the dark? If you are tense, mentally agitated or asleep, none of that will be possible. You cannot access the channel; maybe you lost the remote.

Start simple. Lie down for deep relaxation. Or build a seat with a great deal of care, as you would build the foundation of a house or an altar. Enter the gates to find the Center.

Some questions remain. Can one be undisturbed, completely silent? Silence, stagnation, and immobility could also mean death. Sensory deprivation is a form of torture. Should we welcome the chaos, raise the threshold instead of sorting it out? Clouds and fog have bad press in metaphors as the Vṛttis—masking the clarity of consciousness. But the clouds themselves are so beautiful! Don't they deserve to be the center of your attention as well? How clear is the mind of a cloud?

Sure, the clouds are masking the sun. Just flying above them gives you that experience. If you are above the clouds, you can be warmed by the light of the sun, but you can also surf on a beautiful ocean of cumulonimbus.

Tune into that inner weather channel more often. Don't focus so much on the external one, you cannot control it anyway, same with the stock market. A certain dose of detachment is needed. You can appreciate the beauty of the seasons—especially in Rochester, New York—but also the unique inner season, ever clear, pleasant, stable, sattvic, your first nature.

POSE & COUNTERPOSE

Śavāsana is like a musical fermata, a "point d'orgue." If it had a counterpose, that would be Life-āsana. Or all other āsanas. If we consider the counterpose of the counterpose of the counterpose . . . the practice will have no end, a cycle of life and death.

But actually, Śavāsana can be the counterpose of everything else. A final resolution as in music, returning the fundamental note of the mode or the scale.

Śavāsana's role is to settle down, to digest and assimilate the practice, to experience its resonance. It is a time of absorption, absorbing and being absorbed.

There is pose, counterpose and repose in the pose. Means Śavāsana can be there in spirit and in the background for all āsanas.

RETROACTIVE AWARENESS

Retroactive consciousness works for tensions in Śavāsana and for sounds in Nāda Yoga: we become aware of them when they stop! For example, the noise of the refrigerator or air conditioning in a hotel room is noticed only when it stops. In Śavāsana or some restorative poses with long timing, we experience a jolt when a previously unconscious tension is released spontaneously. So, it is revealed a posteriori.

PILGRIMAGE

In deep relaxation, Yoganidrā or Śavāsana, we may have an experience of the infinite small or the infinite large—a sense of space, lightness and luminosity. As though you had penetrated the heart of matter and the heart of space. It reminds me of the small movie *Power of 10* by Charles and Ray Eames where we travel inside the atom and beyond the Milky Way. Both extremes of the universe look quite similar, lots of emptiness with some vibrating dots in it. By closing our eyes with a reflective mind, we can see that internal image with the telescope and the microscope of the mind. Let it flood and affect how you see everything else. We can see with the eyes of Paul Klee, Max Ernst, Georgia O'Keefe, Georges Mathieu, Hans Hartung, or Jackson Pollock deep inside the object of our attention—again a state of absorption. What they paint may be more realistic than hyperrealism.

DO BE DO BE DO

do

not

let

do

ing

mask

be

ing

WHAT'S LEFT?

Now that you have released all unnecessary tensions, quieted the mind, eliminated the Vṛttis, now that your body has merged with earth underneath and space all around, you are still awake, maybe more awake than ever, a different kind of awakening, what do you see? How do you experience yourself. Is there a Self? Look at what is left on the beach when the tide recedes.

As I guided deep relaxation at the end of my Friday morning advanced class at Open Sky Yoga, during a long silence, after letting go of tensions, old and new, letting go of the social mask, the body's mass, letting go of anything unnecessary, I asked again: what is left? Simply breath, and biological rhythms. What else? What do we have in common in Śavāsana? We have such a deep and wide connection with our supports, the floor, the blankets, the earth. We have a common ground.

Here, it is a tangible reality, not so much a figurative virtual ground for political negotiations. It is always a good way to start and maybe to end as well—find common ground and common space.

You are still alive even though the body is in Mṛtāsana, the pose of death.

You are Viṣṇu sleeping for long periods of time on a bed of snakes floating on the ocean of milk. I saw Him in Buddhanilkanta near Kathmandu when I was in my late teens. It had a profound impact on me. Viṣṇu in his cosmic sleep contains the seeds of creation of a world yet to be manifested, not unlike the mythical story of Noah's Ark.

In Śavāsana, you will be in touch with life at its best, pulsing. As Tagore describes:
The same stream of life that runs through my veins night and day runs through the world and dances in rhythmic measures. It is the same life that shoots in joy through the dust of the earth in numberless blades of grass and breaks into tumultuous waves of leaves and flowers.

You don't have to travel with all your luggage everywhere you go. My first teacher used to say that you had to hang your worries and tensions on the hanger with your coats and jackets in the changing room before entering the class.

Most spiritual traditions will suggest that you empty your cup before filling it up. How can you receive new teaching, change compulsive habits, let go of addictions if you don't? So, garage sales are the best, not just to clear the basement and the attic of your unconscious mind but also of all unnecessary decorations, collections of junk accumulated over the years and no longer relevant but still sticking to the inner walls and inner chambers of our bodies like an antiquity museum. Śavāsana is a way to have a daily garage sale, a cleaning, a clearing, a cleansing so we can start anew the next action, be it an āsana, a public talk, or whatever else we have to do.

SHAMANIC JOURNEY

Tension creates density and definition. To be defined, a muscle has to be tight, or keep a lot of residual tone. In Śavāsana we are looking at muscles' dissolution! To release means to soften, to alleviate, to spread, to go back to our oceanic nature and connect with the part of us made of space. What Ayurveda calls the ether element, Ākāśa and the water element, Jala.

In deep relaxation or meditation, the perception of your body will be less defined in space, more like a watercolor of a full moon with a halo on a hazy night, not a line drawing or a cutout silhouette.

Most people, after fifteen-to-twenty minutes of deep relaxation, if they stay focused inward, aware of all sensations, will experience that merging with the surroundings, be it the earth underneath or the infinity of the space around. What Bonnie Bainbridge Cohen refers to as yielding into earth and yielding into space.

The exhalation and the surrender to the field of anti-gravity create and magnify that experience. Any exhalation-based practice is a release: sighing, yawning, laughing, singing, humming, natural exhalation, deep slow Ujjāyi or Viloma outbreath, or even Kapālabhāti will all create release and an expanded, diffused state of existence.

In Patañjali's *Sūtras*, it is mentioned that prolonged exhalation will be a way to silence the mind (Chapter I, Sūtra 34). Especially the awareness of the silence following the exhalation, in Bahya Kumbhaka—it is not so much a retention, per se, but more of a suspension in time, in anti-gravity. That is where the deepest silence is observed. Some translations suggest in that Sūtra that it is a breathing exercise or even Kapālabhāti, some are more specific with exhalation or exhalation/retention.

It is a peaceful resolution. The resonance of the exhalation, the resonance of the bell, the resonance of the whole sādhanā is in the silence following it. Sometimes we still have the illusion that the sound or the side effects are still there, subliminally, a sort of biofeedback feeding and magnifying the resonance. In that state, we can travel towards the source of the breath or the source of Life, finding that primal unity that we all crave to re-create or access again.

Śavāsana breath is receptive, very quiet but I can recognize already the seed of Ujjāyi inside the cenote. It feels as if the breath has vanished or became so quiet that only the heartbeat is pulsing. That feeling of not breathing should not be confused with anxiety and holding the breath, or the absence of sensation due to a high level of stress, side effects of numbing medication, or past trauma still blocking the natural release of the whole body.

Some yogis may have died in holding their breath for too long. Here they would be labeled insane, there they become a saint in their village!

In mapping the geography of the breath, we feel the periphery of the diaphragm expanding and receding, the centers of its domes, capping the kidneys moving up and down like jellyfish in the water. This is a shamanic journey inside the internal sea.

YAWNGA

If you yawn, do it not loud but privately. And speak not in your yawning
but put your handkerchief or hand before your face and turn aside.
—GEORGE WASHINGTON

I have read most every published book and article written on yawning. Am I a yawn addict?

We yawn about 250,000 times in our lives. Five to ten times a day. Some scholars, biologists, anatomists, psychologists, at PhD level, are still trying to figure out why we yawn. Multiple theories are still considered. "What makes the yawn-ness of the yawn?" asks Dr. Provine in his great book, *Conscious Behavior*. Yawning may accelerate the draining of the cerebrospinal fluid and makes us more vigilant. It generates dopamine and oxytocin, the same neurotransmitters produced by singing and laughing. It can open the door of inner perception, improving our less known sixth sense, the interoception. It helps to preserve lung function.

Most animals yawn. Penguins yawn as part of their mating rituals. Snakes yawn after eating to realign their jaws. The fetus yawns in utero. Many traditional cultures yawn with no inhibition. But it is still a mystery. Schizophrenics yawn very little. Sometimes, at the time of yawning, a hemiplegic can find the ability to stretch a paralyzed limb. So, we know yawning is tapping into a very archaic part of the brainstem, where breathing and stretching centers are located. Yawning relaxes the pelvis. And it may facilitate a baby coming out of the womb by relaxing the jaw and the whole body of the mother. It may improve vision and it also stimulates the production of tears.

Yawning may be another way to release the facial mask. Yawning is an orgasm for the face, wrote Gunver Ingeborg, a psychotherapist specialized in "Yawning therapy." Many people don't yawn any-more due to a high level of stress and anxiety.

If you can have a full organic yawn in an āsana, welcome it and observe it rippling along your spine, for you are in a good space, sukha. It creates a tsunami of release. It is almost a mystical experience to be at the mercy of the Yawn, to be yawned. Follow the whole journey of the yawn inside you. The deep inhalation opening the jaws, expanding the back of the mouth cavity, lifting the soft palate then the long exhalation with the blissful sound of an open vowel, like the beginning of a primitive mantra, AAAAhhh . . . On the other hand, if yawning is not possible in a Yoga posture, you may be blocked, on hold from stress or fear. You are not reposing in the pose.

One of my first teachers, Noëlle Perez, wrote a substantial book on yawning from a mystical and ethnological point of view. It is a brilliant book. Unfortunately, not too many people were interested in yawning. But exorcists were interested! As yawning may be a sign that the devil is leaving the body of the possessed client! By the way, at the time of writing this essay, the current exorcist of the Vatican just died. They are still looking for a new candidate. If you are unemployed, you should consider. But also, be aware that the same chief exorcist is the one who wrote a text claiming that Yoga, Zen and reading Harry Potter are satanic practices. So, you may have to exorcise yourself.

Another connection between yawning and Yoga is Devadatta. The five Vāyus, the five winds of Vāta, the five Prāṇas have corresponding Upavāyus: Nāga, Kūrma, Kṛkara, Dhananjaya and Devadatta. The functions of the Upavāyu are mentioned in *Triśikhi Brahmana Upaniṣad.* Devadatta rules yawning. It says in Ayurveda that Upavāyu functions should not be repressed: sneezing, coughing, burping, eye-blinking—and it's especially true for yawning. It induces high pressure in the body and increases the sympathetic response. In Yoga classes, feel free to yawn, sigh, cough, don't repress them with a muted sound, it is more stressful for all, including the teacher.

In the *Mahābhārata*, every warrior has a conch-shell trumpet that was given a special name. Arjuna's was called Devadatta. Is there a mysterious esoteric connection? Finally, if reading about yawning makes you yawn, don't hold back, it's a blessing.

TO SLEEP OR NOT TO SLEEP?

In Śavāsana, the brain could be confused because you are lying down, eyes closed, in a quiet, soothing, warm environment, especially if you are covered with a blanket. Sensory organs are turning inwards. So, if there is no physical pain, no discomfort, the main obstacles to relax become restlessness, wandering mind and sleepiness. Often the same people will alternate between the two, never finding an oasis of conscious rest in between. The answer to the question of whether it is a service or an obstacle to fall asleep depends on whether the sleep is an escape or a true need for rest.

Sleeping in Śavāsana or restorative poses may be a blessing if you are an insomniac or so agitated that obsessive thoughts run and ruin your life. In my early years of teaching, I always tried to keep students awake so they could follow the whole journey of a guided relaxation, but now I let them sleep if they need to. Unless I see it as a systematic pattern of resistance.

If an airplane-decibel-level snoring student disturbs the rest of the group, I just walk toward the sleeper. Most of the times, by magic, they will feel it and stop as if equipped with a special radar.

In Śavāsana, I am looking for deep release with full awareness, as cooling for the mind as moonbathing

—a timeless, ageless, effortless journey. So, stop fighting falling asleep, welcome it, and see what it's like at the other end of the tunnel when you wake up softly but still in deep relaxation, absolutely receptive and dwelling in the present.

Here is a story I share occasionally if the question occurs in a retreat or a class. This story has changed the way I interact with students who fall asleep in deep relaxation, and it gives me goosebumps each time I read it. It comes from the early Christian mystical tradition of the Desert Fathers. Remember this story next time you are annoyed in a Yoga class or a concert by the person next to you sleeping or by your own sense of failure.

Some old men came to see Abba Poemen (the abbot of the monastery) and said to him: "Tell us, when we see brothers dozing during the sacred office, should we pinch them?" Abba Poemen said: "Actually, if I saw a brother sleeping, I would put his head on my knees and let him rest."

TEARS FOR FEARS

There are tears of grief for the dead, tears of joy for a new birth, tears of release, tears of belonging, tears of laughing and yawning, and tears of life. So many tears lately in so many parts of the world, tears for known and unknown friends. Tears, lacrima in Latin (Lacrimosa in Mozart's *Requiem*) serve to clean and lubricate the eyes. Crying can be associated with strong internal emotions from deep sorrow to intense pleasure or ecstasy, tears of the third eye . . .

Many animals shed tears. Crocodiles really do cry, not because they're sad but thanks to a third eyelid wiping the surface of the eye, the plica semilunaris, a small fold of tissue on the inside corner of the eye. It is the vestigial remnant of the nictitating membrane i.e. third eyelid. "Tears are necessary to keep the eyeball moist, contain proteins and other substances which maintain the eye healthy and help to combat infection," Michael Trimble, author of *Why Humans Like to Cry*, tells *Scientific American*. He adds, "Crying for emotional reasons and crying in response to aesthetic experiences are unique to us."

Some researchers have also suggested that emotional tears, unlike basal or reflex tears, contain stress hormones, which the body is able to physically push out through the process of crying. Another theory is that crying triggers the body to release feel-good endorphins (the same ones you get from exercise or laughing).

To quote the *Sun* magazine: "Just as the Inuit have different words for snow on the ground and snow in the air and snow that drifts, maybe we could have different words for tears: tears we'll forget by tomorrow, tears we never cried but should have, tears that fall from our children's eyes, tears that fall too quickly to wipe away."

Here is a short message I received from one participant in a recent workshop:
"Oh, it was so amazingly nice! And I apologize in advance for my embarrassing confession ahead,

haha, please forgive me. But during Saturday afternoon's Śavāsana, I wept. Ugh. I mean, I cried like a baby. And I was doing my best to hold it in—this involuntary well of sadness and beauty that arose up within me during your teaching."

And from another student:
"During your guided Śavāsana, your mood, your words, the music, the studio space, my own imagination took me up and out of my body, off the studio floor, out into blue skies, and into space, above the earth, out past planets and stars and nebulae, all of it so empty and beautiful, into light, maybe back to the beginning of everything. And so I wept because it felt real, yet it isn't real."

I responded: Please, don't hold in . . . it is always a service if you cry . . . "Crying is one of the highest devotional songs. One who knows crying knows spiritual practice," said Swami Kripalu.

This is why Music, Sound, Nāda is so powerful . . . from the Bhajans of Pandit Jasraj to the *Clarinet Concerto* of Mozart . . . and from the Soundscapes of the Universe to the Music of the Spheres . . .

From another small health magazine recently:
"A study from Free University in Berlin, has determined that listening to 'sad' music may actually lift our mood. The researchers conducted a survey of 772 people, 44 percent of which were musicians, asking each subject about their emotional responses after listening to sad music. While 76 percent felt nostalgic, more than 57 percent of the respondents indicated peacefulness, more than 51 percent felt tenderness, almost 39 percent had feelings of wonder and 37 percent experienced a sense of transcendence. So, the next time you're struggling with something sad in your life, grab your headphones, put on Beethoven's *Moonlight Sonata*, a favorite sad song among the 722 survey respondents and work through whatever's troubling you. Odds are, you'll come out of it in a much better place than when you went in."

Listen to Wilhem Kempff's interpretation, playing in a state of no gravity, as on the moon, the sonata of the same name. Reflecting, like he is not playing. I listened to him a lot in my teens and to Clara Haskil . . . already crying, dreaming awake and opening the Gates!

One student said after a Yoga class where, during Śavāsana, I played *Koyaanisqatsi* from Philip Glass followed by *Mother*, an Armenian hymn sung by Isabel Barakdaryan: "I thought in Yoga class, music should be neutral." Well, there is no *neutral* music or *neutral* art. Emotions have to be impressed, expressed and released. Life has multiple facets and a wide emotional range. For sure, all Doṣas are aggravated by repressing your feelings.

And since we are in the Ayurvedic department, stress literally burns and dries the eyes, Vāta and Pitta combined in excess. So, for some, no more tears are released. Eyes become a desertic field with sensations of dryness and irritation. This leads to a tearless life and a condition known as Keratitis Sicca or Śuṣka Kṣipaka in Ayurveda, a chronic lack of sufficient lubrication and moisture on the surface of the eye.

On the other end, the more we relax the nervous system deep in Śavāsana, as anxiety recedes, the more we can reconnect with the internal sea, our oceanic nature and therefore a huge reservoir of tears! So salivary and lacrymal glands are well irrigated . . . Just by relaxing deeply, you will cry for no reason. So, let's go for bathing the eyes in rosewater and massaging the inner nostrils with organic nasya oil . . . to keep the eyes and the nose nurtured and content. And then we can count on Kūrma Upavāyu to keep moisturizing the surfaces of the eyes by moving the eyelids! Unless you practice the bhāvas, facial expressions in Kathakalī. Those who came to India with us, flying the open skies, know the challenge!

The best is crying and laughing for no reason, rolling on the floor during a Hāsya Yoga session. I have been there a few times.

ANGELS

When I look deeply around the room and observe a whole class in relaxation mode, it is very sweet, very moving! People's faces look like angels. The face is soft, open—a full moon. Mother and daughter, father and son look alike even more, as if this release minimizes and softens the age difference. No need for plastic surgery or Botox injection (especially now that we know that it may spread into the brain!). Just release the skin of the forehead towards the temples! Just let go. Widen between the eyes. Release the outer corner of the lips away from each other, letting half a smile, not even a conscious one, blossom on your lips. If you accept yourself as you let go of tensions, you can see the inside of your face, the beauty of your inner face, the face you had, as they say in Zen, before you were born. And the soft light inside your head glows in this darkness and radiates through your skin. Even if wrinkles and lines are printed on your face, those still visible in deep relaxation are your precious history. Maybe you lived closer to the sun like a Tibetan Shaman. The skin burned and raked by the wind, the rays of the sun and visionary insights. How powerful and beautiful are those faces, ageless, timeless and fully alive.

LESS IS MORE

Nothingness is a word that appears in a book by Thomas DeBaggio, an Alzheimer patient. He asks, "Are we born with a fear of our bodies? Could that be why we pay so little attention to what is inside and so many hours are spent pampering the exterior? If we spent time trying to understand what goes on inside, we'd get nothing done. Might not be a bad idea, doing less and shaping our lives on nothingness."

The legendary poet Pablo Neruda also addresses nothingness in "Keeping Quiet":

> *If we were not so single-minded / about keeping our lives moving, / and for once could do nothing, / perhaps a huge silence / might interrupt this sadness / of never understanding ourselves /and of threatening ourselves with death. / Perhaps the earth can teach us / as when everything seems dead in winter / and later proves to be alive. / Now I'll count to twelve / and you keep quiet and I will go.*

Each shows us the value of deep rest and being contemplative, reflective. Yoga offers sitting meditation, Śavāsana and a few other āsanas as the practices to experience this state. Sure, it can happen in dancing, running, in mindful sun salutations with mantra but there is energy spent; the nervous system is geared for action, so receptivity is more difficult. No output is great. Less is more.

RUN & FORGET

In a Yoga center or in health club Yoga classes, some people want to leave the class before Śavāsana. They paid for action—to sweat, to exercise, to master acrobatic postures, but definitely not for lying down. Actually, some health clubs, under pressure of members, ask Yoga teachers to go easy on Śavāsana. Maybe they fear coming to know where they are at, they fear the "anxiety of having to stop." "Stop and observe" is the original practice of mindfulness meditation. Not "Run and forget." Jay Leno has said he never takes a day off, so he doesn't have a chance to see that he overworks. Sometimes you have to go into deep relaxation to realize how tired you are. And there are so many people who are "underslept" and overworked. Acknowledging fatigue is difficult and scary if you are at the end of a rope already burning at both ends.

ŚAVĀSANA IN THE BIG APPLE

One day, a few years ago, I was teaching in a trendy health club in Manhattan (the one and only time I did, too Kafkaesque!). After asking then to turn down the volume on the twelve TV monitors, stop what seemed to be a turbo-reactor air conditioning (we were freezing and could not even hear someone speaking normally), and also turn down the neon lights, I was finally able to begin Śavāsana at the end of my seminar. Of course, they did not even have blankets to keep people warm. I felt like a missionary on a remote island with a bizarre culture practicing a strange religion of fitness. Still, I went on. Release deep, merge with earth, feel your breath. What is left when you are in deep relaxation . . . slowing down the beat of your heart and the pulse of your breath . . . Dissolve, surrender . . .

Through the glass wall I could see, as I was teaching, a woman going up and down on a Stairmaster, but she was not going up fast enough to read the book or magazine at the top, so she was maybe catching only a few words at a time. Then somebody burst into the room and asked in a loud voice (in France we would say with a voice of a fish merchant at the public market), "What are you doing here? IS THIS YŌGĀ? It looks like they are in a coma!" And suddenly it occurred to me that this was the exact opposite.

Yes, they did appear to be dead (Śavāsana means Corpse pose and is sometimes known as Mṛtāsana, Pose of Death) but I said, "No, they are deeply awake." They are in touch with the Source of life, the pranic flow. In their stillness there is pure consciousness . . . and the guy left, somewhat puzzled, for the locker room. Nothing personal, for the environment of Śavāsana was new to him, but his question does tell us something about the culture at large, where action figures sell well as toys and relaxation figures don't exist.

VACATION

I just came back from Italy. Did absolutely nothing for a week. No agenda, no computer, no phone. Just living, being. Sometimes you have to identify with your primary nature. That is the connection we are usually missing. We are so used to identifying with a second nature, like what we do—I am a Yoga teacher, or I am this or that. Then who are we when not involved in action? Once in a while undoing, completely letting go and going with the flow of life is such a blessing. My parents, who are both eighty, just wrote me that their ultimate pleasure is to garden together, side-by-side, for a few hours. How simple.

I hope all Yoga students or teachers have a chance to experience that for a few days. It usually takes a week to really unwind and realize how tired or tied up you are. Call it positive laziness if you like. Even if you take a week of vacation, you need another week to recover from it. Then, maybe you will begin to reevaluate your list of priorities. Deeper layers of fatigue, especially for those in denial, show when you begin to take the time to rest, repose and reflect. "Doing" more āsana is not the answer. In the early years, to build, yes, but later less is better. Even a Yoga fast would be a good idea for some.

It feels so good to have no schedule, no work, no practice—flowing through. What about designing a special two-hundred-hour vacation training with advanced napping included. Now why is it so challenging for some to rest and be quiet, or take a real vacation?

"We Americans are so active in our leisure that we commonly complain we need a vacation from our vacations . . . Americans are allotted few vacation days, 14 days, on average but ironically, we don't even use them. The average American will leave 4 days of vacation on the table this year. We spend more money than anyone else in the world on leisure—fully one-third of our income—yet we are simultaneously No. 1 in the world at not taking vacations. Bottom line: it is too stressful to relax!" (Po Bronson; "Just Sit Back and Relax!"; *Time Magazine* June 26, 2006)

If the night opens her door of Silence,
And leads one gently to the pilgrim-shore
Where all voices merge into the great Ocean;
If you have inhaled the scent of the lotus,
That floats on the lake of the Mind
As last offering, as last salutation –
Then end the day, and let work rest.
—Rabindranath Tagore

SURRENDER TO G

In order to relax, we must first surrender to Gravity. As my teacher Noëlle Perez used to say, Gravity and God begin with the same letter. It should be simple but, as we know from experience, releasing the body and, more so the mind, is challenging. Lying down in a comfortable position may be the best place to start. After all, this is what we choose for sleeping. I have fallen asleep occasionally while sitting and even once standing, in an overnight overcrowded bus in India, but neither would be my first choice. Supine is best.

SPELEOLOGY

Sometimes it is difficult to be facing up when relaxing. You may feel too exposed or vulnerable to let go of your fears. You may need stronger sunglasses to face the sun. With a history of trauma, from sexual abuse to PTSD, Child's Pose feels better first then Śavāsana. Facing down earthwards is more secure psychologically. Child's Pose or any supported prone position are forms of prostration like kissing the ground, a symbolic gesture but that also feels good as a real sensation.

You can also build a little cave, a hood around your head with a blanket. So, the brain is protected. Dogs take refuge under tables, not because of the rain. It is a shamanic veil of protection. It creates a sort of positive sensory deprivation. Pratyāhāra, the withdrawal of the sensory organs is enhanced. Then brainwaves are slowing down and peace of mind and body come more naturally.

Eyes relax physically by gravity, heavy, passive, soft, cool. Eyes are out of focus with no convergence as there is no more object to see. Light eyebags or Ṣanmukhī Mudrā with eye wrap will help. Optic nerves become silent.

Proper alignment facilitates letting go. Adjust the sacrum-tailbone unit but don't over-tuck, create traction in the spine, support secondary curves and elongate the primary ones. Then, energy will flow along the spine internally. You can play the spine as a flute or the pipe of an organ. The cerebrospinal fluid is an underground river with a soft deep current.

Speleology, snorkeling and scuba diving have Śavāsana in common. Sailing underground lakes with the Vāyus, the five winds of Prāṇa, exploring the caves of the body, the inner chambers, at times we can hear our own heart. And by embryological history, the pulse of the heart comes before the pulse of the breath.

YIN IN THE YANG

Most of us are control freaks. If not all the way, then a part of us is. So, there is interest of controlling the body, controlling the mind. At the same time Yoga philosophy speaks of surrender, releasing, letting go.

Here is the paradox. How can we surrender in Āsana and Prāṇāyāma as there is something to build, to promote, to construct, to shape? Is there a to do list and a to let go of list? Can they coexist?

I'd rather speak of assisting, monitoring, attending to posture or breath. Or finding the yin in the yang. When I was practicing puppetry, the best illusion of life was created by involuntary movements of the puppet, by giving an impulse or controlling a string a subtle way and then the puppet would have a certain response on it's own, yin in the yang, an oscillation or an amplitude that appeared to be the puppet's own expression. If overcontrolled, too yang, it looked like a lifeless object, a machine or a toy. Manipulate the strings of your āsana the same way, being the puppet and the puppeteer. Iyengar Yoga developed practices hanging from ropes. It has been part of my daily practice for decades, better than a warm-up, creating space by letting go. "In Yoga Kuruṇṭa one learns to manipulate oneself in the various Yoga postures by mean of a suspended rope as if one were a puppet," writes Geeta Iyengar in her pioneering book *Yoga: A Gem for Women*.

LE PONT DU GARD

During a Summer 2005 Yoga retreat in the South of France, the group traveled on their day off to visit the Provence of Van Gogh and we stopped at the Pont du Gard, a Roman aqueduct built in year zero and still intact. One of the Wonders of the World. I knew of a secret way to access the river so we could swim downstream under the monumental bridge, a quasi-mystical experience. Mark Schorr, one of the retreat participants and a seasoned yogi, wrote this poem the day after, following a long deep relaxation. Mark was a gifted American poet, the head of the Robert Frost Foundation, and a really good friend.

The sun and summer are at their height
about as far as they can be from night
when, after you, I have just begun
to swim along the limestone-heavy
sources of the Rhône
I think of those before me on this triple arc,
whose sure footings have bridged this way
between their many-layered openings of mind
and the load-bearing arches of their hearts.
The line of arcs above me buoys my chest
neither too high nor too low above the sight lines of the eye
as if in Śavāsana, to bob and to rest.
So, let this well-worn spirit be
Free-floating along this well-washed way.

—Mark Schorr

PART SEVEN

Nāda Yoga

Music of Yoga of Music of Yoga of Music of . . .

NĀDA

All that is visible, clings to the invisible,
the audible to the inaudible,
the tangible to the intangible:
Perhaps the thinkable to the unthinkable.
—NOVALIS

In ancient texts related to Yoga of Sound (Nāda Yoga), it is suggested to practice listening to inner sounds and to meditate on sound or music between midnight and 2:00 A.M. I just had a dream in which I was swimming in an ocean with giant waves and big rocks, and gradually swam to the shore, seeing teepees and fires in the distance. A shamanic dream. It woke me up and here I am at 2:00 A.M. writing about Sound, the sound of Silence, not the beautiful song by Simon and Garfunkel, but the presence of Silence, the vibration of the universe.

Nāda Yoga, or any Yoga, gives you the opportunity to dive into Sound, as you can dive into the essence of matter. These journeys are reflected in the great paintings of Max Ernst, Jackson Pollock, and in great compositions of all times. As you read these words, take a moment to listen to everything around you and within you, just the sound vibrations, as if you didn't know what they were—no words, no labels, no categories—just sound for the sake of it. I hear a trio of distant neighbor's voices, muffled washing machine stopping from time to time, allowing the wind's sound to come in, and a kettle of boiling water . . .

In fact, as Alain Daniélou writes in *The Myths and Gods of India*, a classic work on Hindu Polytheism, "Ancient grammarians and theoreticians of the Sanskrit language considered the separation of spoken language, gestural language and music as a late phenomenon and never completely realized." John Cage said once that when you separate music from life you have art. Nāda Yoga listens to life as music and music as a reflection of life. Everything is music from the audible to the inaudible.

Music is a subdivision of Āhatanāda, the world of "struck" sounds, which includes languages and all sounds produced by striking two objects. Anāhata is the platonic music of the spheres or anything unstruck, always present, self-generated or inaudible, higher or lower frequencies.

For a while now, and since the 1990's especially, Yoga and music have been meeting each other in various ways. Music of Yoga of music of Yoga of music! Some Yoga teachers, depending on the school, play various kinds of music in classes (from Bob Dylan to Enya, from Elvis to Wah!), and argue about the role of silence in Śavāsana. A young couple recently tried one of my beginners classes in which I was teaching āsana in detail. I didn't use music at all that day and at the end they told me: "This is not Yoga, there's no music!" Yoga teacher trainings now address issues like pairing āsanas with songs, as with wines and chocolates. Why not, I say, concerning the chocolate and the wine (after all I am French), but I don't need to take a Yoga workshop to enjoy myself or erase Judeo-Christian guilt. At the same time, doesn't listening to a Mozart concerto or an Indian Rāga require our full attention?

In fitness and health clubs, people are used to multitasking with TV news, reading and listening to music as they exercise, sometimes to inspire and motivate, sometimes to kill the boredom. Yoga is more of an inner dance. It is fascinating, exciting at times, but I am not sure the word fun applies. Yoga practitioners now gather for Kirtans and Bhajans and are deeply moved at times, even though these are mostly devotional practices in India. Imagine if suddenly the Hindus or Muslims or agnostics of another culture's youth were all chanting Hallelujah in fitness classes, or spiritual folksongs in Latin! Something of note (literally!) is clearly happening. Many are experiencing a need for something more than the physical plane, maybe a need to bring back folksong traditions with a modern yogic spin. After all, singing and chanting have left daily life and workplace.

ADVENTURES IN COMPOSITION

Already very early, I thought of a microphone as a musical instrument,
like a bow or like a percussion instrument.
—KARLHEINZ STOCKHAUSEN

Composing professionally for avant-garde puppet shows also opened doors of perception. I played many instruments with varying skill, more like a Tibetan lama, but always for a very specific sound or effect. Experimental, improvised and written, often naïve and minimalist pieces, using gongs, drones on the first generation of synthesizers and sequencers with live music, mixing Middle Age instruments and electronics, taping natural sounds with sophisticated microphones (the early days of "musique concrete" by Pierre Schaeffer and Pierre Henry were not too far off). I tape-recorded the sound of stones rippling over iced over ponds, echoing in stereophony early morning and insects singing unbelievable sounds like woodworms and cicadas. I stand with Salvador Dali who said, "We don't need drugs, we are drugs."

THE SOUND OF MUSIC

Early on I had a chance to meet powerful mentors and to engage in deep listening. I would attend organ concerts on Sunday afternoons. Even though I was not raised Christian, I would go in my early teens to these free concerts, featuring everything from Bach to Widor, to get a dose of celestial vibrations. The Beatles had just come out with *Abbey Road*, which I also listened to on loop. I went to India for the first time when I was nineteen, hitchhiking straight east from Normandy though Europe, Iran, Iraq, Afghanistan, Pakistan and finally India. That was the calling of the times. I got a chance to hear a lot of tribal music on the return trip from Gypsies and nomads. Some left Rajasthan to go west and arrived in Europe. This is described wonderfully in the movie *Latcho Drom*. No words, just music. It will make you appreciate Flamenco even more!

In my teens also I left my parents' house for a little rented room under a roof and I would listen late in the night with my old piano teacher, Marguerite, also a philosopher, to avant-garde music like Stockhausen's *Aus den sieben Tagen*, and different versions of Glenn Gould playing *Bach Partitas* to see how he evolved in his interpretations. Also, we listened to John Cage, Xenakis etc . . . These moments were very precious. Intense meditation for hours. In the course of writing my thesis on Tibetan music I met wonderful teachers at the Guimet Museum and in Parisian universities, again listening to a huge amount of music from all traditions. I would lie down in packed auditoriums listening to the Dagar Brothers or the Trance music of the Pearl Divers of Kuwait. All those sounds remain with me.

DREAM

Peace of mind can be reached through meditation on the knowledge which dreams give.
—PATAÑJALI SŪTRA I, 38

I had a dream of a musical dinner where there were notes and music on my plate and colored feathers on each side instead of fork and spoon . . .

GO EAST, YOUNG MAN!

On one of my first journeys to India and Nepal, I visited an old antique shop in Bhagdaon in the Kathmandu valley, searching for a singing bowl. I didn't know much about resonance or overtones, but the object itself fascinated me—how it was made of shiny golden metals. I traded all my camping equipment for it since I was on my way back from Annapūrṇā basecamp. I brought the bowl back to France where it gathered dust for years. I could have served peanuts in it for all I was using it. Then I began to study Tibetan music as a musicologist, investigating harmonic chanting, diphony and overtones. I also listened to bells of all kinds, in churches and temples, and searched for overtones in contemporary music from Bartok's *Mikrokosmos* and Stockhausen's *Stimmung* to free jazz like Sun Ra and of course the Tibetan lamas themselves. I would not call it Easy Listening. All sounds are in one sound. Like all colors are contained in white light. This is why Indian musicians tune their instruments to the drone of the tambura and its radiating shiny harmonics.

The bowl started to have a life of its own. I could hear how its sounds traveled through space in multiple layers. I touched it, rubbed it with various clappers and sticks to get the best resonance. Later I learned to "drink" the sound, using my mouth cavity as a chamber of resonance next to the edge of the bowl. In Śavāsana, deep relaxation, I was beginning to have deeper experiences of the Prāṇa, the flow of energy moving—what we call in Yoga the Vāyus, the winds of the breath. And I began to explore the space I was projected into after the resonance of the bowl vanished into silence. It felt like being suspended in time or in Bahya Kumbhaka, the silent state following the exhalation, which Patañjali refers to in Sūtra 1.34.

Back on the Indian continent again, I listened to Pandit Jasraj twice in concert. Once in Pune when B.K.S. Iyengar suggested we go on a Sunday morning and Jasraj sang for five hours non-stop. Trance, deep emotion, meditation. A few years later I heard him sing in Rishikesh, where we were having a Prāṇāyāma intensive on the banks of the Gaṅgā. He sang for us and our guru in the evening, Rāgas under the tent . . . reminiscent of our nomadic roots and literally common ground as Proto Indo-Europeans. The presence of the Gaṅgā nearby and the transcendent voice of the singer after a day of intense Prāṇāyāma are still interwoven in my mind decades later.

DEEP LISTENING

What I teach often in meditation—while sitting at the beginning or lying down at the end of class—is to listen deeply to whatever there is to be listened to. This could be internal sound, whatever is in the room (light frequencies, the heater, or the cracking of the wood etc.), the sounds of other people, the sounds of the city, the sounds of nature, near and far, subtle and not so subtle; a "global" listening, the live soundtrack of life's movie. Just receive and absorb, making our whole body a microphone. This is a powerful experience. I've done it in all kinds of different places, way lost in the jungle, in the middle of the city, in a crowd or by myself. With no pre-existing labeling agenda, listen with the innocence and wonder of a child seeing the ocean for the first time.

I have the pleasure to recognize overtones/harmonics in every sound, soundscape or when any group of Yoga students chant the mantra OM. Overtones are a bridge between the unmanifested and manifested world and it is possible to hear them, but most people don't know what to listen for! (Watching the film *Genghis Blues*, a documentary about a blues singer traveling to Mongolia for a throat-singing contest, is a good start.) I have for decades investigated so-called meditation music, sacred music of all periods and cultures, "prehistoric" music, free jazz, acoustic and electro-acoustic, "world" music, new and old age music, classical Indian, contemporary, Gregorian chant, and, best for me, "unclassifiable." In every category I have found a soundscape that is able to create a yogic state of mind, maybe even a glimpse of Samādhi. It recalls " Enlightenment is a Bitch," a poem by Dane Cervine:

Meditation becomes oddly redundant,
Attention now like water, absorbed in tree root,
Plumbing; even fire hydrants with their red
Stubby arms become maṇḍalas, and, worse
The police siren revving its wail behind
My slow-moving car sounds like a mantra.

INHALE MUSIC, EXHALE MUSIC

Listen first to slow movements, Adagios and/or music that has loops, "repetitive" music, because it will be closer to our biological rhythms, the heartbeat, the breath, walking, and will create a sense of timelessness. Any music that waves, cycles, loops, or breathes within the breath will be more likely to induce a state of trance or absorption. Any drone-based, and therefore modal-like, music will also play better through you, just as life is also repetitive but never the same from moment to moment. If the drone can be seen as the ground, the ocean, the river, the melody would be the flight of the musician. If the music has substance, it will create a pranic awakening. If the music (a song, or anything from Ave Maria to OM) touches and moves you, the upper cakras will be highlighted, especially the fontanelle or a bit above it.

As Levon Helm says, "If you give it good concentration, good energy, good heart and good performance the song will play you." You may feel a kind of buzzing, something like pins and needles in the fascia and skin; this means the sounds have resonated deep into your whole being. Whether it's a slow piece or a fast piece, no matter what you do with your breath, you're going to feel like it's somewhat in sync with the musical sentences, the flow of the music. This works particularly well with Mozart; if you practice deep, slow yogic breathing, you are always in sync with the melodic or harmonic wave patterns. You are part of the same play. Some small bits of melodies just make you cry and your whole being is swept by deep waves of music.

Often, music's breath and my own will merge. Like sometimes heart and breath beat do. Great music, regardless of its classification (including unclassifiable), has undertow waves. With the magic of entrainment, my own breath will end up in phase with the music. When Ujjāying, I am inhaling and exhaling the music as if I was composing it or playing it as it unfolds from the now to the next now. The music itself is riding along with the glottic sound. Inhale music, exhale music: a new Ghaṭa.

A few suggestions for that specific experience: Adagio from Ravel's *Piano Concerto in G Major.* Keith Jarrett's *Köln Concert, Part 1*. Mozart's Adagio from *Piano Concerto 23, K.488. Crossing Dark Rivers* by Stephen Micus. Djivan Gasparian, *I Will Not Be Sad In This World.* Philip Glass' *Second Movement of Tirol Concerto. The Guardian Angel* by Heinrich Biber and so many more you will discover on your own!

MUSICAL MEDITATION

Oh wisest ones!
This body—a splendid Tambura!
—KABIR

First, choose a Posture. Of course, it has to be comfortable and suitable for long timing from ten to forty-five minutes. Make sure you're warm enough. Cover yourself with blankets, if needed.

These are the options:

Sitting meditation poses: as long as the knees are lower than the hip joints and the natural spinal curves are respected. So Sukhāsana, Siddhāsana, Vīrāsana, Ardha Padmāsana, Padmāsana, sitting on a chair.

Supine positions. All variations of lying-down poses suitable for Śavāsana, with the chest and head supported, or calf muscles on the chair. Even Supta Baddha Koṇāsana with a bolster.

Inverted poses like Sarvāṇgāsana, supported Halāsana and Śīrṣāsana if they are functional and effortless. As a musicology and Yoga student, I used to listen to Mahler and Bruckner symphonies in Head Balance and Shoulder Stand (a Pitta-induced idea). In those days we had to turn the LP every twenty-five minutes or so; it was a perfect inversion and Nāda Yoga practice combined!

Listen with eyes closed. If lying down, cover them with an eye bag or some cloth. Eyes, being the windows of the brain, have to be completely soft, receptive, introverted, relaxed, as must all sensory organs, including the skin, so that the whole body can become a giant listening ear. Volume should be moderate but intense enough so frequencies can reach your fluid body. If you find one piece you like in particular, listen to it on loop. If you have a computer, click on Controls, then on Repeat, and on One!

Quite a mystical agenda! Enjoy the ride, let yourself go. In an article by B.K.S. Iyengar in Yoga Journal, he ended with: "You have to lose yourself to find yourself." A challenge, sure, but one with a payoff!

Second, choose the music:

I offer a list I have selected from thousands of possibilities over the years. It could have been much longer, and the choices are somewhat subjective. You may want to create your own version someday. Having a list does not mean that I do not listen to other sources like Joan Baez, Emmylou Harris, Neil Young, French singer-songwriters, the Beatles or Reggae. Good music is something that moves you and you are moved by. In every category of music there is a wide range of material: gems, good finds, less exciting pieces and things not worth listening to. The following suggestions would not do well in a nightclub, unless the definition of a nightclub is a Yoga center in the dark with candles!

CONTEMPORARY, REPETITIVE, MINIMALIST

We cannot avoid Philip Glass, like it or not, because he practices meditation and his music is very open-ended, with a concept of time not unlike ritual Tibetan music. Even though he's been prolific, it's not always interesting. There are two CDs I recommend by Glass. One is *Glassworks*, featuring a piece called *Facades*. Then there is the music he wrote for the silent movie *Koyaanisqatsi*, based on a Hopi revelation text. This work includes a deep voice (bass) organized around a Chaconne structure, a type of musical composition used for variations on a short, repeated bassline. The piece is powerful, abyssal and works well with Śavāsana. As far as Steve Reich, who is part of the same group of so-called minimalist composers, I recommend *Music for Mallet Instruments*, which is very hypnotic. I also recommend *A Rainbow in Curved Air* by Terry Riley; it's nice for an early-morning rise, if you can transcend the outdated synthesizers. And there is the mythical *String Trio* from La Monte Young.

ETHNIC/FOLK

I'm a big fan of Armenian music. There's an instrument called the duduk, an ancestor of the oboe, also a double reed, and it's heartbreaking. The main duduk player is Djivan Gasparyan. Some of his disciples, like Levon Minassian, are also mind-blowing, literally and can take you into deep otherworldly space. Early polyphonies and water drumming of the Aka and Baka Pygmies, South African tribal music from the Xhosa women, Amazonian Indians, 'Are'are Melanesian people . . . a very rich field of exploration resonating in the collective unconscious layers . . .

CLASSICAL WESTERN MUSIC

There are several Concerti that work well; stick to the slow movements. Listen to Baroque composers such as Marcello, Albinoni, Locatelli and Vivaldi. You will find gems. Making a big jump in time, the

Adagio in Ravel's *Piano Concerto* in G is beautiful and extremely meditative.

Back to Mozart, his music can be a little bit too nice and peppy sometimes, so you have to search for pieces more on the spiritual, introverted side of the spectrum. His compositions for glass harmonica are ethereal, rich in overtones and quite wonderful. They're played on wet glasses that turn, creating a singing bowl kind of sound. On the Concerti side, best are the *Piano Concerto No. 23* (Keith Jarrett recorded it and improvises wonderfully in the final cadenza) and, of course, his pieces for the clarinet or for flute and harp. Check out the *Andante* from the *40th Symphony,* the *Adagio* from the *Gran Partita*, conducted by Pierre Boulez, and the dark *Masonic Music* he wrote for his friend's funeral. Mitsuko Uchida has recorded all the Mozart sonatas. As a yogini, she masters the art of silence and has laser-beam precision, reminding me of Iyengar, who likewise possesses sharpness, precision, and so much spirit and presence. Clara Haskil and Martha Argerich also have stunning interpretations.

Then you have Arvo Pärt, a Christian mystic. His music sounds like it is from the Middle Ages or Early Renaissance but with a twist and some surprises. Actually, it was composed in the last twenty years. He retains the purity of the Cistercian Abbeys. I particularly enjoy *Für Alina, Spiegel im Spiegel,* and *Lamentate.*

Synesthesia is invoked in the composer's words: "I could compare my music to white light which contains all colors. Only a prism can divide the colors and make them appear; this prism could be the spirit of the listener."

CLASSICAL INDIAN

It is a form of Yoga, actually, and by essence meditative; the Rāgas are very long, several hours, though producers usually shorten them when exported to the West to an hour or less. Pandit Jasraj, the best-known classical singer in India, has recorded almost everything from Rāgas to Bhajans to the Upaniṣad verses. These recordings will keep you content for several years. Search for Rāgas for the surbahar (a bass sitar), the sanṭūr (ancestor of the cymbalum), the flute, the shennai, all great Indian instruments. I have a soft spot for the jalatarangam, an instrument resembling the glass harmonica, which uses small bowls filled with water played with little sticks. There's also a group called Ghazal, more on the Persian side of the spectrum, that has recorded *Lost Songs of the Silk Road.* Rāga-like meditative improvisations on the Oud in Iran, Iraq and North Africa create deep soundscapes and bring us close to the Birth of Music. These are extremely shamanic in feeling, very suitable for restorative practice and Nāda Yoga.

Great music, as its sound vibrates through all cells, generates an emotional response. It can make you cry. I've had experiences like this in many sacred places, like the Temple of the Sea in Mahābalipuram or in small chapels like the one at the top of the Pic Saint Loup in the South of France. At moments like these you just cry out of nowhere, because it's so beautiful and you know it is tapping into a very deep, primal, preverbal, prereligious, prehistoric layer of yourself. It's a cry of joy or ecstasy, generated by the overtones of your own voice, the quality of the silence, the sacred music and pipe organ of the cathedral, the accordion of the beggar in the subway, the song of a little boy in the Rajasthani desert. It's powerful because something is reaching deep into the nervous system and into the heart center. Anāhata Nāda into Anāhata Cakra?

A.M. & P.M.

Just a few suggestions!

Wake up with John Mayall and the Bluesbreakers, *Blues from Laurel Canyon*, Bach's *Double Violin Concerto*, Haydn's *Allegro of the Harp Concerto*, Terry Riley's *Rainbow in Curved Air*, and *Good Morning* with The Beatles.

Drift gradually into heavenly sleep with Mozart's Adagio for Glass Harmonica, an instrument invented by Benjamin Franklin and rich in overtones, *Lullaby to Mother Earth* by Luzmila Carpio, *Path 5* of Max Richter, *Spiegel in Spiegel*, Arvo Pärt, and *Good Night* with The Beatles.

Good morning equals Viloma 1 Prāṇāyāma (long interrupted inhalations) equals double espresso.

Good evening equals Viloma 2 (long interrupted exhalations) equals chamomile.

ETHNOCENTRISM

1931. Paris invited the famous Indian musician Timir Baran Bhattacharya for a recital in a concert hall, where usually Chopin and Liszt were played. After all, it was called "classical" Indian music. He received tomatoes and eggs on stage. Most in the audience that day labeled the performance as, "not music." They had the impression that it was all the same because of the drone and the modal quality and what appears to be repetitive and a lack of harmony in the Western sense—no development like a symphony or a sonata. And they were lost! Western culture is so ethnocentric. What it doesn't understand, it rejects—it rules as boring or noise or too simplistic. It is actually the same for most contemporary music, from Pierre Henry to Stockhausen. The American minimalist composers deeply influenced by the East and by Africa manage to be accepted by some, at least, thanks to their neo-classical harmony—and maybe because times have changed, finally.

In 1981, I presented my Master's thesis on ritual Tibetan music in the University of Normandy. The concept "World Music" did not really exist yet. The jury was made up of professors specialized in Berlioz or Italian Opera. They had no clue. They were asking me questions on how to deal with high altitude when recording instead of addressing the content of the thesis. They gave me the diploma *cum laude*. A positive side effect of ethnocentrism, as for them Western classical music was the only music they knew.

MOZARTIANA

Since my early teens, Mozart has been my close friend. For some, it could be the Rolling Stones or Bob Dylan. When I got sick with hepatitis in 1989, Mozart was my main prescription. I had hallucinations; I would see Mozart music in three Dimensions.

Since then, I listened even more to all his music and played some. Recently, I read again Joseph Campbell's and Dr. Alfred Tomatis's research on the powerful impact of Mozart music on the brain, the verticality and more. How it is deep nourishment for your whole being. I am a believer in Mozartherapy. Sure, I have doubts as well, but only two percent like the milk.

"And it's so joyful when it works. It's that intersection of math, instinct and musicality that just makes me so happy," —wrote the composer Nico Mulhy about the music of Philip Glass, but for sure Mozart would qualify.

In a self-imposed retreat in the foothills of the Himalayas a few years ago, I listened in the dark—on repeat mode—to all slow movements of the String Quartets and try to find out if the Mozart Effect introduced by Dr. Tomatis was real. I discovered that one of the *Adagio* themes of the first string quartet is also present in the *Concerto for Flute and Harp*, a deep musical caress, goose bumps guaranteed.

Oh, imagine if you were in utero listening to Mozart, as he was himself listening to his mother singing and other musicians around him during the whole pregnancy, being nourished by ecstatic harmony and melody!

EVERYTHING IS MUSIC

Music—received or played, voice or instrument, sounds of nature or culture—is essential to human beings. Everybody is a musician. Everybody can sing. "Everything is music," Kabir says.

Don't worry about saving these songs!
And if one of our instruments breaks,
It doesn't matter.
We have fallen into the place
Where everything is music.

AURAL TRADITION

If you were playing, as a musician, the written composition of the ongoing universe's soundscape, you would just have to meditate and listen to it. It would unfold by itself as if you were composing it from moment to moment.

Music as we usually define it is included in Sound, Nāda.

The world of Sound includes everything that vibrates, Anāhata Nāda and Āhata Nāda, unstruck or struck sound. Music is struck as it is produced by playing consciously.
The sounds of nature are unstruck, they are just composing themselves in the now.
Listen to music, any kind you like, preferably without words as pure Sound, as if it was random or just sounds happening in nature with no specific intention.
Listen to the vibration of the sound mass not what it is according to names, category of music, tonality or mode, chords, notes. Just the organic resonance, like a deaf listener can feel bass in bones or lower torso, and treble in the head.
Music as soundwaves going through you, being filtered by the body and its various layers…

Listen to all sounds. A global listening, far, near, inside and outside yourself.
Listen to the soundtrack of the world without the images, without the movie.
Listen to Nature sounds of all kind, environmental sounds but just the sound of it, not labeling what it is. So, airplane or bird sound, just as sound, as if it was the first time you heard it. No references.
Echoing parts of a poem by Jorge Luis Borges:

> *Everything happens for the first time.*
> *I saw something white in the sky. They tell me it is the moon,*
> *But what can I do with a word and a mythology.*
> *Whoever lights a match in the dark is inventing fire.*
> *Whoever goes down to a river goes down to the Ganges.*
> *Everything happens for the first time*
> *But in that way it is eternal.*
> *Whoever reads my words is inventing them.*

Listen to images imagining the sound associated with them. That will become music! Sometimes it is obvious, sometimes it is abstract. Realism, hyperrealism. symbolism, romanticism, lyrical abstraction, cubism, fauvism, impressionism, we can re-create everything.

Listen to your own voice chanting.
Listen to your own voice reading poetry out loud.
You can label, define, categorize, name, like or not like, before or after, but not during the deep listening of Nāda Yoga meditation.

FUGUES

Listen to the first few minutes of *The Idea of North* from Glenn Gould—human voices telling stories superposed as a weaving of musical instruments, just sounds of conversations recorded in a café, as music with dynamics, melodic patterns, no meaning, a fugue of multiple human voices speaking simultaneously. And then listen to Gould playing J.S. Bach's *Three-Part Inventions* (2, 9, and 13) or

Keith Jarrett playing Shostakovitch's *Prelude and Fugues* (5 and 22 are stunning). Listen to separate voices in the fugues. No words here but each voice is telling a story with the mantra-like theme of the fugue and the "stretto," where voices are knitted closer together towards the end. It feels as if several people were talking at the same time, hence *The Idea of North* reference. Stretto means tight and has the same root as stress!!! Thanks to Sarasvatī, it is resolved—not unlike Śavāsana, in the last chord, and sustained, usually including the sound of God, a perfect fifth with a fermata.

STAIRS TO HEAVEN

A few years ago, I arrived in Rochester from Europe late at night but with time zones still early morning. Brahma Muhūrta is the most suitable time for meditation. I opened the Gate of the Zen Center garden. Like the one from the Ramamani Iyengar Institute in Pune, it is a rite of passage to open a Gate and walk on the other side, beyond fear, opening the door of a yogic Narnia, opening the gate of an invisible maṇḍala. When the town is still asleep it feels like before sunrise in India—something special in the vibration, the colors, the atmosphere. The transpersonal Buddha in the Japanese garden sits there no matter what, tropical weather or blizzard.

In the sky right above the Gate, the belt of Orion. It seems that I always see Orion no matter where I am. My father was pointing it to me as a child. Also reminds me of the great mythical album of the French singer Gérard Manset, *La Mort d'Orion*. It was quite visionary.

So, I chanted and practiced a few āsanas on my circular mat in the center of the Buddha Hall. No music, no fitness in mind, just for the sake of it, singing and moving. Mental and physical health are side effects of the practice, not a goal. They are also side effects of life choices, dharma connections.

Then, still in sitting meditation, sitting in the middle of the purple circular mat, I listened to the Philip Glass *Tirol Concerto Second Movement*, one of his most inspired pieces. Absorbing the sound like a sponge, traveling inside the sound. Tears came with those ascendant and descendant scales spiraling, melody and rhythm interwoven. Clearer, now that I know that he studied with Ravi Shankar and Alla Rakha numerous times. Philip Glass also studied Yoga and Tibetan Buddhism very seriously and really did his homework. His biography, *Words Without Music*, is phenomenal. I could have met him on the road to India or at the Golden Temple of Amritsar in the 1970's, or at the Festival d'Avignon where I performed with the avant garde troupe known as *Theater in the Sky (Théâtre-en-Ciel)*, along with the *Bread and Puppet Theater*, still based in Vermont, in their underground barn. I could also have bumped into him at a John Cage happening or a Steve Reich performance in Paris, where he studied for a few years with the legendary music teacher Nadia Boulanger in the Conservatoire de Paris. The last movement of his opera on Gandhi, *Satyāgraha* has the same feeling. Ascending scales composed on verses of the *Bhagavad Gītā*. Now I fully understand why I have such a deep connection with his musical language. Stairs to Heaven.

CONVERSATION

Last night I had a great conversation with Mordecai Lipshutz, a great musicologist, who used to be a pillar of a Classical public radio station. I invited him for dinner so we could compare our playlists. At one point we were saying that Guillaume de Machaut and early Renaissance choral music like Pierre de la Rue were influences on Arvo Pärt's sacred music. Then we commented on the repetitive aspects of Ravel's *Bolero*. Apparently, Ravel wrote it toward the end of his life, when a creativity-unleashing form of dementia was rewiring the circuitry of his brain and chronic migraines were banging in his head. The theme sounds like a haunting, desperate, obsessive thought, like a stubborn Vṛtti, louder and louder, a loop with different textures and colors, an ascending drama. Pierre Boulez has directed a laser-like interpretation. Then if you want to go all the way, listen to Steve Reich's early electro-acoustic piece *Come Out*. You will go crazy, but the mind is like that at times, hyper-rajasic. Relaxing music may be overrated!

GHAZAL

Ghazal in Urdu language refers to a form of lyrical poem. It is also the name of a small group of musicians from India and Persia, improvising together. It has the feel of an Indian Rāga, but with a different architecture. A Rāga develops very gradually toward a climax, where in ghazal music, we see endless variations on a verse, more like a song or a poem.

The classical music of Ghazal has the color of the early pre-Islamic shamanism of Central Asia: Hypnotic and wide-open loops bring you from the steppes and deserts of Central Asia all the way to the Tibetan kingdoms of Ladakh and Zanskar. You are part of the caravan.... If you were walking on the Silk Road, this would be the soundtrack of the Journey.

GLASSICAL

Philip Glass and Leonard Cohen met a few times. Leonard gave Philip a big stack of his poems and illustrations, which Glass organized into five categories, then he picked five or six poems from each and composed a series of song cycles. Ultimately there were twenty-two poems for the World Première *Book of Longing: A Song Cycle Based on the Poetry and Images of Leonard Cohen*, performed in Toronto on June 1, 2007.

In a public discussion afterwards, Leonard was asked whether he thought Glass's work was classical music or musical theater. He replied, "Glassical!"

MINIMALIST TO THE MAXIMUM

Philip Glass, Steve Reich, Terry Riley, Arvo Pärt, La Monte Young, Michael Nyman, John Cage,

Pauline Oliveros, Laurie Anderson, Baird Hersey; so many names have shaped the soundscape of the century and have deeply resonated in me from the mid-'70s until now. They share a strong interest in the nature of Sound itself. The repetitive cycles, the loops, the overtones, the silences are Mantras and Sūtras to open our minds, the inner skies and the doors of Perception. They evolve gradually from moment to moment, sometimes with no beginning and no end. Distant cousins to Tibetan ritual music, Pygmies tribal polyphonies or medieval organa.

A meditative state is required to appreciate those secret languages and their references to Rāga, African drumming or nature's harmonics and harmony.

In the late seventies in Paris I heard John Cage, as well as Steve Reich, when he was experimenting with electronics. I composed "minimalist" music for theater for a decade, mixing medieval instruments like lute and duduk with synthesizers. I have listened to those composers' repertoire, sitting or supine, over and over again as a kind of spiritual practice. A visionary experience where synesthesia rules, where you can see or touch the Sound like Evelyn Glennie, a deaf percussionist, does when she makes love to her marimba at the end of the movie *Touch the Sound.*

POSTURAL RĀGA

Modal music with a drone, a continuous sound, whether it is a chord or a single note—such as in the Armenian duduk or Indian tambura—is not unknown to the West. In fact, most early medieval music in Europe is modal, as are Gregorian chants and the songs of the troubadours and trouvères. Each scale has a certain feel and emotional content, as does the mode of a Rāga. Lyrical jazz of Keith Jarrett, Michel Petrucciani and Abdullah Ibrahim thrives on modes, eolian, myxolydian and more.

A Rāga in Indian classical music begins with an alap, a long meditative improvisation establishing the scale, the melody and the mood of the piece. Two notes, the Vādī and the Saṃvādī, become the base of the melody. Then the percussion comes gradually, structuring the composition in a very complex rhythm known as the Tāla. The main soloist and the drummer gradually engage in a dialogue, which culminates in an orgasmic trance and is ultimately resolved into the drone and into silence.

Sometimes I envision a Yoga class or a Yoga practice having the same evolution, the ālap and dhrupad of a postural Rāga, opening poses searching to create space to be more in touch with the inner tuning and retuning, then gradually adding complexity and rhythm towards a peak experience—what would be the highest notes of the melody in the Rāga—and then restorative inversions and Śavāsana to bring back the silence in which the whole practice resonates. Is Śavāsana the cause of all āsanas? Does action follow being, as Saint Augustine writes, or are they coexisting? The Tāla in any case is the underlying Vinyāsa, the sequencing, the mindful repetitions; a stable structure even if not visible at first glance. Music of Yoga of Music of Yoga.

VIVA VIVALDI!

I have been to Venice many times to track the prints of Vivaldi's life and music. From the church where he was baptized to the one where he had almost daily rehearsals with his orchestra. One year I got the keys to the abandoned Santa Maria Della Croce. Grass is growing on the steps, not far from Piazza San Marco, near the hotel where James Bond has his daily Spritz. After climbing up the stairs inside the church I could touch the organ Antonio played, but I also realized most of the "orphaned" girls and young women from the orchestra were not orphans, per se, as most biographies would have it to keep it politically correct. Every story has a shadow. Baby girls born out of wedlock to priests, cardinals and aristocratic families were dropped in a giant mailbox at night. The sisters would take them in the morning and later each little girl would be given the name of the instrument she played as her family name. Your name would be Anna della Viola, if you played the viola and mine could have been Francesco del Flauto.

Vivaldi has been in my life since my early teens, as much as Mozart and the Beatles. Something so alive, from the dark drama of the Stabat Mater to the pure ecstatic joy of the Piccolo recorder Concerto that François Truffaut used in his movie *The Wild Child.* It has a kind of pre-pop music vibe with almost disco-like bass lines. It has so much energy. Antonio Lucio Vivaldi would have been a rock star in this century with his group, Red Priest and the Orphans or Antonio and the Ragazze!

SYNCHRONICITY

A few years ago, I was teaching a private lesson to a mentally ill student. Yes, we all are at some level, but this particular person was deeply agitated, the result of a traumatic karma. So, she would not consider resting or practicing Restorative Yoga, what she needed most, as she was an insomniac. I finally succeeded by surprise after asking her if she would consider listening to music I really loved. I played this wonderful piece of Armenian music by Djivan Gasparian called *I Will Not Be Sad In This World* as she was lying down. She fell asleep in Supta Baddha Koṇāsana. A step in the right direction, surrendering. But here is the magical part of the story: In the beginning phase when she was still awake and thinking about resting, my cell phone rang right next to us. I forgot to turn it off. But my ring tone, believe it or not, was programmed to be a melodical fragment, a short loop of that very same song played by Gasparian on the duduk, an apricot wood traditional Armenian oboe. I had changed it from the annoying original programmed ringtone everybody knows. So, when the phone went on, we heard the same music playing simultaneously at almost the same volume as the quadraphonic sound system in the Yoga studio. Actually, I did not hear it at first because it was the same exact piece, and of course she did not realize it because she would think the second voice was in the original piece! Wow! Because it is a modal music with a drone, it sounded like an echo or a perfect canon with two parts, two duduks with the same tuning. I did not realize right away what was going on and had a Samādhi-like moment. Later, I lost that particular phone. It flew out of a rental car roof in New Mexico. (Open Sky indeed.) The new one has a stupid standard ringtone again. If I forget to turn off my phone before teaching, everybody is annoyed, rightly so, and the teacher (me) has a little guilt trip as we usually ask the students to turn their phones off before class. Oh, and what about our agitated student? She woke up and came back gradually to the present moment. A little oasis of peace in a troubled life.

You can reproduce the experience by having two sources of sound like one phone and one computer or CD player and play the same song on repeat mode on both devices ten or fifteen seconds apart. I have done it later with Hildegard von Bingen's *O Quam Mirabilis Est*. Find your own!

MUSIC HISTORY

Chanting, the voice of a group often resonates like the one of early Christians, hiding in caves, like the psalmody of the monks in Ajanta or Ellora caves. It reverberates. If we begin without a dronic reference like a śruti box or a tambura, the sound cluster of the group gradually comes into unison by the magic of entrainment and sympathetic resonance. From atonal to modal in a few minutes, it re-creates music history backwards!

Chanting OM in a group starting with no reference, no drone, no śruti, and no tambura will re-create music history in a few minutes from unpredictable Penderecki-like clusters of sounds to unison Gregorian chant, and anything in between, sometimes consonant, sometimes dissonant but over time tending towards harmonic convergence, sympathetic resonance and law of entrainment, ending all in unison! From vertical to horizontal organization. Listen to early medieval songs like organa.

THE BELL AND THE CELL

This happened on Long Island, near New York City, in the early '90s, during the opening ritual of a weekend seminar, sponsored by an association of Yoga teachers. I was inviting the Tibetan bell to ring at the end of the closing meditation. We were all sitting in a circle, deeply listening, dwelling in the present moment and right during the last bell resonance with beautiful overtones, the phone of the young teacher sitting next to me in the circle rang with a loud synthesized *Für Elise, Tatatatata tatata ta, tatatatata, tatata ta*, you can sing it with a nasal, high-pitch techno sound and an accelerated tempo to get the idea. Well, she felt mortified, was in shock, all stressed out, apologized afterwards again and again on the way out, almost crying. But believe it or not, I had some kind of ecstasis-enstasis moment like opening the door of Narnia, a surprisingly blissful instant. I did not get disturbed, nor destabilized. I forgave her instead of giving her a lesson, the sharp Pitta way, about turning phones off before class. Forgiveness is the way.

I experienced it more like I was in a dream, a satori-like moment. A small sattvic shower. It reminded me later of a piece I composed way back for a string quartet, voices, symphonic gong and a live radio. During the swelling waves of the gong playing, bubbles of sounds and clouds of voices were coming from the live radio or from other composed fragments. They could not be heard very clearly as they were covered or absorbed by the sonic tsunami of the gong. The listeners had doubts, not sure if other sounds occurred or not while the gong was fading. They were hearing sounds in the Sound. Did the gong itself have a musical dream?

TAJ-MONTRE-HAL

In Montreal for the harbor festival, they programmed a "boat horns" outdoor concert. Somebody composed a musical happening for all the boats and they played their horns following the written plan. Some chords, simple harmonies and some solo parts, from a distance, sounded like pipe organ, brass and marine trumpets. Usually, those horns are used in the fog. Here it turned into a concert!

I was teaching at the same time a Nāda Yoga afternoon session in Old Montreal, just a few hundred feet from the harbor. Students were in Śavāsana. So, I just had this idea to play Paul Horn's recording *Inside the Taj Mahal*. Paul was granted permission by Rajiv Gandhi to play alone in the Taj Mahal. His saxophones sounded like the boats, with more echoes, silences, reverberation. The space within the Taj Mahal holds a tone for twenty-eight seconds with near infinite echoes. It created a tapestry of sound and was a perfect match. Students were happily confused between what was coming live from the harbor and what was coming from the speakers in the Yoga studio. Made my day. Blissful.

HERE COMES THE SUN

The correspondence is mind-blowing between the *Canticle of the Sun* (Saint Francis of Assisi, 1224) and Gāyatrī Mantra (*Ṛgveda* between 1400 et 1000 BCE). Listen to Donovan, who wrote a folk song based on it for the movie *Brother Sun, Sister Moon*. The mantra Gāyatrī comes from the *Ṛgveda* (III, 62, 10). The most sacred mantra in Vedic literature is an invocation to the Sun. It can be sung in the river, at sunrise or sunset.

Notice the resemblance of the texts, both dedicated to Sun Power as Source of Life. This is deep ecology way ahead of its time!

BROTHER SUN, SISTER MOON (Donovan)

Brother Sun and Sister Moon
I seldom see you seldom hear your tune
Preoccupied with selfish misery
Brother Wind and Sister Air
Open my eyes to visions pure and fair
That I may see the glory around me
I am God's creature, of Him I am part
I feel His love awakening my heart

CANTICLE OF THE SUN (translated by Marty Haugen)

The heavens are telling the Glory of God

And all creation is shouting for joy
Come, dance in the forest. Come, play in the field,
And sing, sing the Glory of the Lord
Praise for the Sun, the bringer of day,
He carries the light of the Lord in his rays,
The moon and the stars,
Who Light up the way unto your throne.

GĀYATRĪ MANTRA (translated by Douglas Brooks)

The eternal, earth, air, heaven
That glory, that resplendence of the sun
May we contemplate the brilliance of that light
May the sun inspire our minds.

Oṃ bhūr bhuvaḥ svaḥ
Tat savitur vareṇyaṃ
Bhargo devasya dhīmahi
Dhiyo yo naḥ pracodayāt

THE CREATION

Dedicated to those driving with me that morning.

PART ONE:
May 2016: In a newsletter to my students, I suggested listening to *The Creation* by Haydn. Beautiful harmonic shifts, a sudden change of chords will project you, in a nanosecond, somewhere else, in time and space.

In the opening of his Oratorio, Haydn is evoking the sunrise with dramatic loud chords and the birth of the whole Creation. Licht, Licht, Licht . . . Light, Light, Light . . . sings the choir . . .

PART TWO:
June 5th, 5:00 A.M. South of France. In the parking lot of the Hameau de L'Etoile. Last day of the graduation weekend of the Brussels teacher training. We have a six-car procession in the dark to be able to reach the summit of the Pic Saint Loup by 7:00 A.M. after a twenty-minute drive and a ninety-minute hike, to catch the sunrise at the top and practice our Prāṇāyāma "routine." That is the plan.

Well, in my small rental car, I turned the radio on to France Musique, classical music radio station, and guess what? Right when we started driving, *The Creation* of Haydn began on the car stereo, the whole Oratorio, as the light gradually appeared in the Sky. Haydn refers to the Beginning of the Creation of the World. We were just having the soundtrack of a real Sunrise movie. At the top of the mountain, we were above a Sea of clouds. Sun rising on one side, moon still present on the other side of the Open Sky, Ha and Ṭha. I rang a bell, the Prāṇāyāma practice began for the group in silence. Everyone practiced at their own pace a simple Prāṇāyāma Vinyāsa: Bhastrikā, Ujjāyi, Bhramarī, Om, Silence. Another bell closed the ritual.

PART THREE:
Down the mountain, after a one-hour hike downhill, we had breakfast at the local "Café des Touristes" with a giant fougasse d'Aigues Mortes, orange-flower-water-and-almond-syrup-flavored local brioche that I special ordered for the group a few days before. Great beginning of the graduation ceremony of another Open Sky Yoga Teacher Training (retraining, untraining . . .).

THE FIFTH

The pituitary gland and the sellar diaphragm can be symbolized by the archetypal image of Aladdin flying on his magic carpet.
—JOHN BEAULIEU

It can be helpful when chanting to practice with a base frequency or a drone with a śruti box, a tambura or even an application on your phone. I often use a śruti box. A drone with the octave and the fifth gives you a ground from which to practice over-toning.

In the harmonic series we find the octave, the fifth above, the second octave and the third above it. Together this constitutes the basis of all modal music. The interval of fifth (C & G for example) was seen as a manifestation of God in the middle ages and the interval of the tritone (C & F#) as the devil, diabolus in musica. So, when you travel from a tritone or a micro interval above or below the fifth to the perfect fifth itself, the dissonance is resolved. It turns a dramatic tension into divine pure harmony. Well, later on, Carlo Gesualdo, J.S. Bach, John Coltrane and Jimi Hendrix, to name a few, used the tritone quite a bit in their compositions. Don't get me wrong—I love the Fifth. I am a devotee of the Fifth and the music of Ars Nova, but I also welcome white noise, Webern and all other intervals!

Tempered tonal music, which we all currently enjoy, came later in music history. The octave was divided artificially into twelve notes. Though I worship at the altar of Bach, Vivaldi and Mozart, there's a potency to the harmonic series that gets lost in tempered music. We can experience it within Indian Classical Rāga, in which melody based on a natural harmonic scale manifests out of and returns to a drone.

Why does all of this interest us as practitioners of Yoga? When we chant or hear overtones they cause certain parts of us to vibrate. They recognize themselves in us by sympathetic resonance. Harmonics are at the border between Āhata and Anāhata Nāda. They are not directly sung. It sounds like a strong wind is blowing in a windpipe. Our voice is a single pipe organ. As we move away from the fundamental pitch, the sound multiplies itself into partials, which resonate in us, releasing endorphins, opioids substances from the pituitary gland. I like to think that Music, especially high frequency overtones and the interval of the Fifth make the lesser wings of the sphenoid bone vibrate. Between those wings, the pituitary gland sits on the sella turcica. On that small trampoline, you can imagine a mini string quartet playing, taking the pituitary for a ride, having fun, dancing and singing along, sending a pleasant message to its pineal friend, keeping us in an uplifted mood. *Good, good, good, good vibrations* . . . as the song says.

7TH

The Allegretto of Beethoven's 7th could be the soundtrack of 2020, year of drama and hope worldwide. I got the piano transcription by Liszt and played the opening measures every day of the confinement as best I could. Jean-Claude Pennetier on YouTube has a fabulous version of it. There is something infinite and eternal in that obsessive mantra japa, that abyssal bass line. 7th Symphony and 7th cakra correspondence? Played with too slow of a tempo changes it into a funeral march, too fast makes it lose its meaning and emotional impact. At the right tempo, tears of hope and ecstasy may come. I was teaching in Montréal a few years ago and during a long Śavāsana, as it was the fifth anniversary of my father's passing, I played that piece of music he loved. I was lying down with the students, which is atypical for me, guiding as I was traveling inside. Images and visions, described in the following poem, came to me during that session.

ALLEGRETTO *(for my father)*

Pom Pom pom pom Pom Pom Pom pom pom . . .
(Sing softly the theme of the *Allegretto*)
On the memory Highway
Driving towards the Thousand Islands
In the sky, wild geese and heavenly swans
Haṃsas over the valley of the Gods
Fly towards another shore
As secret and subtle signs
Above the Himalayas
Beyond the Maya of the coming days
In a luxurious jungle
With crazy trees and plants
Appears a river so blue
That it floods and illuminates me
Haṃsa . . . So'ham . . . river flowing from the Source
Exhale, inhale
And suddenly a big lightning
Takes my breath away
A tsunami of light
Projects me in the world of Darkness
Among Luxor and Thebes mummies
Recumbent statues of baptisteres and cathedrals
I am now a living dead
Levitating in space
Wrapped into an imaginary wingsuit
Suspended in time like a bat
A giant sphenoid

At the confluence of the Ganges and the Styx
It is there that I met my father
Forever asleep
Taking, as he said just before passing, his longest holiday
I had forgotten the date of the departure for his last vacation
But the Allegretto of this seventh symphony
With its obsessive mantra
Its inexorable march
Revealed it to me again.
Pom Pom pom pom Pom Pom Pom pom pom . . .
(Hum or murmur the theme again.)

ALLEGRETTO *(pour mon père)*

Pom Pom pom pom Pom Pom Pom pom pom . . .
(Chanter doucement le thème de l'Allegretto)
Sur l'Autoroute du Souvenir
En route vers les mille îles . . .
Dans les cieux, les oies sauvages et les cygnes célestes
Signes secrets et subtils
Haṃsas survolant la Vallée des Dieux
Volent vers un autre rivage
Vers un autre avenir
Au dessus de l'Himalaya
Au dela de la Maya des jours à venir
Dans une jungle luxuriante
D'arbres fous et de plantes
Apparait une rivière d'un bleu si clair
Qu' elle vous inonde et vous éclaire
Haṃsa . . . So'ham . . . Une rivière qui coule de Source
Expire, Inspire
Et puis soudain un grand éclair

À couper le Souffle
Un tsunami de lumière
Qui me propulse dans le monde des ténèbres
Parmi les Momies de Luxor et de Thèbes
Les gisants des baptistères et des cathédrales
Me voilà mort-vivant
Lévitant sur l'air
Volant dans un wingsuit imaginaire
Suspendu dans le temps
Comme une chauve souris
Un sphénoïde géant
Au confluent du Styx et du Gange
Et c'est là que je rencontre mon Père
Endormi a jamais
Prenant, comme il le disait lui même, de grandes Vacances
J'avais oublié la date de son départ
Mais l'Allegretto de cette septième symphonie
Avec son mantra obsédant
Sa marche inexorable
Me l'a révélée en ce jour
Pom Pom pom pom Pom Pom Pom pom pom . . .
(Murmurer le thème comme au début du poème)

POPE GREGORY I, 540-604

The normalization of modes for Gregorian chant by Pope Gregory destroyed the preexisting beautiful ornaments of Eastern Orthodox Church, too sensual I guess for his taste. It got disconnected from archaic liturgies of Babylonian and Yemenite Hebrews, and the rich Jewish psalmody tradition. At the same period, Christian monasteries stopped being co-ed with the dark consequences we are all witnessing now centuries later. Those Gregorian rules paved the way for the birth of the tempered scale, for the best and the worst of it. We moved from horizontal modal music to vertical tonal harmonies, adding layers and voices. It evolved from Ars Nova to Johann Sebastian Bach to the atonal composition of Anton Webern, to blues, jazz and the Beatles. Then it exploded with free jazz,

Xenakis, and Stockhausen. Oh well, as long as there is Presence, direct perception and that we are touched by the Sound, it's all good! But Mozart, on his deathbed, regretted not to have composed a Gregorian chant.

OM FOR ALL, ALL FOR OM

These are various ways to play OM.

OM alone! Listen to your self chanting.
Listen to yourself AND the group chanting.

Baird Hersey, a virtuoso overtone singer, leader of the group The Year of the Ear, and more recently composing for a collective of nine singers, Prana—and a yogi himself— once said that it is perfect when you chant not so loud that you can hear the group but not so soft that you could not hear yourself, tuning the channels on a human mixing sound board.

Listen with the shield of your hands in front of your mouth or cupping one hand behind your ear, highlighting harmonics.

MOM: Chant Om backward almost like Bhramarī. MOM is a palindrOM!

Call and answer: Leader chants one Om, a cappella or with drone, group responds.

All together now: Everybody chants at the same time the first Om without a reference.

Om for all, all for Om: All participants chant following the rhythm of their own breath, superimposing voices over the drone, tiling with different pitches up and down, hoping for the best. So, there are no silences and it creates layers, superposed sounds like tiles on a roof.

Bhramarī is unmanifested OM.
Ujjāyi is unmanifested Bhramarī.
Natural breath is unmanifested Ujjāyi.
Natural breath is silent Om.

Practice the following Vinyāsa with Ṣanmukhī Mudrā or earplugs.
Silence.
Ujjāyi with glottic sound. A few slow cycles.
Bhramarī Prāṇāyāma. Bumblebee sound. A few slow cycles.
MOM. Om backwards. Few cycles.
Back to silence.

Three major shifts can happen after chanting Om.

The Soundscape is vivid. The doors of perception have been opened. From very near to far away. Inside the body as well. Listening is deep, in a state of absorption like becoming a sponge. We can hear the Silence and sounds very far away or deep inside us.

The pranic shower. An inner shower . . . tingling sensations in the scalp, the arms, the skin of the face . . . Signs that Prāṇa has been moved and we have been touched by the sound.

The phosphenic activity in Ājñā Cakra. Very consistent star-like patterns appear, solar eclipses, bindu of light, pulsing over a night sky background, a virtual screen. Simple geometric design, primitive yantra. This may be one Source of all maṇḍalas. The blueprint of the floor map for future temples, stupas and cathedrals.

WORSHIPING THE VOWEL

Ahh, Awe and Aha!
—JAYME STONE

I'm in love with vowels. All of them. Wow!
Vowels are defined by their harmonic layout. They are the melody. Consonants are just percussions, diving boards for the vowels to have a good time.

There is a secret harmonic scale of the vowels, even poetry based on it . . .
In American English the vowels are listed by the frequency of the second formant, the higher of the two overtones.

Upward, going up the scale of harmonics:
O love, be fed with apples while you may . . . (Robert Graves)

or downward—
When lilacs last in the dooryard bloom'd . . . (Walt Whitman)

Stimmung by Karlheinz Stockhausen is written for six singers over-toning, whispering and chanting colored vowels, God and Goddess names from all religions. There is something special, magical about it. I used to listen to *Stimmung* with my old piano teacher with a good level of intensity in the dark. The original version of 1969 and the new one of 2018 by Paul Hillier and the Theatre of Voices ensemble are both stunning. It was composed before overtones and Tibetan monks diphony went in fashion. To follow *Stimmung's* path, chant only the vowels of your name or the verse of a poem on the same fundamental frequency. Take all the consonants away. Your name vowels, a powerful mantra, will shine in a rainbow of harmonics.

Baird Hersey has recorded *Waking the Cobra, The Eternal Embrace* and *Gathering the Light* (with Krishna Das). I guarantee you will dive in oceans of vowels and fly the skies of stratospheric harmonics.

OM is actually AUṂ. This is also why the sound AU in French is pronounced O and OU is OO. All Indo-European languages and Sanskrit have a common ancestor as Proto-Indo European. Pārśva Uttānāsana becomes PārśvOttanāsana. When we chant OM we are sweeping though several vowels one by one and all the interstitial vowels that have no name. Between them, windows open for overtones to appear spontaneously. One of my friends used to say that A is an outward projection of the voice to the horizon, O individualizes, gives a container, OU is digestion and M, humming is for appreciation. Overtones often appear between the OU and the M of OM.

Several mystical texts, *Nāda Bindu Upaniṣad* and *Brahmavidyā Upaniṣad*, break down the mantra into smaller units. They describe in great detail the components of the OM, A, OU and M in symbolic and esoteric ways.

Practice chanting long drones of vowels on different frequencies, with a śruti box, a tambura or a small synthesizer. You will be amazed and may not recognize your voice if you record it. Has no age and no gender. It is your natural primal voice. All voices are beautiful as Maya Angelou reminds us:

I thought of myself as a giant ear which could just absorb all sound, and I would go into a room and just eat up the sound. I memorized so many poets. I just had sheets of poetry; still do. I would listen to the accents, and I still love the way human beings sound. There is no human voice which is unbeautiful to me.

MAGICAL CONCHES

If you open the door to Open Sky in Rochester, New York, you may see some conches on the windowsills or in a center of a sand mountain. In fact, the maṇḍala downstairs is the spiral of spirals! A trail of shells and conches leading to a stupa of clay, a replica of Boudhanath Stupa in Kathmandu, a place I stayed when traveling to Nepal way back. You may also notice in the Yoga room a little statue of Patañjali that holds a conch in one of his four hands.

The conch is one of the most beautiful seashells and a musical instrument. If you listen to it, covering your ear, you will hear the sound of the breath like Ujjāyi and the soft drone of the ocean as an echo in the distance. If you blow into it as a marine trumpet, the sound of OM is evoked. A deep, dense, organic tone, more like a trombone or a tuba. The conch is used in Tibetan music and in Indian rituals, sometimes with circular breathing as a continuous sound.

The body is an instrument, an emitter-receiver. The conch is the symbol of the origin of existence. It has the shape of a spiral, a vortex. Look at them closely, take them in your hands. Larger and larger rings originate from a center. Coming from water, it is associated with the primordial ocean. In Indian mythology, it is an attribute of Viṣṇu and, therefore, of Patañjali as his incarnation. I recently asked Dr. Douglas Brooks, professor of religious studies, about the symbolism of Devadatta, the conch blown by Arjuna in the *Bhagavad Gītā*:

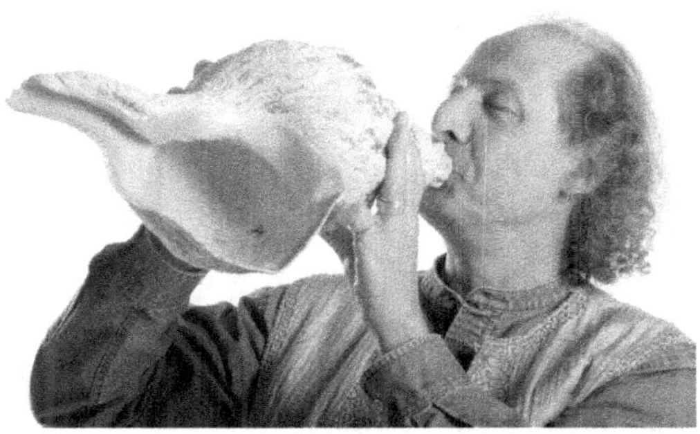

> "The shankha's (conch's) meaning is always connected to the relationship between individual and universal identity. The conches have proper names, not just symbolic ones. That is important too because, whatever the name means, the conch is an entity, a discrete presence that holds its own consciousness. In a certain way, the individuality of the conch and the hero it possesses reveals that the universal, the ultimate is taking on particular forms endlessly: each conch possesses its own sound, and simultaneously all conches participate in the same sound, the eternal, the AUM.
>
> So, the point is that the individual is a form of the universal and yet the universal chooses to express itself individually, all the way down to the level of achieving a personal identity in the form of the conch. Certainly, the conch is the manifest form of the AUM. The conch's own song, its own voice, its AUM never ceases and blowing the conch simply amplifies what is 'already present' in it. One AUM, many forms, all real, all distinctive, but all the same and different."

The spiral reflects our life journey, in the way we are always evolving but still connected to the core, the center of the labyrinth. The labyrinths of the floors of the cathedrals, Chartres near Paris being the most known, are nothing but life journeys towards awakening, projected in the marble or the stone. In India I often saw Sādhus playing the conch, absorbed in a deep listening of that resonance. Originally the conch was an instrument to call for war. In the *Mahābhārata*, an Indian epic, Arjuna's mighty conch scares the hell out of the enemy. Later, it became an instrument to create peace, or to call the Gods, in New Caledonia, for example. In Vajrāyana Buddhism, the conch is the symbol of the truth of the dharma. It appears as a tattoo, an auspicious mark on the soles, palms and forehead of a divinely endowed being.

On the roofs of the Tibetan monasteries, early morning, two monks tile the sounds and create a drone.

It resonates like a giant halo of sound through the mountains, waking up all creatures and the monks for their early morning rituals. I had a chance to be awakened at sunrise by these pure sounds when traveling in the Kingdom of Zanskar in the early '80s. It is actually surprising to find an oceanic instrument in Tibet, but the Tibetan plateau was once an ocean floor.

In Indian or Mediterranean mythological tales, Viṣṇu and Triton are playing conches. Is it not fascinating that shepherds from Corsica, Celtic farmers from Brittany and Creta used them until the end of the nineteenth century?

We have in our practice the sound of the breath and mantras, especially during Bhramarī Prāṇāyāma. The humming resonates in the whole body as a string instrument played by the bow of the breath. Ṣanmukhī Mudrā creates a deeper, introverted state, moving inward into the shell of the skull, releasing the sensory organs into Pratyāhāra. Conches are a reflection of such a beautiful practice. We still don't really know, in the protohistory of music, if human voices imitated instruments or if instruments were imitating human voices.

This is why I have loved to gather shells since childhood. The ocean, early on, invited me to explore the Yoga of Sound, and through Nāda, I was allowed to enter the kingdom of Breath.

Postlude: SILENCES

A painter paints pictures on canvas.
But musicians paint their pictures on silence.
—LEOPOLD STOKOWSKI

Listen to silence or what you think is silence. Is it the absence of sound or when whatever was making a sound before stops? Listen to both silence and sound simultaneously. Silence and sound are not mutually exclusive. What is silence? It is a construct of the mind. So if you are looking for absolute silence, you will always be disappointed or annoyed. Life has vibration. We want to sleep in relative silence. How can we make abstraction of existing sounds? Is that a form of Yoga? Or is it the silence behind the sound?

At times, silence is needed to receive, like a blank tape can record new music. Becoming a microphone membrane to record objectively, a sponge to absorb or a satellite dish to receive waves. Is there a Vinyāsa of consciousness, a Vinyāsa of Silence, a Śavāsana Vinyāsa, deeper and deeper stages, from superficial to deeper silence? *Silere* is a verb in Latin, *to silence*. When it is silent in practice, is it the silence of beatitude or the silence of repression? True silence is deeper after screaming, laughing or crying in such a manner that you become who you are. Remember John Lennon's song *Mother.*

A common concept in classical Yoga is to stop the thinking mind to reach a state of silence. Nirodha, found in the second Sūtra of Patañjali, could mean "to stop something from growing," not necessarily cessation or annihilation. It may be the continuous release of all experiences. Śaṇkarācārya calls this "tyāga" or to let be. So, thoughts are released not cancelled by force into silence. If we repress anything it will pop up later in other ways, thanks to Sigmund!

John Beaulieu, sound healer, and John Cage, composer, both had experiences in an anechoic chamber where there is no echo, so it is absolute silence. Beaulieu used it to explore intervals. Some people visiting the chamber lost their mind after twenty minutes and went mad. Absolute silence can be a form of torture. John Cage meditated on inner sounds which he describes in his book *Silence:*

It was after I got to Boston
that I went into the
anechoic chamber at Harvard
University.
Anybody who knows me knows
this story.
I am constantly telling it.
Anyway,
in that silent room,
I heard two sounds,
one high and
one low.
Afterward I asked the engineer in
charge why, if the room
was so silent, I
had heard two sounds,
He said,
"Describe them." I did.
He said,
"The high one
was your nervous system
in operation.
The low one was
your blood in circulation."

John Cage composed a conceptual piece titled *4.33* which is made of three movements of complete silence. Funny story: I purchased the MP3 online for ninety-nine cents per movement. So, I bought literally nothing. A blank book is still a book, but a piece of silent music is nonexistent. I played it afterwards. And of course, the rest of the world's inner and outer sounds are highlighted in a special way. Sounds crazy, yes. Absurd yet powerful experience.

This is how René Daumal, a surrealist poet and Sanskritist describes sound-silence relationship in the play of a sitarist: "The agility of his fingers modulates, with precise palpitations, the spectrum of resonances; he lets the sound die, sculpting it again until its death, until Silence. And, it is believed that he continues to sculpt the silence. At that moment music becomes almost visible around the musician; his fingers appear to play with luminous and silent veins."

Silence is the Source of all sounds.

PRELUDE TO THE BIBLIYOGRAPHY

I have read, digested, assimilated, re-read, re-re-read and sometimes forgotten most of the books listed below. I go back to them, over and over again—some since the early '70s. They create a fertile soil for explorations, metaphors, visions and revelations. It does not matter if you already know or if you think you know everything, if you don't know anything, if you don't know how much you know or if you know how much you don't know. You will have to welcome the feeling of being lost in a deep fog and suddenly have an epiphany or see the Light. We need to keep learning and be curious.

I've learned over the years: where cool things are located; to answer a student's question; to be inspired for a future workshop or to double-check information, such as a name, a date, a story, a quote. I have the secret access code to find the page or the paragraph. Sometimes I read four or five books simultaneously or open a classic text randomly and always discover something new. I used five or six copies of *Light on Yoga* and other seminal books until they fell apart. I read between the lines or look at the photos upside down to see better the vertical cosmic axis in Tāḍāsana, as Ūrdhva Śīrṣāsana.

Yoga is a multi-faceted diamond. All life experiences—immersions in nature, art, music, travel, meeting with remarkable beings—will make you a true seeker, an inner trekker towards Mount Meru or a real traveler towards Mount Kailash.

Then we have to rewrite some of the books from our own experience. Everyone is trying to sell their interpretation of the Urtext, manipulating the timelines to serve their beliefs. You need to be a linguist, a scientist, archaeologist, ethnologist, musicologist, pranalogist and asanalogist to dig deeper and find more questions about the questions. You may be disillusioned, disappointed or angry that you have been manipulated but you will be closer to the Truth, the Roots, the Essence of the Essence, Ur, the Origin.

Reading the books inspires your practice and practice leads back to the books. Repeat the cycle. Life and Yoga will become a luminous Weave.

BIBLIYOGRAPHY

ĀSANA

Broad, William J., *The Science of Yoga: The Risks and the Rewards*, Simon & Schuster, 2012.

Clennel, Bobby, *The Women's Yoga Book*, Shambhala, 2007.

Farhi, Donna, *Yoga Mind, Body & Spirit*, Holt Paperbacks, 2000.

Holleman, Dona, *Yoga Darśana of B.K.S. Iyengar, Vol I, Vol II,* Self-published, Italy, 1987.

Iyengar, B.K.S., *Light on Yoga*, HarperCollins Publishers, 1964.

Iyengar, Geeta S., *Yoga, A Gem for Women*, Allied Publishers Pvt. Ltd., 1983.

Kaivalya, Alanna & Van Der Kooij, Arjuna, *Myths of the Āsanas*, Mandala Publishing Group, 2010.

Mehta, Mira, Silva & Shyam, *Yoga the Iyengar Way*, Alfred A. Knopf, 1990.

Newell, Zo, *Downward Dogs and Warriors*, Himalayan Institute Press, 2007.

Perez-Christiaens, Noëlle, *Être d'Aplomb*, Institut Supérieur d'Aplomb, 1983.

Raman, Krishna, *Matter of Health*, East West Books, 1998.

Schatz, Mary, *Back Care Basics*, Shambhala, 1992.

Sjoman, Norman E., *The Tradition of the Mysore Palace*, Abhinav Publications, 1996.

Van Kooten, Victor, *From Inside Out: A Yoga Book Note I, II, III*, Ganesha Press, 1998, 2000, 2003.

PRĀṆĀYĀMA

Antoni, Charles, *Yoga De La Puissance*, L'Originel, 1984.

Cosseron, Corinne & Leclerc, Linda, *Le Yoga du Rire*, Trédaniel, 2014.

Cuvilliez, Joëlle & Medjber, Martine, *Rire pour les Nuls*, First, 2013.

Farhi, Donna, *The Breathing Book*, Holt Paperbacks, 1996.

Iyengar B.K.S., *Light on Prāṇāyāma*, HarperCollins Publishers India, 2013.

Kataria, Madan, *Laughing for No Reason*, Madhuri International, 1999.

Perez-Christiaens, Noëlle, *Le Bâillement*, Poche, 1980.

Perez-Christiaens, Noëlle, *Praṇāgnihotra : Le Sacrifice du Quotidien du Prāṇa*, Institut B.K.S. Iyengar, 1977.

Provine, Robert R., *Curious Behavior*, Belknap Press, 2014.

Rosen, Richard, *The Yoga of Breath*, Shambhala, 2002.

Rosen, Richard, *Prāṇāyāma: Beyond the Fundamentals*, Shambhala, 2006.

Van Lysebeth, André, *Prāṇāyāma*, English Language Edition by Harmony Publishing 2012, French Edition Published in 1971 and 2017 by Flammarion as *Prāṇāyāma, la Dynamique du Souffle.*

ŚAVĀSANA

Axt, Peter & Axt-Gadermann, Michaela, *The Joy of Laziness*, Bloomsbury, 2005.

Benson, Herbert & Klipper, Miriam Z., *The Relaxation Response*, William Morrow, 2000.

Lasater, Judith Hanson, *Relax and Renew*, Rodmell Press, 1995.

Perez-Christiaens, Noëlle, *Śavāsana, Harmonie des Profondeurs*, Institut B.K.S. Iyengar, 1978.

Piquemal, Michel, *Paroles de Paresse*, Albin Michel,1996.

Walker, Matthew, *Why We Sleep*, Scribner, 2017.

NĀDA (SOUND/MUSIC)

Anderson, Laurie, *Nothing In My Pocket : A Diary*, DIS Edition, 2003.

Beaulieu, John, *Human Tuning*, BioSonic Enterprises, 2010.

Berendt, Joachim Ernst, *The World is Sound: Nāda Brahma*, Destiny Books, 1991.
Cage, John, *Birds*, Marion Boyars Publishers Ltd, 2000.
Cage, John, *Silence*, Ed. 1939 by John Cage, 50th Anniversary by Wesleyan.
Cousto, Hans, *The Cosmic Octave*, LifeRhythm, 1988.
Daumal, René, *Bhārata*, Gallimard, 1970.
Daumal, René, *Les Pouvoirs de la Parole*, Gallimard, 1972.
Gauquelin, Michel, *Rythmes Biologiques, Rythmes Cosmiques*, Poche, 1973.
Glass, Philip, *Words Without Music*, Liveright, 2016.
Goldman, Jonathan, *Healing Sounds, the Power of Harmonics*, Healing Arts Press, 2002.
Hersey, Baird, *The Practice of Nāda Yoga*, Inner Traditions, 2013.
Jenny, Hans, *Cymatics*, MACROmedia, 2001, 1st Edition Basillus Presse, 1967.
Kornblum, Nestor, *Overtone Chant—The Practical Book*, Copyright @ Kornblum Nestor, 2003.
Kriyananda, Goswami, *The Kriya Yoga Upaniṣad and The Mystical Upaniṣads*, Published in 1993 by The Temple of Kriya Yoga, Chicago.
Mann, Thomas, *Doctor Faustus*, Vintage Books, 1999.
Massin, Jean & Brigitte, *Wolfgang Amadeus Mozart*, Fayard, 1970.
Menuhin, Yehudi, *Unfinished Journey*, Brown Book Group Limited, 1978.
Michaël, Edward Salim, *The Law of Attention*, Inner Traditions, 1983.
Miller, Terry E. & Shahriari, Andrew, *World Music A Global Journey*, Routledge, 2009.
Oliveros, Pauline, *Deep Listening*, iUniverse, 2005.
Ono, Yoko, *Grapefruit*, Simon & Schuster Ltd, 2000.
Padoux, André, *L'Energie de la Parole*, Le Soleil Noir, 1980.
Padoux, André, *Vac : The Concept of The Word in Selected Hindu Tantras*, Translated by Jacques Gontier, State University of New York Press, 1990.
Schaeffner, André, *Origine des Instruments de Musique*, Mouton Editeur et Maison des Sciences de l'Homme, 1968.
Schafer, Murray, *The Soundscape and the Tuning of the World*, Destiny Books, 1993.
Shankar Ravi, *My Music, My Life*, Mandala Publishing Group, 2008.
Van Tongeren, Mark C., *Overtone Singing*, Fusica, 2002.

ANATOMY

Bainbridge Cohen, Bonnie, *Sensing, Feeling and Action*, Wesleyan University Press, 1993.
Calais-Germain, Blandine, *Anatomy of Breathing*, English Language Edition in 2006 by Eastland Press, Inc, *Respiration: Anatomie* – Geste Respiratoire, French Edition Published in 2005 by Désiris.
Calais-Germain, Blandine, *Anatomy of Movement*, English Language Edition in 1993, 2007 by Eastland Press, Inc – French Edition Published in 1985 by Désiris revised 1991 and 1999 as *Anatomie pour le Movement*.
Calais-Germain, Blandine, *The Female Pelvis*, English Language Edition by Eastland Press, Inc – French Edition Published in 1999 by Désiris as *Le Périnée Féminin et l'Accouchement*.
Colangelo, Joy, *Embodied Wisdom*, iUniverse, 2003.
Conrad, Emily, *Life on Land*, North Atlantic Books, 2007.
Franklin, Eric, *Dynamic Alignment Through Imagery*, Human Kinetics, 2012.
Franklin, Eric, *Pelvic Power for Men and Women*, Elysian, 2003.
Hartley, Linda, *Wisdom of the Body Moving*, North Atlantic Books, 1995.
Johnson, Will, *The Posture of Meditation*, Shambhala, 1996.
Johari, Harish, *Chakras*, Destiny Books, 1988.

Kapit, Wynn & Elson, Lawrence M., *Anatomy Coloring Book*, Pearson, 2013.
Keleman, Stanley, *Emotional Anatomy*, Center Press, 1985.
Lasater, Judith Hanson, *Yogabody: Kinesiology and Āsana*, Rodmell Press, 2009.
McHose, Caryn, *How Life Moves*, North Atlantic Books, 2006.
Myers, Thomas, *Anatomy Trains*, Churchill Livingstone, 1st Edition 2001, Elsevier, 2021.
Myers, Thomas, *Body^3: A Therapist's Anatomy Reader*, Anatomy Trains, 2014.
Obert, Kerrie & Chicurel, Steven, *Geography of the Voice*, Vocal Innovations, 2005.
Olsen, Andrea, *Body and Earth*, University Press of New England, 2002.
Olsen, Andrea, *Body Stories, A Guide to Experiential Anatomy*, Station Hill Press, 1991Wesleyan University Press, 2020.
Robin, Mel, *Physiological Handbook for Yoga Teachers*, Fenestra Books, 2002.
Rolf, Ida P., *Rolfing, The Integration of Human Structures*, Harper & Row, 1978.
Shubin, Neil, *Your Inner Fish,* First Vintage Books, 2009.

AYURVEDA

Frawley, David, *Yoga & Ayurveda*, Lotus Press, 1999.
Lad, Vasant, *Ayurveda, The Science of Self-Healing*, Lotus Press, 2004.
Lad, Vasant, *Ayurvedic Perspectives on Selected Pathologies*, The Ayurvedic Press, 2005.
Lad, Vasant & Durve, Anisha, *Marma Points of Ayurveda*, The Ayurvedic Press, 2008.
Svoboda, Robert, *Prakriti*, Lotus Press 1988 - Sadhana Publications, 1998.
Svoboda, Robert, *Life, Health and Longevity*, the Ayurvedic Press 2004, 1st Edition Penguin Arkana, 1992.
Svoboda, Robert & Lade, Arnie, *Tao and Dharma. Chinese Medicine and Ayurveda*, Lotus Press, 1995.

PHILOSOPHY

Bouanchaud, Bernard, *Essence of Yoga*, Rudra Press, 1998, *Yoga Sūtra de Patañjali*, 1st Edition Agamat, France, 1995.
Bryant, Edwin F., *Yoga Sūtra*, North Point Press, 2009.
Brooks, Douglas, *Poised from Grace*, Anusara Press, 2008.
Danielou, Alain, *Hindu Polytheism*, Princeton University Press, 1964.
David-Néel, Alexandra, *Journey to Lhassa*, Harper Perennial, 1999, 1st Edition Harper and Brothers Publishers, 1927.
Desikachar, T.K.V., *The Heart of Yoga*, Inner Traditions, 1999.
Eliade, Mircea, *Patañjali and Yoga*, Funk & Wagnalls, 1969.
Eliade, Mircea, *Images and Symbols*, Princeton University Press, 1991.
Eliade, Mircea, *Yoga: Immortality and Freedom*, Princeton University Press, 2009.
Francis of Assisi, Saint, *Canticle of the Sun*, Andesite Press, 2015.
Hamilton, Sue, *Indian Philosophy*, Oxford University Press, 2001.
Harding, Douglas, *On Having No Head*, Shollond Trust, 2000.
Hesse, Herman, *Narcissus and Goldmund*, Bantam, 1984, *Narziss und Goldmund*, 1st Edition, Fischer Verlag, Berlin, 1930.
Iyengar, B.K.S., *The Tree of Yoga*, HarperCollins Publishers Ltd, 1994.
Iyengar, B.K.S., *Light on the Yoga Sūtras*, Thorsons, 2002.
Jung, Carl G., *The Psychology of Kuṇḍalinī Yoga*, Princeton University Press, 1996. 1st Edition, Sonu Shamdasani, 1932.
Kapleau, Roshi Philip, *The Zen of Living and Dying*, Shambhala, 1998.
Kornfield, Jack & Feldman, Christina, *Stories of the Spirit, Stories of the Heart*, HarperCollins, 1991.
Kornfield, Jack, *A Path with Heart*, Bantam, 1993.
Krishnamurti, Jiddu, *Notebook*, KPublications, 2008.
Lama Govinda, Anagarika, *Foundations of Tibetan Mysticism*, Martino Fine Books, 2012.

Lanza Del Vasto, Giuseppe, *Return to the Source*, Pocket Books 1993, *Le Pélerinage aux Sources*, 1st Edition, Denoël, France, 1943.
Lasater, Judith Hanson, *Living Your Yoga*, Rodmell Press, 2000.
Lebedynsky, Iaroslav, *Les Indo-Européens*, Editions Errance, 2006.
Mallory, James Patrick, *In Search of the Indo-Europeans*, Thames & Huston, 1989.
Parpola, Asko, *The Roots of Hinduism*, Oxford University Press, 2015.
Perez-Christiaens, Noëlle, *Etincelles de Divinité/Sparks of Divinity*, Institut B.K.S. Iyengar, 1976.
Safransky, Sy, *Sunbeams: A Book of Quotations*, North Atlantic Books, 2012.
Sanford, Matthew, *Waking*, Rodale Books, 2006.
Sargent, Winthrop, *The Bhagavad Gītā*, Excelsior Editions, 2009.
Satyananda Saraswati, Swami, *Yoga Kuṇḍalinī Tantra*, Yoga Publications, 2002.
Shearer, Alistair, *Effortless Being*, Unwin Paperbacks, 1989.
Shearer, Alistair, *Upaniṣads*, Harper, Colophon Books, 1978.
Sivananda Radha, Swami, *Kuṇḍalinī*, Timeless Books, 2010, 1st Edition Motilal Banarsidass UK, 1996.
Smith, John, *Mahābhārata*, Penguin Classics, 2009.
Svātmārāma, *Haṭhapradīkipā*, Kaivalyadhama S.M.Yoga Mandir Samiti, 1970.
Svātmārāma, Yoga Swami, *Haṭha Yoga Pradīpikā*, Aquarian/Thorson, 1992.
Thakar, Vimala, *Glimpses of Rāja Yoga*. Rodmell Press, 2004.
Thich Nhat Hanh, *Peace is Every Step*, Bantam Books, 1992.
Thich Nhat Hanh, *The Blooming of a Lotus*, Beacon Press, 2009.
Trautman, Thomas R., *The Aryan Debate*, Oxford University Press, 2005.

POETRY

Baudelaire, Charles, *"Correspondances," Les Fleurs du Mal*, Gallimard, 2005, 1st Edition, M. L. Paris, 1857.
Daumal, René, *Le Contre-Ciel*, Gallimard, 1970.
Dickinson, Emily, *"The Brain—is Wider than the Sky—" The Complete Poems*, Back Bay Books, 1976.
Kabir, *Unstruck Music: Spiritual Poetry*, Jim O'Neill, 2009.
Merton, Thomas, *"In Silence," In the Dark Before Dawn*, New Directions Books, 2005, 1st Edition 1946.
Mirabai, *Ecstatic Poems*, Beacon Press, 2004.
Mitchell, Steven, *Enlightened Heart*, Harper Perennial, 1993.
Rilke, Rainer Maria, *"Breath," Duino Elegies & The Sonnets to Orpheus*, Vintage; Bilingual Edition, 2009.
Rilke, Rainer Maria, "*Buddha in Glory," New poems*, North Point Press, 2014.
Rimbaud, Arthur, *"Voyelles," Poésies suivi de Les Illuminations*, Editions Ararauna, 2020.
Roberts, Elizabeth & Amidon, Elias, *Life Prayers from around the World*, HarperOne, 1996.
Rumi, Jalal Al-Din, *The Essential Rumi*, Coleman Barks, 2004.
Shorr, Mark, *"At the Pont du Gard," Heart's Ladder*, Bookmarkpress, 2009.
Supervielle, Jules, *Gravitations*, Gallimard, 1966.
Tagore, Rabindranath, *Last Poems*, HarperCollins India, 1960.

ART /SACRED ARCHITECTURE

Cunningham, Bailey, *Maṇḍala, Journey to the Center*, DK Adult, 2003.
Goldsworthy, Andy, *Collaboration with Nature*, Abrams, 1990.
Graumont, Raoul & Hensel, John, *Encyclopedia of Knots*, Cornell Maritime Press, 1939.
Jamme, Franck André, *Tantra Song*, Siglio, 2011.

Jumel, Chantal, *Kōlam Kalam*, Geuthner, 2010.

Kalman, Tibor & Maira, *(un)Fashion*, Abrams, 2000.

Letscher, Jean, *Le Temple Intérieur*, Editions Trigramme, 1991.

Livingston, Morna, *Steps to Water, The Ancient Stepwells* of India. Princeton Architectural Press, NY, 2002.

Mookerjee, Ajit, *Tantra Art*, Rupa & Co, 1994.

Mookerhee, Ajit, *Tantra Art: Its Philosophy and Physics*, Ravi Kumar, 1966.

Mookerjee, Ajit & Rawson, Philip, *Yoga Art*, New York Graphic Society, 1975.

Morrison, Philip & Morrison, Phylis and the Office of Charles & Ray Eames, *Powers of Ten*, Scientific American Library, 1982.

Olsen, Scott, *The Golden Section*, Walker & Company, 2006.

Purce, Jill, *Mystic Spiral*, Thames & Hudson, 1980.

Rawson, Philip, *The Art of Tantra (World of Art)*, Thames & Hudson, 1985.

Terryl, Nancy & Heald, David, *Architecture of Silence*, Harry N. Abrams, 2000.

Tucci, Giuseppe, *The Theory and Practice of the Maṇḍala*, Rider & Company, London, 1961.

PRELUDE TO THE DISCOGRAPHY

The list below will play you. It is a playlist after all. The list is subjective—it could have been less or more. It's still evolving. For a deeper experience, listen in the dark with a good level of intensity and a good sound system. Listen in a meditation state if possible, in a quiet environment. I've played most of these pieces hundreds of times, sometimes in a loop, over and over again, for hours as I was writing this very book, forgetting it was the same piece playing. Repetition is not boring, it adds layers and surprises, it can induce a trance. Listening to music can be a spiritual experience or a casual one, while cooking, cleaning or doing the dishes. Always the same and always different. Music is in our blood. Music is multifunctional. Feel free to add to this list compositions close to your heart. Make your own universal playlist.

The german romantic poet Christian Morgenstern got It:

Der Himmel die Partitur	*The Sky is the musical score*
Die Sterne lauter ganze Noten	*The Stars, all but the notes*
Der Mensch das Instrument	*The Man, the instrument*

DISCOGRAPHY

Albinoni, Tomaso. *"Adagio, Concerto #2 In D Minor, op. 9/2," Albinoni's Adagios*. Claudio Scimone & Solisti Veneti. Warner Classics International, 1988.

Accentus. *"Immortal Bach, Komm Süsser Tod," Transcriptions*. Laurence Equilbey. Naïve Records, 2017.

Allegri, Gregorio. *"Miserere," Sacred Treasures II.* Hearts of Space Records, 1999.

Anthologie de la Musique des Pygmées Aka. Harmonia Mundi, 2016.

Anthologie des Musiques Traditionnelles. Ocora. Outhere, 2018.

Anthology of Indian Classical Music. *A tribute to Alain Daniélou*. EMI, 1997.

Anthology of Vocal Expression. *Voices of the World*. Various Artists, Le Chant du Monde, 2010.

Arpegiatta (L'). *Complete Alpha Recordings*. Christina Pluhar. Alpha, 2013.

Bach, Johann Sebastian. *The Well-Tempered Clavier Books I & II*. Glenn Gould. Sony Classical, 2012.

Bach, Johann Sebastian. *"Partita in A minor for solo flute BWV 1013," Sonates pour Flûte et Clavecin*. Marc Hantaï & Pierre Hantaï. Mirare, 2018.

Bach, Johann Sebastian. *"So Ist Mein Jesus... /Sind Blitze..." St. Matthew Passion*. Nikolaus Harnoncourt. Teldec, 2001.

Bach, Johann Sebastian. *Morimur.* The Hilliard Ensemble. ECM New Series, 2006.

Bachan, Kaur. *"Agua de Estrellas," Magdalena Mariposa*. Bachan Kaur, 2015.

Back, Hans de. *"Hans de Back in Concert," Ancient Treasures: The best of singing bowls healing sound.* Samuel Weiser, 2002.

Baez, Joan. *"Farewell Angelina."* Vanguard, 2002.

Baka Forest People of Southeast (The Music of). *Heart of the Forest.* Hannibal Records, 1993.

Bauer, Andrea. *Cello Sounds for Silence.* Silenzio, 2012.

Bayrakdarian, Isabel. *"Where are you, O Mother," Joyous Light.* Alliance, 2006.

Beatles. *"Get Back," Let It Be*. From the motion picture Let It Be, 1970. Capitol, 2012.

Beatles. *"Here Comes the Sun," Abbey Road.* Apple Records, 1969.

Beethoven, Ludwig Van. *7th Symphony*. Herbert Von Karajan. Deutsche Grammophon, 1978.

Beethoven, Ludwig Van. Liszt, Franz. *Symphonie N° 7, Piano Transcription.* Jean Claude Pennetier. Harmonia Mundi, 1995.

Berneville, Gillebert de. *"De moi doleros vos chant," Troubadours, Trouvères, Minstrels*. Studio der Früher Musik, 1985. Thomas Binkley. Teldec, 2007.

Biber, Heinrich. *"Passacaille," Les Sonates du Rosaire*. Patrick Bismuth. La Tempesta. Zig-Zag Territoires, 2004.

Bley, Carla & Swallow, Steve & Sheppard, Andy. *"Útviklingssang," Trios.* ECM Records, 2013.

Cage, John. *"4'33," Silence Happening.* Mis, 2012.

Calchakis (Los). *El Condor Pasa.* Mercury, 1999.

Carpio, Luzmila. *"Lullaby To Mother Earth," The Song of the Earth and Stars*. Harmonia Mundi, 2004.

Clemencic Consort (The). *Carmina Burana.* Oehms, 2009.

Central Asia and Siberia. *Epics and Overtone Singing*. Inedit, 1983.

Chandra, Sheila. *"ABoneCroneDrone 1," ABoneCroneDrone*. Real World Studios, 1996.

Chukchi. *Russian Far North.* Playasound, 2007.

Cielo Y Tierra. *"El Día (Remix)," Heaven and Earth.* Artes de Mexico y del Mundo, 2006.

Copland, Aaron. *"Suite - 1. Very slowly," Appalachian Spring.* Los Angeles Philarmonic. Decca, 1996.

Corelli, Arcangelo. *"II. Adagio - Allegro – Adagio," Concerto Grosso in G Minor op. 6 n° 8, Christmas Concerto.* Christopher Hogwood, Academy of Ancient Music. Decca, 1983.

Couperin, François. *"Troisième Leçon," Leçons de Ténèbres*. René Jacobs. Harmonia Mundi, 1970.

Dagar Brothers. *Golden Rāga Collection III.* Times Music, 2017.

Darling, David. *"Minor Blue," Eight String Religion.* Hearts of Space Records, 1993.

Donovan. *"Everlasting Sea," Sūtras*. American Recordings Catalog P&D, 1996.

Dufallo, Cornelius. *"Suite for Electric Violin," Dream Streets*. Innova, 2010.

Einaudi, Ludovico. *"Passagio," Le Onde*. BMG Records, 1996.

Einaudi, Ludovico. *Seven Days Walking*. Decca Records, 2019.

Gabrieli, Giovanni. *Sacrae Symphonae*. His Majestys Sagbutts and Cornetts. Hyperion, 1997.

Garbarek, Jan. *"Beata Viscera," Officium*. The Hilliard Ensemble. ECM, 1994.

Gasparian, Djivan. *"A Cool Wind Is Blowing," I Will Not Be Sad In This World*. Opal Records, 1989.

Ghazal. *Lost Songs of the Silk Road*. Shanachie Records, 1997.

Glass, Philip. *"Facades," Glassworks*. CBS, 1982.

Glass, Philip. *"Koyaanisqatsi," Koyaanisqatsi*. Nonesuch Records, 1983.

Glass, Philip and Shankar, Ravi. *"Channels And Winds," Passages*. Private Music, 1990.

Glass, Philip. *"Movement II," Tirol Concerto for Piano and Orchestra*. Dennis Russell Davies. Orange Mountain Music, 2004.

Glass, Philip. *"Part 3," Satyagraha*. New York City Opera City Orchestra & Chorus, Christopher Keene. Sony, 2009.

Global Meditation. *Authentic Music from Meditative Traditions of the World*. Ellipsis Art, 1992.

Gould, Glenn. *The Idea of North*. Sony, 2012.

Gundecha, Brothers. *Tears of Lotus*. Sense World Music, 2007.

Gyurme, Lama & Rykiel, Jean-Philippe. *"Hope For Enlightenment," The Lama's Chant Songs of Awakening*. Narada, 2005.

Hadra (El). *The Mystik Dance*. Akasha Mundi, 1991.

Haydn, Joseph. *The Seven Last Words of Our Savior on the Cross*. Delmet Quartet. Hyperion Records, 1993.

Haydn, Joseph. *"Part 1: Ouverture," The Creation*. William Christie & Les Arts Florissants. Erato 2020.

Haydn, Joseph. *"Andante/Allegro," Harp Concerto in B Major*. The Stuttgart Chamber Orchestra. Brilliant Classics, 2015.

Henry, Pierre & Schaeffer, Pierre. *Symphonie pour un Homme Seul*. Philips, 2009.

Hersey, Baird. *The Eternal Embrace*. Bent Records, 2004.

Hersey, Baird. *Waking the Cobra*. Bent Records, 1999.

Hersey, Baird & Prana & Krishna Das. *Gathering in the Light*. Satsang Music Inc, 2007.

Horn, Paul. *Inside the Taj Mahal, Vol. 2*. Wounded Bird, 1972.

Ibrahim, Abdullah. *"Untitled," Echoes from Africa*. ENJA, 1979.

I Muvrini. *"Terra," Platinum Collection Disc 2*. EMI 2007.

Indigo Girls. *"Closer to Fine," Indigo Girls*. Epic, 2006.

Inlakesh. *"Dwelling Place of the Radiant Mind," The Gathering*. Inlakesh Music, 1999.

Inuit. *55 Historical Recordings*. Subrosa, 2004.

Izadi, Kamyar. *Santour*. Cinq Planètes, 1996.

Jarrett, Keith. *The Köln Concert*. ECM Records, 1975.

Jarrett, Keith. *Book of Ways*. ECM, 2006.

Jasraj, Pandit. *Ragas Triveni & Multani*. Navras Records, 2007.

Jasraj, Pandit. *"Om Namo Bhagavate Vāsudevāya," The Best Bhajan Collection: 83 Tracks for Divinity*. Music Today, 2003.

Joy. *"Om Ananda Mayi," Hymns and Songs in Sanskrit*. CD Baby, 2012.

Keyrouz, Soeur Marie. *Chants Sacrés Melchites*. Harmonia Mundi, 1994.

Khan, Ustad Imrat. *Sitar and Surbahar*. Lyrichord, 1991.

Kornblum, Nestor. *Overtone Chant - The Practical Guide*. Harmonic Sounds, 2003.

Krishna Das. *"Om Namo Bhagavate Vāsudevāya," Breath of the Heart*. Razor & Tie, 2006.

Latcho Drom. *"Sat Bhayan Ki Ek Behanadli."* Music from movie. AllMusic, 1993.

La Monte Young & Pandit Pran Nath. *The Rāga Cycle*. Śrī Moonshine Music, 2006.

Léonin, Pérotin. *Sacred Music from Notre Dame Cathedral.* Antony Pitts. Naxos, 2005.
Li, Wang. *Guimbarde: Jew's Harp.* Cinq Planètes, 2013.
Los Calchakis. *El Condor Pasa.* EPM, 2009.
Machaut (De), Guillaume. *"Kyrie," La Messe de Nostre Dame.* Ensemble Gilles Binchois. Cantus Records, 1999.
Machaut (De), Guillaume. *Motets.* The Hilliard Ensemble. 2004.
Madosini. *"Wenu Se Goli," Power To the Women.* Melt Records, 2000.
Malgoire, Jean Claude. *Musique au Temps des Croisades.* Le Florilegium Musicum de Paris, 1973.
Malicorne. *"Marions les Roses,"* Le Mariage Anglais. Griffe, 1975.
Marcello, Alessandro. *"Adagio," Concerto in D minor, Oboe, Strings and Continuo.* Geoffrey Burgess. 2006
Mayall, John. *Laurel Canyon Home*, DECCA Records, 1968.
McFerrin, Bobby. *Circlesongs.* Sony Classical, 1997.
Messiaen, Olivier. *"Louange à l'Immortalité de Jésus," Quatuor pour la Fin du Temps (Quartet for the End of Time).* Daniel Barenboim. Deutsche Grammophon, 2006.
Minassian, Levon. *"Ar Intch Lav Er," Songs From a World Apart.* Long Distance, 2006.
Moffett, Karma. *Golden Bowls of Compassion.* Padma Music, 1995.
Monk, Meredith. *Our Lady of Late.* Minona Records, 1973.
Mozart, Wolfgang Amadeus. *Concerto for Flûte and Harp K.299.* Nicanor Zabaleta, Deustche Grammophon, 2015.
Mozart, Wolfgang Amadeus. *Piano Concerto K.488 (n° 23).* Hélène Grimaud. Deustche Grammophon, 2011.
Mozart, Wolfgang Amadeus. *"Fantasia in C Minor, K.475," Mozart Piano Sonatas.* Mitsuko Uchida. Decca Music Group Ldt. 2006.
Mozart, Wolfgang Amadeus. *"Adagio for Glass Harmonica in C, K.356."* Bruno Hoffman, Vox allegretto, 1987.
Mozart, Wolfgang Amadeus. *Adagio & Rondo K.617; 12 Canons.* Archiv Productions, 1991.
Mozart, Wolfgang Amadeus. *Masonic Funeral Music K.477.* London Symphony Orchestra. Decca Music Group Ltd, 1968
Natural Sounds. *Dolphins & Whales.* New World Music, 1998.
Ockeghem, Johannes. *"36-Voice Canon: Deo Gratias," Da Vinci: Music from His Time.* Sony/CBS, 2008.
Oliveros, Pauline. *Deep Listening.* New Albion Records, 1989.
Pachelbel, Johann. "*Canon," Baroque Favorites.* Jean Claude Malgoire. CBS Records, 2015.
Papua New Guinea (Manus, Bougainville). Occra, 1975.
Pärt, Arvo. *"Spiegel im Spiegel," Alina.* ECM, 1999.
Pärt, Arvo. *Lamentate.* ECM, 2005.
Parry, Richard Reed. *Music for Heart and Breath.* Deustshe Grammophon, 2014.
Pena, Paul "Earthquake" & Kongar-Ol Onda. *Genghis Blues. Music From The Motion Picture.* Six Degrees, 2000.
Penderecki, Krzysztof. *Threnody to the Victims of Hiroshima.* Warner Classic, 2012.
Perez Cruz, Silvia & Goldschmidt Ravid. *"Lullaby for Yali," Llama.* M.A. Recordings, 2007.
Pergolesi, Giovanni Battista. *Stabat Mater* Philippe Jaroussky. Naïve, 2017.
Pérotin. *"Viderunt Omnes," Fragments.* Paul Hillier and the Theatre of Voices. Harmonia Mundi, 2005.
Piffaro. *Canzoni e Danze : Wind Music for Renaissance Italy.* Archiv Production, 2016.
Polnareff, Michel. *Complainte à Michaël.* Disc'Az, 1967.
Primeaux, Verdell & Mike, Johnny & Attson, Robert. *Healing and Peyote Songs in Sioux and Navajo.* Canyon Records, 1994.
Ragunathan, Sudha. *"Visalakshim Vishveshim II," Shakti.* Accords Croisés, 2005.
Ramos, Uña. *El Arte de la Quena.* Pata del Gato Music, 2015.
Rautavaara, Einojuhani. *Cantus Arcticus op. 61, Concerto for Birds and Orchestra.* Hannu Lintu. Naxos, 1998.
Ravel, Maurice. *"Adagio assai," Piano Concerto in G Major.* Martha Argerich. London Symphony Orchestra & Claudio Abbado. Deutsche Grammophon, 1988.

Reich, Steve. *Music for 18 Musicians.* ECM Records, 2015.
Reich, Steve. *Proverb.* Nonesuch Records, 1996.
Reich, Steve. *"Drumming Part 3," Drumming.* Deutsche Grammophon, 2000.
Reimann, Michael. *Light Sound (Overtone Harp and Monochords).* Acron Music, 2013.
Reznikoff, Igor. *"Liturgie Fondamentale: Grand Magnificat," Le Chant de Fontenay.* Studio SM, 2005.
Richter, Max. *Recomposed by Max Richter: Vivaldi, The Four Seasons.* Deutsche Grammophon, 2012.
Riley, Terry. *A Rainbow in Curved Air.* Columbia Masterworks, 1969.
Riley, Terry. *"Song in G," Cadenza on a Night Plain and other String Quartets.* Kronos Quartet. Grammavision, 1985.
Rossini, Gioachino. *Petite Messe Solennelle.* Michel Corboz. Erato, 2000.
Savall, Ariana & Udland Johansen, Peter, Hirundo Maris. *Chants du Sud et du Nord.* Edition of Contemporary Music, 2012.
Savall, Jordi. *Ostinato.* Alia Vox, 2001.
Schaeffer, Pierre. *Anthology of Noise & Electronic Music.* Sub Rosa, 2006.
Sedlacek, Ivo. *Barvy Listi. Colour of the Leaves.* Savita Music, 2011.
Sedlacek, Ivo. *"Temple," A Garden of Silence.* Prikosnovenie, 2008.
Shankar, Anoushka. *Live at Carnegie Hall.* Angel 2011.
Shankar, Ravi. *"Gāyatri ," Chants of India.* Angel Records, 1997.
Shostakovitch, Dimitri. *24 Preludes and Fugues, Op.87.* Keith Jarrett. ECM Records, 1992.
Schubert, Franz. *"I. Allegro moderato," Piano Sonata in F Sharp Minor D. 571.* Patricia Montero. Pavane Record, 2019.
Silk Road Ensemble & Yo-Yo Ma. *A Musical Caravan.* Smithsonian Recording, 2002.
Somei, Sato. *Birds in Warped Time II.* Theresa Salomon & Kathryn Woodard. Sonic Crossroad, 2011.
Stivell, Alan. *"Marv Pontkalleg," Renaissance of the Celtic Harp.* Universal Music, 1971.
Troubadours & Trouvères. *The Boston Camerata.* Joel Cohen. Erato, 1991.
Turner, Tina. *"Svarvesham Svastir Bhavatu," Children Beyond.* Igroovemusic, 2011.
Vellard, Dominique & Chauduri, Swapan. *Two Worlds of Modal Music.* Harmonia Mundi, 2004.
Vias, Manish. *Ānanda Nāda: Blissful Sounds of Santoor.* Vias, 2019.
Villa-Lobos. *Bachianas Brasileiras N°5.* Kiri Te Kanawa. English Chamber Orchestra. Universal Music, 1995.
Vivaldi, Antonio. *The Four Seasons.* Nikolaus Harnoncourt. Elektra, 2007.
Vivaldi, Antonio. *"Largo," Recorder Concerto in C Major RV 443.* Michala Petri. RCA Red Seal, 2018.
Vivaldi, Antonio. *Four Seasons.* Yehudi Menuhin. EMI Classics, 2005.
Vivaldi, Antonio. *"Andante," Concerto for 2 Mandolines.* I Solisti Veniti. MSI Erato/Warner, 2006.
Von Bingen, Hildegard. *"O Quam Mirabilis Est," Chants de l'Extase.* Sequentia. Sony Music, 1994.
Webern, Anton. *6 Bagatelles for String Quartet, op. 9.* Emerson String Quartet. Deutsche Grammophon, 2000.
Widor, Charles Marie. *"Toccata de la 5e Symphonie pour Orgue," Toccatas pour Orgue.* Jean Guillou. Philips, 2013.
Who, The. *"See Me, Feel Me," Tommy,* MCA, 1996.

RESOURCES

For classes, workshops, teacher training and international retreats in India, Crete, Italy, Mexico and more, visit www.openskyyoga.com

François Raoult can be contacted at yogawave108@gmail.com

BIYOGRAPHIES

François Raoult, M.A., ERYT 500, C-IAYT, is the Founder and Director of Open Sky Yoga Center in Rochester, New York, and has taught Yoga since 1975. He first felt called to Yoga at age nineteen on a pilgrimage to the sacred sites of India. For a decade, he toured Europe with an avant-garde puppet theater and composed music for the plays. The manipulation of string puppets led him to explore Yoga and Tai Chi. A graduate of the École Nationale de Yoga in Paris and among the first French Yoga instructors to study in India with Śrī B.K.S. Iyengar, he conducts seminars, international retreats and teacher training worldwide. François also has studied meditation, Ayurveda and experiential anatomy. Certified in Gong and Laughing Yoga (!), François completed the International Sound Healer program and also holds a Master's degree in Ethnomusicology.

Karina Alvarez obtained a PhD in Art (2015) from the University of Guanajuato, Mexico and an MFA (2009) from L'École Supérieure d'Art de Grenoble, France. Her work is a multidisciplinary exploration, combining video, sound production and drawing. Karina lives in San Miguel de Allende, Mexico.
www.tragiclandscape.com

www.ingramcontent.com/pod-product-compliance
Lightning Source LLC
Chambersburg PA
CBHW081655120626
46550CB00010B/2905
* 9 7 9 8 9 8 5 3 7 0 5 0 8 *